John Flynn

Of Flying Doctors and Frontier Faith

Ivan Rudolph

Central Queensland
UNIVERSITY
PRESS

Very Rev. John FLYNN, O.B.E., D.D.

Celebrating John Flynn by Phillip Bosua

First published by HarperCollins in 1996

This second edition published in 2000 by
Central Queensland University Press
PO Box 1615
Rockhampton
Queensland 4700

Phone: 07-4922-8144
Fax: 07-4922-8151
email: d.myers@cqu.edu.au
website: www.outbackbooks.com

National Library of Australia
Cataloguing-in-Publication entry:

Rudolph, Ivan

John Flynn: of flying doctors and frontier faith
ISBN 1 875998 90 X
1. Flynn, John, 1880–1951.   2. Royal Flying Doctor Service of Australia.
2. Presbyterian Church-Missions.   4. Missionaries - Australia - Biography.
5. Aeronautics in Medicine - Australia - Biography.   I. Title.

266.5294092

The double-page collage on the frontispiece is entitled "Celebrating John Flynn"
and was created by Phillip Bosua for PAB Productions.
email: contactme@optusnet.com.au

Printed and bound by Watson Ferguson & Co, Moorooka, Brisbane.

Celebrating John Flynn by Phillip Bosua

First published by HarperCollins in 1996

This second edition published in 2000 by
Central Queensland University Press
PO Box 1615
Rockhampton
Queensland 4700

Phone: 07-4922-8144
Fax: 07-4922-8151
email: d.myers@cqu.edu.au
website: www.outbackbooks.com

National Library of Australia
Cataloguing-in-Publication entry:

Rudolph, Ivan

John Flynn: of flying doctors and frontier faith
ISBN 1 875998 90 X
1. Flynn, John, 1880–1951.   2. Royal Flying Doctor Service of Australia.
2. Presbyterian Church-Missions.   4. Missionaries - Australia - Biography.
5. Aeronautics in Medicine - Australia - Biography.   I. Title.

266.5294092

The double-page collage on the frontispiece is entitled "Celebrating John Flynn"
and was created by Phillip Bosua for PAB Productions.
email: contactme@optusnet.com.au

Printed and bound by Watson Ferguson & Co, Moorooka, Brisbane.

CONTENTS

FOREWORD

I was with John Flynn up in the Cape York cattle country. His easy-going habit was to sit on a log, on a fence, on a swag, on anything, and talk to men of the bush. He was a gifted story teller – and his yarns always got to the point of sharing his ideas about what makes life real. That's the way he got me into his team.

I was a young minister full of zeal but I hadn't expected a happening like this. He came and sat beside me on the sand at Southport beach. I was in my surf-life-saving gear. At first I had little interest. I had other dreams for my career. But the compassion of the man grabbed me. There was a simple warmth in his slow voice. His eyes lit up with an inward enthusiasm. He was no pretender: flying doctors, bush nurses, pedal wirelesses were God's gifts. Flynn knew this, and claimed no personal credit. "God supplied the rations," he said. A miracle happened that day on Southport beach. It was the beginning of my life-work beside this man and his Australian Inland Mission.

That Ivan Rudolph has had the mind to research the life and work of John Flynn gladdens my heart. His book speaks for itself. His research is authentic. He brings out Flynn the man who, like no other, revolutionised the lives of people in the "Never Never" country of Australia.

Rev. Dr Fred McKay OBE

To those men and women who still carry the flame
of Flynn's love to brighten up the bush.

Some will be struggling along dusty inland tracks, some will be in
the air, still others will be serving in sweltering inland towns.

This very day, all will face difficulties and be
required to make personal sacrifices.

You are the heritage of which Australia is proud.

PREFACE

John Flynn has had more memorials dedicated to him than any other Australian. His presence still pervades the Australian bush. Why was he so special? Who was this extraordinary man? He never wrote his autobiography – never had the time. Many others have written about him, though. In my search for Flynn, I have blended their historical accounts with original and unpublished source materials and Flynn's own letters, pamphlets and articles. I have reconstructed the events, conversations, thoughts and details of his life as best I can. The result is neither a history text nor a detailed biography, but as you move with Flynn through the action and drama of this life story, you will experience the man and his times in a fresh and authentic way.

I am indebted to a number of people who have graciously helped me in my research.

Special thanks are due to Mrs Valerie Helsen and staff at the National Library in Canberra, who searched out valuable material and produced copies of several hundred documents.

I am grateful to the Vickers family for giving interviews and allowing me to use Dr Allan Vickers' unpublished manuscript.

Most of all, my heartfelt thanks go to Dr Fred McKay, who was Flynn's close friend and successor. Dr McKay, in his eighties, willingly granted me an all-day interview, which left me exhausted while he went off to dig in the garden until darkness fell! Since then, he has corrected the book for accuracy and provided fresh material. When faced with several versions of an incident, I have taken Dr McKay's advice on what to include. I am privileged to have had his help.

Dr McKay directed me to a number of good books about John Flynn and his times. Although none of the authors had set out on the specific search I was on, to find "Flynn the Man", they all supplied useful historical information. I particularly recommend:

John Flynn – Apostle to the Inland by Scott McPheat.

The Flying Doctor Story 1928–78 by Michael Page.

Traeger – The Pedal Radio Man by Fred McKay.

The Man From Oodnadatta, originally by R. Bruce Plowman, and updated by his daughter, Jean Whitla.

IN FLYNN'S FOOTSTEPS ...

John Flynn travelled to most parts of Australia.
Here are some of the places mentioned in this book.

Conversion table

For the sake of historical authenticity, various imperial weights and measures have been retained in this book. Approximate metric equivalents are given below.

1 foot	0.3 metre
1 mile	1.61 kilometres
1 acre	0.4 hectare
1 gallon	4.55 litres
1 pound	0.45 kilogram
1 ton	1.02 tonnes
110° Fahrenheit	43° Celsius
120° Fahrenheit	49° Celsius

Australian currency until 1965

1 pound (£) = 20 shillings (s)
1 shilling = 12 pence (d)

1

HALLS CREEK, AUGUST 1917

Jimmy Darcy sat on a log, head bowed, all too aware of the nagging pain in his side. It was a chilly dawn in the Kimberleys and his mug of hot tea was steaming. Unusually for him, he was not looking forward to riding that day. From the time he had sat on his first heifer in the stockyards as a child and felt its writhing, heaving body, he had loved riding. From heifers to horses to breaking in brumbies, Darcy had become an expert rider and respected stockman. Since a recent bout of malaria, though, this dull pain was always there and it grew worse on horseback. In true Outback fashion, he did not complain, believing that if he ignored it, it would eventually go.

Suddenly Jimmy Darcy stiffened, his practised ear picking up a rumble on the early morning air. He got to his feet, head turning towards the noise. Then he dropped his mug and ran towards the horses. "Stampede!" he yelled.

There was no time to saddle up. Jumping straight onto his horse bareback, he rode at full gallop towards the mob. If he could turn the leading steers he could turn the lot before the stampede was beyond the control of one lone rider. He felt truly alive again. This was what he loved! "Yee-ha!" he yelled, as his horse galloped alongside the flank of the herd and strained to reach the fleeing leaders.

A large hole, hidden by tufts of spinifex grass, went unnoticed until too late. The horse stumbled, flinging Darcy through the air. He crashed into the ground with a sickening thud. Of course he had often fallen off horses before, yet instinctively he knew this heavy fall was different. Tentatively, he tried to wriggle his fingers, then his toes. Despite the flush of pain this caused, he was relieved to find he could move them. At least his spine was not broken. Gingerly, he attempted to sit up but swooned as a red cloud swept over him.

It took his mates a while to find young Jimmy, who looked like a rag doll lying broken on the ground. After some hesitation and debate, they decided to lift him. Supporting him carefully, they carried him to Ruby Plains homestead, laying him out on a table. His ashen features worried them, as did the fact that his injuries were obviously internal and beyond their ability to treat. They drew aside to discuss their strategy.

"He's hurt real bad."

"I think he's bleeding inside."

"We've got to get him to a doc."

They nodded at each other in consensus.

"The only doc I know is at Wyndham, near to 300 miles from here. He's hurt too bad to travel that far."

"There is also a doc at Derby, but that's closer to 500 miles away."

"I reckon we take Jimmy to Halls Creek first. The postmaster there, Fred Tuckett, he's patched up some of my mates before. He's no doc, but he knows first aid, and at least he's only 50 miles away. If he can't fix Jimmy up, he'll give us good advice."

"Let's go."

It was now two in the afternoon. They harnessed a springless buggy, placing Jimmy Darcy gently in the back on a blanket. One man sat with him, watching his facial contortions whenever they hit a bump. The ridged and rutted track had been scored out by heavy bullock carts with their metal-rimmed wheels. When Darcy started to moan, his mate placed a hand on his shoulder.

"How's he doing back there?" the driver called out.

"He's suffering real bad." His mate bent down slightly to catch Darcy's mumbled words, then straightened to ask the driver, "Do you think we could stop for a few minutes? He's too cramped and wants to straighten himself."

Gently, they laid Darcy on a blanket on the track, the flattest ground around. He writhed and twisted in pain, rolling this way and that for several minutes. Finally he stopped squirming and, setting his face like flint, whispered through tight lips, "Right, let's go." Within five miles they needed to place the cramped stockman on the ground again. He writhed once more until composed. The procedure was repeated time and again during that nightmare journey.

It was 2 a.m. when the buggy clattered to a halt in front of the telegraph building in Halls Creek. Fred Tuckett was soon roused and quickly took control. He was a good man, used to dealing with emergencies. He instructed that Jimmy Darcy be laid out on a large table in the telegraph office, where he examined the young man by the flickering yellow light of oil lamps.

When he had finished, he drew the men aside. "Your friend is seriously injured internally. He has only one hope, which is to see a doctor. I can't do anything for him because my training is in first aid only. Unfortunately, the nearest doctor is at Wyndham and I doubt that the patient would survive a buggy ride of 230 miles. Our best chance is to ask the doctor to ride out to us."

"Could we use the telegraph to ask him to come?"

"Yes. I'll make Jimmy as comfortable as I can and then get onto the wire. Most telegraph offices are manned soon after daybreak and some even answer at night. I'll start trying in a few minutes and I'll keep trying."

Tuckett tapped out his message in Morse code. Tiny bolts like blue lightning crackled and leaped the spark gap of the coil as he worked his Morse key, the acrid smell of ozone filling the tiny building. The first few attempts drew no response. Then the key started to clatter away as if moved by some strange, invisible spirit. Tuckett wrote down the reply: the doctor in Wyndham was out of town and likely to remain so for some days.

"I'll try Derby next." But Derby also drew a blank. The men studied Tuckett's face, trying to read his thoughts, sensing his feeling of impotence. One of them asked awkwardly, "How much training did you have in first aid, Mr Tuckett? Could you do something yourself, if we can't raise a doc?"

"No. Definitely not." Even as he replied Tuckett's mind flashed back to Dr John Holland, his St John's Ambulance lecturer eight years before. Could Dr Holland help, even now? It seemed a crazy question: the man was in Perth in Western Australia, 1 700 miles away. Desperate, lacking an alternative, Tuckett decided to try to raise him by wire.

Telegraph messages in 1917 needed to be copied down at a series of relay stations, then sent again, because the wire distance to Perth was 2 283 miles and Leclanche's cells were not able to produce electricity to carry messages that far. This greatly slowed the whole process. There were long minutes of silence between the sending of the message and the arrival of the clattering replies. However, dawn had not yet lit up the sky in Halls Creek when a message came that Dr Holland was standing by in the telegraph office in Perth!

Tuckett described the patient's symptoms and answered questions. There followed a delay. Then the tapper began once again, breaking the tense silence. Tuckett scribbled furiously, first frowning, then looking completely startled. The men stirred uneasily. Tuckett blurted: "He says it's a ruptured bladder and that I'm to operate! I can't operate. I'm not a surgeon."

Tuckett sent this response to Dr Holland. This time the answer was not long in coming. Tuckett reported, "He says I must do the operation." His face had started to shine in the oily light and he was visibly agitated.

The telegraph messages buzzed to and fro:

"I have no scalpel."

"Use your penknife and razor."

"I have no drugs."

"Use permanganate – Condy's crystals."

"I'm not qualified. I might kill the man."

"You must do it or he will die. If you don't hurry, he will die before you start. I will send you exact instructions for the operation. Get everything prepared."

The operators of relay stations between Perth and Halls Creek cleared the telegraph lines of other traffic. Little knots of men and women gathered around at stations along the way as the word spread. They realised that this drama stood at the edge of history – nothing like it had ever been attempted before.

By chance, Jimmy Darcy's two brothers were in Wyndham that day and heard the news. Immediately, they made plans to leave their mob of cattle and ride to their brother's side, despite being exhausted from the previous night's watch. They rode slowly at night and much more quickly during the day, taking only a minimum of rest. Was Jimmy still alive? They pushed themselves and their horses as hard as they dared.

Tuckett sharpened his penknife against a whetstone until it sliced easily through sheets of paper. Soon it would serve as his scalpel and have to cut through a man's skin and muscle. He taped it up until only the pointed end showed, checking it carefully for flaws. Then he got Darcy's mates to scrub up by dipping their hands into a bucket of permanganate solution. They helped him shift an old wooden table next to the telegraph desk so that he could keep in contact with Dr Holland while he worked. The table was washed down carefully and covered with a bed-sheet. There was no anaesthetic, so the men attached belts to the table so that the patient's legs, arms and upper body could be held steady during the operation.

Tuckett received by wire detailed surgical procedures from Dr Holland for a "perineal cystostomy". About noon, he was ready to make the first incision. Nervously he looked at Darcy, wanting to reassure him. "I'll do my best," he said lamely. Darcy's eyes met his and he said slowly, "I'll do my best, too, mate. Cut away. I'm ready." Encouraged by his patient's inner strength, Tuckett steeled himself to begin.

The skin parted readily beneath his scalpel-knife as he made the first cut. Expecting some kind of shout or gasp but hearing none, Tuckett glanced at Darcy's face. The stockman's eyes were tightly closed, his mouth set in a determined line. He made no sound at all. Tuckett looked back down to the abdomen and concentrated on his next incision.

The primitive conditions, the difficulty of keeping the flies away once they had scented blood, the problems with sterilisation, the delays caused by stopping to send questions and then waiting for answers from Dr Holland – all these factors added to the trauma, which went on for seven hours. At last, exhausted, Tuckett wiped down the abdomen with permanganate for the last time, commenting tersely as he did so, "Now it's up to time and nature." As far as he could tell, every step of the operation had been performed successfully.

His mates kept a vigil at Jimmy's side, following Dr Holland's instructions for after-care to the letter. As the hours passed, Jimmy seemed to be improving. But certain worrying symptoms remained which Tuckett described to Dr Holland. Eventually, the telegraph chattered out the reply Tuckett dreaded. Another operation, a "suprapubic cystostomy", was imperative.

This was performed under the same ghastly conditions. Despite its apparent success, Darcy appeared to be weakening, though his stoic bravery never wavered. When further complications arose the next day, an incredible third operation was performed.

Eighty hours after setting out from Wyndham, the Darcy brothers finally rode into Halls Creek. Very relieved to find Jimmy still alive, they sought out Tuckett for his prognosis. The postmaster was less than optimistic. He told them, "Jimmy should be recovering quickly by now, but he isn't. I've sent a description of his latest condition to Dr Holland. Right now I am waiting for his reply, which is taking longer than usual. My greatest fear is that he will order another operation. Jimmy is too weak to survive that, in my opinion."

When Dr Holland's reply arrived, it startled them – he would come to Jimmy himself on a mission of mercy! He intended to leave Perth as soon as he could organise his affairs.

Seven days after the first operation on Jimmy Darcy, Dr Holland boarded a cattle-boat bound for Derby. It took six days to arrive, followed by the frustration of a twelve-hour delay waiting for the tide to rise before the boat could enter the port and dock. Dr Holland paced the decks impatiently.

At the quayside he was met by well-wishers. The manager of a cattle station had made a powerful Model T Ford available to transport him to Fitzroy Crossing, the next leg of his journey. The men carried the news that Darcy's condition was slowly worsening.

The road to Fitzroy Crossing was in reasonable condition and they made good time, taking only a day-and-a-half to complete the 165 miles. En route, his companions told the doctor that there was now a new-fangled telephone link between Fitzroy Crossing and Halls Creek. A telephone! This would enable him to talk to Tuckett and even to Darcy, to encourage the young man.

The phone line between the two settlements crackled and was faint. Tuckett told Dr Holland that the stockman was in constant pain, and weakening. The patient was put on the line.

"Dr Holland here, Darcy. Can you hear me?"

After a short pause, Darcy spoke. "Yes, I can." His voice was hard to catch.

"I'm coming to help you. I'm at Fitzroy Crossing already."

"Fitzroy Crossing. That's not too far, but it's a bad road from there."

"It's not very far at all. When I get to you, I'm going to fix you up and get you back in the saddle. So wait patiently for me, do you hear?"

"Yes, Dr Holland. I will. Thank you."

A well-seasoned station tourer with men to drive it was provided for the trip, the Model T being unsuitable for the roads ahead. The road out of Fitzroy Crossing began promisingly, but soon degenerated into a track. The going was very slow. At times a man had to walk ahead through the bush or wade over a creek to check the best path for the vehicle to follow. Dr Holland tried to be patient, but the knowledge that Darcy was hovering between life and death was foremost in his mind. His fear was that a motor accident would bring their progress to a halt.

Skidding down a sandy slope one morning, the driver lost control of the car and thumped heavily into a blackened tree stump. No one was hurt, but the tourer would not restart. Dr Holland joined the men in looking underneath the car. He was appalled at how much of the vehicle was held together with thick twists of fencing wire! A couple of hours later they were on their way again.

Some miles on, the car jerked a few times, then stopped. One man jumped out with a crank handle and whirled it furiously, to no avail. "It sounds to me like it could be out of petrol," Dr Holland observed. Everyone got out and pushed the car gently from side to side while one man lay on the ground and listened.

"I think I can hear a little petrol slushing around in the tank," he told them. "It doesn't sound like much. I don't think there's enough to reach the carburettor."

The jerry cans of petrol they had brought with them were dry. What to do? One of the men had a suggestion: "We could drain the tank into a tin and feed it directly into the carburettor."

"We'd need a pipe of some sort for that."

"I've got some hose for you," said Dr Holland. He reached into his black bag and withdrew a stethoscope. Stripping the ends off, he presented the men with the resultant thin rubber hose. By tilting the car, all of the remaining petrol in the tank was drained into a tin. With the ingenuity of men of the bush, they succeeded in setting up a gravity feed from the tin to the carburettor and off they set once again. At the next cattle station, they replenished their petrol and struggled on. Three further breakdowns, however, were to cost a further 30 valuable hours.

The men had been cooped in the car for five endless, frustrating days when iron roofs glowing in the late afternoon sun came into view. "That is Moola Bulla Station, Doctor. We're only twenty miles from Halls Creek." Night would soon fall, but Dr Holland was impatient. "I know it's tricky driving in the dark, but we should push ahead and reach Darcy tonight." Only a few miles past Moola Bulla, however, a loud tearing screech told them that the gearbox had finally succumbed. There could be no further travel in that car.

Resignedly, the group trudged back to Moola Bulla in the dark. Here there was no car for loan, but there was a home-made sulky. Some men went out in the dark to catch two horses – any horses would have to do, whether they had been in harness before or not.

"What's the news of Jimmy Darcy?" Dr Holland asked anxiously.

"Last I heard was a few days back," said the station manager. "He was still alive."

The sulky gave the party a wild ride because of frisky, untrained horses and difficult vision by moonlight. Several thumps and crashes could have toppled them, but miraculously didn't. Dawn was just splashing the sky in pastel pink when the vehicle clattered into Halls Creek, thirteen long days after Dr Holland had set out from Perth.

Tuckett heard it coming and stepped out of the door of the Telegraph Office as it drew up. Dr Holland dispensed with social niceties to call down to Tuckett, "How is Darcy?"

"He died yesterday," Tuckett replied.

Something inside Holland seemed to collapse at hearing this. He sucked in a deep breath and shook his head slowly, very sadly. "Time wins," he said.

Darcy's red-eyed brothers sought him out later that morning to thank him for his efforts. They asked whether he would do an autopsy, to settle their minds about what had taken their much-loved brother. Dr Holland began by inspecting the site of the operations and then the bladder itself. He was surprised, and gratified, by his findings: Tuckett had done a fine job, no infection had set in and healing had been on course. What, then, had killed the young stockman? He would investigate further.

The autopsy uncovered an enormous spleen, blown up like a balloon. Severe malaria prior to the accident was the main cause of death: it would have been a lingering condition that took advantage of post-operative weakness to kill its host. "What a man," Dr Holland thought to himself. "To have ridden a horse in his condition must have required enormous grit."

Dr Holland was more than usually affected by his findings. He said to Tuckett, "That boy ought not to have died. You had done a magnificent job. If there had been a doctor available to diagnose and treat the other problems, he would have been right as rain. Even half-decent roads would have let me reach him in time. It was a totally unnecessary death. Why are things so backward out here? The government should be doing something about it. It's a blight on our nation."

"Politicians don't appear to care much about us," Tuckett told him. "I guess we don't count for too many votes; at least that is what most of the bush believes. There's another problem. Politicians are mainly city folk and have no real idea what conditions are like out here."

There was no minister of religion within hundreds of miles of Halls Creek, so his brothers buried Jimmy Darcy. They used the simple burial service to be found in that most practical of books, *The Bushman's Companion*. This book was written by the Reverend John Flynn, of whom the community of Halls Creek was soon to hear much more.

2
ENTER JOHN FLYNN

Unknown to Dr Holland, Australian newspapers gave prominent coverage to the events at Halls Creek. For a few days in August 1917, even the Great War was upstaged while a nation waited to see whether one brave stockman lived or died.

A tall, 36-year-old minister named John Flynn told everyone, "It shouldn't have happened. Brave men like Jimmy Darcy shouldn't die because of lack of facilities in the Outback. Some of our finest men are struggling to open up the interior of our nation and it is up to us to help them."

Flynn was the Superintendent of the Australian Inland Mission (AIM) of the Presbyterian Church and his burning desire was to help the pioneers. In the Mission's quarterly magazine of which he was editor, *The Inlander*, Flynn wrote passionately concerning the Halls Creek saga. "Is Providence to blame? Some men will say so: most of us will be mute, pause to wonder further – and look nearer." In other words, let's not shift responsibility elsewhere when we can do something about a problem ourselves – a typical Flynnian sentiment.

He also referred to the tragedy in his speeches and letters, trying to stir the rich and influential to do something. Many listened, but were discouraged by the enormity of the problem. Flynn would not quit though. "Can any good come out of a tragedy like this?" he asked repeatedly.

The men of Halls Creek met informally after the burial of Jimmy Darcy to discuss the situation. Each knew that he could have been in Darcy's shoes.

"I heard Dr Holland saying he would not come here again unless by aeroplane," one told the others.

"Yeah, he also said Jimmy need not have died if there had been proper medical attention in this area," another observed.

The rumblings of dissatisfaction grew in the district. Three local men of influence, Fred Tuckett, Fred Booty and Arthur Haly, manager of Moola Bulla Station, decided to make informal approaches to John Flynn to see if he could help in any way, perhaps by supplying a trained nurse. Booty wrote to Flynn in Sydney in February 1918:

> We are not ignorant of your work in this back country and have considered consulting you on a question which has become much more urgent.
>
> Halls Creek is one of the furthest outposts of Australia today. There was recently a hiatus of five months in our mail service and there is a flour and sugar famine on, as is usual in the "big wet" season.
>
> The town consists of post office and courthouse, one pub-and-store combined, another store, two cottages and a police station. It is situated centrally for cattle stations, which are just beginning to flourish, and is visited chiefly by cattle punchers and diggers. There are only two ladies and three children here.
>
> THE DARCY INCIDENT IS BUT ONE OF MANY SUCH WHICH HAVE OCCURRED HERE.
>
> The population is insufficient to support a medical man, but we thought it might be possible to keep up a cottage hospital in charge of a nurse or two, where those who are at times so sadly in need of help could be cared for ... We might have to borrow to build the accommodation, but this does not dismay us. It is the staffing of the place that has got us guessing, and upon which we would like your advice. The staff we could engage would only be "stragglers" or "pikers", while yours would come from a recognised "herd" controlled by the AIM. One nurse and a companion is at present our ideal. We intend to hold a meeting here in a month or so and, as the course of post is so very long, perhaps you could kindly wire Mr Tuckett your views, or whether your Mission would take such an institution under its wing.

To keep up the momentum, Tuckett called a public meeting at Halls Creek three months later. His audience was rowdy to begin with and Tuckett gave them time to blow off steam, most of it directed against the government. When there was calm, Arthur Haly addressed them: "There is one man who understands our needs and who would be willing to help, not just with words but in practical ways. I am speaking of the Reverend John Flynn. Most of you will have heard of him or used his book, *The Bushman's Companion*. We used it when we buried Jimmy. Frederick Booty wrote to him in February and I went and spoke with him when I was in Sydney recently, to sound him out. He is genteel and quietly spoken, sort of a gentleman, but is greatly upset by our situation. He is heart and soul in his desire to make the backblocks habitable and safe, not just for men but for families. He gave me an undertaking to help us."

"Yeah, but what can he do?" one of the men called out.

"He has a very practical proposal. Providing we band together and put up a hospital, even a crude one, he will send out a trained AIM nurse, with an assistant. Flynn has nurses serving elsewhere in the bush and they enjoy the highest of reputations. I believe we should accept his generous offer. What of it, men?"

A hush greeted Haly's words. Then an excited hubbub broke out. Someone in the cities cared enough to help! Suggested plans and enthusiasm spread like a flame.

The meeting decided, after much discussion, to take over the obsolete and ramshackle old Miners Institute, and to refurbish it as a nursing home. That way it would be ready to open within a few months. They would erect a permanent hospital later on. Men committed their time, materials and money to the enterprise. When Tuckett passed a hat around, £200 was raised!

Back in Sydney, John Flynn was delighted. His next move was to search for the right nurse to pioneer the hospital at Halls Creek. It was the roughest of areas: she would need courage, commonsense, expertise, good humour and the capacity to improvise and "make do" on every level. He broadcast the need through church news-letters and among AIM staff and supporters. Weeks slipped by without a volunteer for the task.

Finally, Sister Muriel Rogasch stepped forward. She had already proved her worth at the AIM nursing home at Oodnadatta. Flynn told her about the Kimberley region and the myriad problems she could face there. "You will be away from home for more than two years and isolated for months during each 'big wet' season. In that time you will be carrying sole responsibility for the health of that vast area. You will face food shortages and lack of equipment ..."

"I look forward to the challenge, Mr Flynn," was her quiet response when he paused for a breath.

Flynn's eyes shone with approval behind his round-rimmed spectacles. "Good girl," he smiled, and went to wire the news to Tuckett.

In the frantic process of organisation that followed, Flynn wrote a long letter to Halls Creek to inform the community of progress. He used the correspondence to state clearly some principles on which the AIM nursing home would operate, in the hope this would forestall problems.

> Sister Rogasch is a Baptist lady, Miss Madigan [her companion] is an Anglican, and many of our friends helping to make a success of the hospital are, I understand, Roman Catholics. We can cheerfully agree to differ on some points and work like blazes together to make Kimberley a splendid corner of the Commonwealth.

> Our anxiety is not to make Presbyterians. Our aim is to get a fair deal for all our citizens, to make our country prosperous and healthy in the best sense of the word – which starts with the body and ends with the spirit.

> Our theory is that one of the first necessities, apart from health and tucker, is that a man should have respect for that Faith which made a good woman of his mother: we may have our own opinions over various brands of Faith, but these are just details.

> As to the finances of the nursing home, the AIM would do more than supply the nurses if needs be – the battlers up your way seem determined to find all the cash needed and good luck to them. But our Board will be cheerful enough if we need to put in some oil and petrol at times, for our work is to help ...

Within days, Flynn was at the railway station in Adelaide saying farewell to Sister Rogasch and Miss Madigan, her companion. Miss Madigan was to act as housekeeper and general helper to Sister Rogasch. Flynn offered them some parting advice: "Be ready for anything. Don't expect to do everything yourselves, though. They are good men out there and very willing to help. Remember, too, that whomsoever God calls, he also empowers."

" 'Be ready for anything!' Do you think the Superintendent was over-dramatising? Rural life moves slowly, after all," Miss Madigan said to Sister Rogasch as their railway carriage lurched this way and that.

The nurse thought back to her time at Oodnadatta before replying. "I think his advice is very good. We must be prepared for anything."

Dr Holland met the pair at the station in Perth, and looked after them while they were in the city, taking an intense interest in the plans for Halls Creek. Knowing the conditions there first-hand, he was able to advise them what to take, and helped them purchase medicines and equipment for their dispensary. He also arranged a "hot line" for emergencies between Halls Creek and himself in Perth.

"I hope I never need to operate by proxy as Tuckett had to," Sister Rogasch told him.

"Had you been there, Darcy would not have died," Dr Holland observed soberly. "The good thing is that you will be there from now on."

The journey to Halls Creek took several more weeks. Sister Rogasch wrote to John Flynn while waiting at Point Samson:

> On board is a lady going to Halls Creek. Her husband heard of our going and wired for her. She makes one more home in the land that needs them …

Flynn was especially pleased to receive this news because it was his intention to encourage families to live in the "Never Never". Here was an example of how the promise alone that an AIM nurse would be in the vicinity was sufficient for a man to send for his wife, and was enough for her to respond to his call: secure in the knowledge that child-bearing would be safer, that a young family could receive medical help, and that there would be a nurse to talk to about womanly problems.

As the women disembarked at Port Wyndham, they were met by a policeman who handed them a telegram. Sister Rogasch tore open the brown envelope and read it quickly, frowning as she did so. She relayed to Miss Madigan, "The storekeeper at Halls Creek has been shot and is seriously wounded. They fear for his life. They ask us to get there urgently." To the young policeman, who had been listening, she said, "We're booked to take the horse-drawn buggy service from here to Halls Creek. Is there any faster means of travel available? A man's life hangs in the balance."

The man thought for a moment before replying. "Not officially, and the buggy service is rather slow. I'll put the problem to my superior. Please gather your luggage and wait here for me to return." Within an hour, a car and driver had been arranged to take them express to Halls Creek, a distance of 230 miles along rough roads.

"Is this a repeat of the Darcy tragedy?" Sister Rogasch wondered. The parallels were striking. She had plenty of time to ponder the question as they were thrown this way and that. "Motoring in the Kimberleys is a severe form of punishment," Flynn had told her. It was a good description!

At last they were able to clamber out of the car at Halls Creek and stretch their cramped limbs. Tuckett and some other local men were on hand to welcome them, then they were rushed along to the new hospital to examine Mr Ward, the wounded storekeeper.

After twenty minutes, Sister Rogasch delivered her prognosis. "He should live, but needs to be shifted at once to the doctor at Wyndham. Miss Madigan and I will nurse him along the way. How was he shot?"

"It was the result of an argument," Tuckett told her. "The man who did it killed himself immediately afterwards and has been buried already. It's a strange life out here – we had to knock up his coffin from old packing cases we found in his victim's shop."

Using blankets and cushions, the women made Mr Ward as comfortable as possible in the car that they had just arrived in. As they drove, they discussed their first impressions.

"The hospital is very, you know, basic. Makeshift. At least I thought so."

"That's true, but we'll scrub it up and equip it," Sister Rogasch replied.

"The men were, well, you know, different from city men, don't you think? I mean, they didn't say much, just stood around and looked at you."

The driver, originally from Wyndham, intervened here, saying, "You must forgive the men for staring, ladies. You two are a novelty to them. Very few women come to the Outback and you are the first two they will have seen in uniforms."

Thanks to Sister Rogasch Mr Ward survived both the journey and the bullet wound. The Reverend John Flynn's interventional planning had enabled an exact reversal of the Darcy tragedy, a contrast that was not lost on the men of the Kimberleys.

Once their charge was safely on the mend, the women returned to Halls Creek, this time in a horse-drawn buggy at a more sedate pace. They enjoyed the breathtaking scenery as they swung gently up steep mountain roads and onto the Kimberley Plateau.

Back at Halls Creek they found the new hospital filled to overflowing due to an outbreak of fever. The two women immediately set about nursing the sick. There were plenty of surprises. For instance, when Miss Madigan went out to the washroom to collect a bucket of hot water, she stumbled into a mattress on the floor, hidden in the semi-gloom. The very pregnant woman lying on it explained, "They didn't want me to have my baby where the fever is, in case the baby catches it. They put me out here in the washroom to wait for your return. Now that you're back, you can decide what's to be done with me."

"Be ready for anything," Flynn had said. Miss Madigan was beginning to comprehend what he had meant! Her understanding deepened during the busy night that followed in the fever ward: some men became delirious on account of their high body temperatures and the heated blood coursing into their brains; some yelled and threw their arms about wildly.

When morning finally arrived, Sister Rogasch felt washed out. Glancing out the window, she saw a man holding a blood-soaked rag to his head, staggering towards the hospital. When she went out to meet him he stopped, and holding himself stiffly erect, asked nonchalantly, "May I see my daughter, please? You have her in here someplace. She came in to have her baby."

"What happened to your head? Take that cloth away and let me see," demanded Sister, ignoring his request.

"Oh, it is nothing serious, but I suppose I wouldn't mind if you took a gander at it. My horse kicked me just a short while ago."

On examining his head, she found that most of the man's ear was missing!

Once the fever epidemic had been defeated, without loss of life, the newcomers set about improving the nursing home. They knew Flynn wanted it to become a wholesome focus for community life as well as a centre of healing. His concept included ministry to the soul and spirit as well as to the body.

Sister Rogasch bullied the men into making a simple tennis court on the clay outside the hospital. It was soon in regular use. Next, she put up wooden bookshelves, lining them with zinc to try to discourage the voracious termites. She established a "library" of books and magazines supplied by Flynn's Mail-bag League. These were free for the taking and carried the invitation, "Read and pass on". "It sure beats reading the labels on jam tins," one man told her appreciatively. "In my little hut, that is all I've had to read this last year, labels on tins. You get to know them quite well."

Flynn's nursing home fulfilled a real need, providing a focus for an otherwise dispersed community. Soon a stream of visitors came in to chat, or to sit and read. Musical evenings with phonographs and records proved popular and often the locals would sing or play musical instruments. Everyone seemed to enjoy themselves. A sense of community was growing.

Extracts from the letters of Sister Rogasch and Miss Madigan paint a vivid picture of the difficult and colourful life they were now leading.

> Our cane chairs, and lounge, and deck chairs, that we bought in Perth arrived two months after we did, per donkey team, and sadly in pieces. The lounge didn't arrive at all. The teamster told us cheerfully that he thought it was back on the road three or four miles, as a bough had dragged it off, and he didn't know whether the wheels had run over it or not as he was working the brake at the time and didn't look. However, an ingenious old man has mended our chairs. With them our corner looks nice and comfortable and we keep it fresh with green leaves ...

No glass is put in small windows, a swing board affair serves instead ...

We put the lounge and easy chair stovewards in the winter evenings and it was quite nice to see a tired mailman resting there before he started away off to his final destination for the night. He had just come in from his 198-mile track and had to go nine miles further on where feed was good for his horses. His own bed was to be a trough filled with grass ...

A drover came in last Wednesday, he was delighted to take some books away with him. He told me a harrowing story. He and some mates were attempting a new stock route to the southern markets when he became too ill with malaria to continue, so returned home. His mates failed to arrive down south with the cattle. The mystery was cleared up some weeks later when their remains were found near the carcasses of their horses. They had been speared by blacks, along with many of the cattle. The remaining cattle must have been scattered as they have not been found as yet. I was appalled by his story and I must say I was most surprised to learn that dangers of this sort still existed in the Inland ...

An old prospector visited us. I found him staring into a cot at a white baby, whose mother was at that moment being examined by Sister Rogasch. He looked up at me and I noticed tears running down his cheeks. "It must be sixteen years since I've seen a white baby," he explained, then strode out of the hospital without further comment ...

Flynn was disturbed by the report of the bushman who hadn't seen a white baby for so many years, asking "What kind of a frontier have we allowed to develop?" He yearned to produce a more civilised Inland, fit for babies. He wrote poignantly on behalf of the bushmen, "Will you not help us to help them to become grandparents?" This concern for family life was despite the fact that Flynn himself was a bachelor with no home to call his own.

Halls Creek, meanwhile, had taken the AIM hospital and its staff right into their hearts. The staff, in turn, had to accept the new culture as they found it. For example, in the extreme heat of summer, the locals dragged their beds out of doors and slept under the stars. Hospital patients did the same if they were strong enough and there would have been no point in Sister Rogasch objecting.

Many facilities were lacking at the hospital, but an active local committee set about raising funds. When they wrote to Flynn asking how he saw the long-term future of the hospital, his reply surprised and pleased them.

> Once your Local Committee is self-sufficient, you can take over the hospital yourselves, we are quite happy for it to float out of our control. We will give you any equipment of ours there as a gift, and the title deeds to the hospital also if that is appropriate. Our nurses will continue to staff the hospital, as long as you want them, and we will pay their salaries, but you will run the hospital yourselves. *Our intention is to serve, not to control.* We believe Outbackers are, by nature, self-sufficient and operate best like that. However, if there are financial problems either end, we will pick up the tab.

One of the fundraising ventures, in December 1918, was a "carnival" organised by the local committee. The main events were supposed to be the "horse races", although there were few of these; most people came for the sociability and fun. Almost the whole district gathered and lived in tents for up to a week. Sister Rogasch and Miss Madigan were the centre of attention and were asked to be judges of various competitions. The chairman's report sets the scene.

> The pavilions, judges' box etc. dressed out in new coverings of green boughs, and the spic and span appearance of the course indicated that Billy Solanders had put a lot of ginger into keeping his end up. Generally, the meeting passed off very satisfactorily and we are gratified to announce the funds of our local hospital will benefit to the extent of about £450.
>
> However, on the 19th December, tragedy struck, a tragedy that removed Sister Rogasch and Miss Madigan from the remainder of the meeting.
>
> Charles Diedrich, a recent arrival from Fitzroy Crossing, was thrown heavily from a horse, sustaining serious injury to the brain. Fortunately, Sister Rogasch was present on the ground and was quickly in attendance and did all possible to alleviate

the sufferer. In the cool of the evening, he was removed to the local hospital, accompanied by Sister Rogasch and Miss Madigan. Medical aid was summoned by telegraph and it was ascertained that his case was hopeless. He lingered until Sunday evening 22nd, when he died without having regained consciousness. He was buried in the local cemetery early the following morning.

Sister Rogasch stayed behind at the cemetery as the mourners moved away. Despite Dr Holland wiring from Perth that death had been inevitable, she was upset at having lost a patient. She spoke sternly to herself: "Pull yourself together. You have lost one patient, but have saved others and will save still more in the future. That's what's important."

As she strolled by the graves, she noticed one headstone in particular. It read, "SACRED to The Memory of JAMES DARCY who Died at Halls Creek 22nd August 1917, Aged 29 Years. RIP." Could good come out of that tragedy? Flynn had asked. Sister Rogasch looked up from the headstone in the direction of her makeshift hospital at Halls Creek and she sighed. She had better be getting back.

As she left, she passed several mounds which had no headstone at all – unmarked graves, covered with rubble and spinifex tufts. What tragedies lay behind each of those graves? There was much work for her to do in the Kimberleys.

Jimmy Darcy's headstone is still on his grave at old Halls Creek. His brother Charlie is buried beside him, having reached the mature age of 52 years, thanks in part to Flynn's work in the Kimberleys. They lie in a graveyard that is far smaller than it would have been if John Flynn had not established a hospital there.

A plaque in the old town honours "Russian Jack", who pushed a sick mate hundreds of miles along the rugged track from Derby to Halls Creek in a wheelbarrow! It was to help brave pioneers like Darcy and "Russian Jack" that Flynn established his hospital.

Who was this John Flynn? Why did his heart beat in time with the "Great Red Heart" of Australia, where desert dust blew and dingoes howled?

3

YOUNG FLYNN

A tall, gangling youth knelt in the shadows and took careful aim. The rabbit nibbled at the grass, its whiskers dancing. It had not scented the hunter and was unconcerned. A shot cracked out through the crisp evening air, knocking it sideways off its feet as though hit by an invisible fist. Up in a flash, red already staining its fur down to its belly, the rabbit darted into the dry stone walling, disappearing from view. The lad, still grasping his rifle, broke from cover and loped forwards. As he did so, two or three other rabbits fled from their grazing and scattered.

John Flynn pulled aside some of the rocks where the rabbit was hiding, caught him by the back legs, yanked him free and smacked his head on a nearby stone with a swift, efficient thump. His fourth one that evening! As he straightened, holding the limp rabbit by its legs, he saw a thick-set man on a horse who had reined up to watch.

The man urged his horse forward until he and Flynn could converse comfortably. "I'm glad you're shooting the rabbits. They're vermin and a great nuisance. What do you do with them? The shot ones, I mean."

"My family eats them, sir," Flynn replied. He easily recognised Hugh Victor McKay, famous for designing and manufacturing Sunshine Harvesters, forerunners of today's combine harvesters. McKay had visited local properties in the past, to get orders for his machines.

"And what might your name be?" McKay asked.

"John Flynn, sir."

"Is your father the Flynn who is a schoolteacher and also a lay preacher?"

"Yes, he is, sir."

"Ah, I have heard some good reports of his preaching." McKay was known as an ardent Christian and loyal Presbyterian.

That evening, John moved the blade of his penknife backwards and forwards across a smooth stone he reserved for this purpose. The skin of the first rabbit parted easily beneath his sharpened blade. He peeled it back, gutting each rabbit in turn. His sister, Rosetta, would make them into a stew with the potatoes they all enjoyed, perhaps shades of their Irish ancestry.

Rosetta was the only woman in the home after the death of the children's mother in 1883 in Moliagul, the tiny Victorian town in which John had been born two-and-a-half years before that tragic event. John's father had given each child a silver locket containing a picture of their beautiful mother. John carried his locket with him everywhere, often opening it and staring at her face, wondering what she had been like. He couldn't remember. His older brother Eugene told him that she had been "kind and gentle" and John noticed tears in his eyes as he said it.

There had been a period of four years following their mother's death during which their father could not support them and the children had been looked after by kindly relatives. John had been the special charge of his mother's teenage sister during that uncertain time. Once reunited, the three children and their father made a close-knit family, happy to be together again.

When Thomas Flynn arrived home that night, Rosetta told him rather grandly, "John spoke to Hugh Victor McKay today. He's heard of you."

"Has he now? How did you meet him, John?"

John told his father and summed up McKay with the words "He didn't say much, but he saw everything."

Thomas said, "I heard he might be purchasing land in this area for a factory. If so, we could become neighbours."

This turned out to be the case. Hugh McKay built a factory complex at Baybrook, later renamed "Sunshine", on land where John had hunted rabbits. A friendly, neighbourly relationship developed between the families. "H. V." took a special interest, over the years, in what John was doing.

Thomas always worried about his dreamy younger son. He once expressed this concern to their family doctor, saying "I don't know what to make of John, if anything."

"John may not be as outstanding a scholar as Eugene," the doctor had replied, "but he is a fine lad nevertheless. He has a sharp mind and takes an interest in everything. When he was in here a while back, he made me explain how each of my instruments worked." They both chuckled. Thomas left, reassured by the doctor's words. How he wished his wife were still alive, though! She would have understood the children better than he did: he understood books better than people.

Thomas Flynn had loved his wife deeply and never remarried. As the years went past, he became increasingly reclusive, retreating into books and studies. Materially speaking, he could not give his children a great deal, but he imparted his Christian faith and its vision of life and eternity. The virtues of honesty, hard work and service were also drilled into his young family.

There was little physical affection between father and children, which was the norm in that era. Thomas took great interest in each child, though, and conversation in the home was intelligent and lively. Little family rituals like the Saturday spoonful of medicine "for the liver" gave the children the security of knowing that they were cared for.

Although gregarious and sociable, John took to spending hours by himself in the beautiful countryside near their home. He marvelled at the magnificence of nature, and dreamt dreams. During this period, his belief in God deepened. He decided to serve Him by becoming a minister in the Presbyterian Church. This Protestant denomination, the official Church of Scotland, had been brought to Australia in 1822 by the colourful John Dunmore Lang. By the 1880s the Presbyterians were a respected and conservative church, spread right across Australia and numbering many thousands of members.

Prior to theological training at Melbourne University, John attended University High School, Parkville, to obtain the necessary entrance qualifications. He worked hard at high school, matriculating in only 16 months, and receiving a glowing reference from his headmaster, who said John's success was "due to his commendable industry and perseverance, as well as to his intellectual ability. He is one of the most trustworthy, painstaking and upright pupils this school has had for some time."

But an obstruction stood in John's path to university: the family lacked the funds to send him. He would have to get a job and save first. And so early in 1899 he became at the age of 18 a "pupil teacher" with the Victorian Education Department.

John enjoyed his newfound independence and lived life to the full at a hectic pace. A number of new hobbies fascinated him, including first aid and photography, which were to become lifelong involvements. He also bought a new rifle, which he slung over his shoulders when he went on bicycle trips into the countryside.

Despite being a dreamer, John was also highly involved with people of all ages. He formed a successful Sunday school among his pupils, took on the leadership of the Footscray Young Men's Bible Class, and arranged a series of outings as well as organising Bible studies. He also helped at the local church in other ways.

The pittance he earned was hardly enough to keep body and soul together, let alone support such an active lifestyle. But an unusually compassionate nature began to find expression in his management of his money. He hated to hear about parishioners who were down on their luck and he often bought a bottle of medicine here or a few groceries there to help where he could. One storekeeper remembered Flynn saying to him, "Please don't present my cheque at the moment, as there might not be enough money in the account to cover it. But don't worry, the money will come in eventually." And it did.

That same year, 1899, John's beloved brother Eugene died, aged twenty-two. His death knocked the family sideways. The talented, handsome Eugene had been the one on whom most hopes of success had been pinned.

During this time of mourning, John's conviction grew that his own destiny lay in serving God. But as the years slipped by, so did any money that came John's way. Did God really want him to train for the ministry? If so, why was there so little progress in that direction? Doubts began to assail him, as can be seen in the letter John wrote to his father on 11 November 1901.

> Dear Father,
>
> I will be 21 this day fortnight, and have been thinking that I should give you my thoughts concerning the future. It is four

or five years since I first got the idea of becoming a minister. Since then, of course, my views have changed considerably, but the more I think the more I see the grandeur and beauty of Christianity, and the hollowness of human life considered complete in itself ...

I do not lose sight of an aspect illustrated by an anecdote given by Dr Todd. It runs something like this – A certain broom-maker was anxious to become a minister, and communicated this to a clergyman of some eminence. The clergyman heard him in silence, and then said: Friend, God intended some men to be ministers and some to be makers of brooms. I feel convinced that He intended you to be a maker of brooms.

I would not care to take up the responsibilities of the position if I were not fitted for them, and I am not altogether capable of gauging my own abilities ... I will be very glad to hear any comments you may have.

And now I must thank you for all your love and care through all these years. It is not much to utter thanks, but I feel I have been deficient in this respect.

Your affectionate son,
John

His father's reply to this was noncommittal, leaving Flynn to agonise in prayer as to his future.

During the long school vacations of 1902, he decided to tour the drought-stricken farmlands of Western Victoria. The intention was to make money by taking photographs and writing about his experiences for Melbourne newspapers. He would camp out in his home-made tent and travel by bicycle.

John wrote wittily for the media in the course of his journey, using the pseudonym "Sprocket", and accompanied his writings with excellent photographs. A real journalistic flair was apparent in his descriptions of the people, the crop failures, sand drifts and burnt countryside. He recounted a minor accident that occurred when cycling one night:

Seeing ahead of me a horse tethered near a tent, I slackened my pace considerably, but no sooner had I passed the animal than

I went over the handles. The cause proved to be a temporary fence of wire netting stretched across the road, which was, the sleepy drover explained, during a conversation somewhat warm on my side, to keep the sheep off people's crops!

Some weeks after his return, John counted the expenses of his bicycle trip against the money he had been paid for his articles. He found he came out even. Journalism was not likely to solve his financial dilemma, not when his photography was so expensive.

Should he abandon his dream of becoming a minister? Flynn conferred in some despair with trusted friends who suggested an alternative path to the ministry, that of becoming a "home missionary".

The Home Mission Department was a response by the Presbyterian Church of 1903 to a great need: pioneering communities were mushrooming all over the nation, far more than could be reached by the small number of trained ministers. The plan was to use young men thinking of training for the ministry. These enthusiasts could prove themselves first by "taking the Gospel of personal salvation through commitment to Jesus Christ" to these communities. The Church, in return, would give on-going academic training culminating in full-time study at Ormond College, Melbourne University. Some funding of students would still be required, but not as much.

The scheme sounded like an answer and a challenge, so Flynn applied to become a home missionary. He was accepted in June 1903, and appointed to Beech Forest, high up in the rugged Otway Mountains near the southern Victorian coast. Here he found himself in a pioneering community of timbermen and settlers. At once his photographer's eye was enchanted by the beauty of the Otways with their mammoth ash trees, so huge that the Governor and his party had danced on a single stump to celebrate the opening of the railway line! The resinous smell of cut wood was everywhere. It permeated the homesteads, the splitters' camps, the timber mills and even the roads, because offcuts and sawdust were used as packing to stabilise the sticky black soil.

How could a youngster get a fair hearing from the hard-working, hard-swearing, hard-drinking, hard-everything timbermen and settlers? Initially, Flynn did not try to speak about God, but rode around his parish getting acquainted instead.

It was on one of these rides that he fell off his horse and tore his upper lip badly. A crude job was done when the wound was stitched and he carried the scar for the rest of his life. His mobile and expressive mouth drew attention to the scar, which looked like a hare lip that had been repaired surgically.

On one morning ride, he noticed a circle of agitated men outside a timber mill. They surrounded a man lying on a blanket.

"What's wrong?" Flynn asked the closest person.

"He had a bit of an accident. A log rolled onto him," was the man's reply.

No one seemed sure what to do, so Flynn took control. "I know some first aid. Let me have a look at him, please. Don't crowd him, move back and give him some air."

His examination revealed that the man had a break in his left arm, which he had presumably lifted to protect himself against the falling log. Apart from that, there seemed to be only bad bruising. Flynn collected bandages from his saddlebag and splinted the arm, telling his workmates they should take the man to the nearest doctor.

"Nice job you did there," the manager said to him afterwards. "We keep having minor accidents, and unfortunately none of us knows much about first aid."

"That's a pity. Do you think your men would be interested in learning the basic principles? I'd be prepared to give some talks on it."

"That'd be worthwhile. I'd attend myself. We don't have a hall but we could clear the dining room after the evening meal, if that would suit you."

"That'll do fine."

John Flynn's first-aid lectures attracted a good turnout. The men liked his practical approach and the fact that he used different members of the audience to demonstrate on. Flynn's teaching experience had made him a good communicator in this type of situation: he interlaced the important information with anecdotes and light-hearted banter.

He concluded his final talk on the Saturday evening by saying, "Men, I want to thank you for being such an attentive group. I have enjoyed my time with you, teaching you how to patch up your bodies. Friends, you all know that we are more than just bodies, and that our souls need patching up as well. It happens that I am in the business of teaching men first aid for the soul as well as for the body, and I'll be having a simple church service right here tomorrow morning at nine o'clock. I invite you to attend and I hope to see you then." They did not all come along, but a good number did because they had come to like and respect the young minister. Some even responded to the love of Christ that Flynn told them about.

Other opportunities opened for the friendly Flynn because he was helpful, even getting his hands dirty by working alongside the men he was talking to. He also taught in the local school when the teacher was away sick.

John Flynn's other great asset was that he had inherited a touch of Irish blarney. He spoke slowly and with a twinkle in his eye, and was always ready to have a laugh. Farmers and timbermen the world over love a yarn, and Flynn soon established himself as a good mate despite never resorting to the coarse language they used. He was amused, though, to find the men sometimes understood one another better if they swore.

"What does one man one vote mean?" a timberman asked about democracy.

"It means each bloody man gets one bloody vote," his mate explained.

"Oh, is that all? Why didn't they say so then?"

If the chance arose, Flynn would yarn quite naturally about God and his goodness, without getting preachy. He held services wherever he was permitted: in homes, camps and public halls. Attendance grew steadily as he became known and liked.

One day a timberman rushed over to him, calling urgently, "Come quickly, please! A man is injured, badly injured." John followed his companion along an overgrown path to a group of men standing at the base of a cliff. Blood dribbling from the corner of the mouth of the injured man and the extreme pains in his chest suggested more serious injuries than Flynn's level of first aid could deal with. "We'll have to get a doctor," he told the group.

"There ain't one hereabouts. Nearest is in Colac."

"We'll have to take him to Colac, then."

Flynn directed the making of a "bush stretcher": two poles laced together with the men's belts and a couple of blankets spread over the top. Gently, very gently, the men carried their mate out of the forest on it. He was then made as comfortable as possible in a buggy and Flynn and a driver set off.

"The road to Colac is real bad," the driver told him, "on account of the rain and the bullock carts turning the mud into slush." This was no exaggeration. Their patient moaned as they slithered and skidded about and several times became bogged. The able-bodied had to use the shovel and their shoulders to heave the buggy free. Once they failed and needed assistance from a team of bullocks.

Flynn winced each time they jolted, feeling for the injured man. The driver noticed his agitation and tried to encourage him, saying "You're doing a great job, young fella, don't you worry about that. I remember hauling a mate with a broken back some years ago. He screamed when we thumped him about. Poor old Jake – he was in a coma before we reached Colac. He passed away soon after."

"It shouldn't be this way," Flynn said, his mouth in a tight line. "No man should have to suffer like that. What is needed is a doctor and clinic up in the forest."

"Management looked at that after Jake's death, but it would have cost too much without government help. They tried offering a doctor facilities for a private practice, but there isn't enough work here to attract anyone. You would need a doctor to see it as a personal mission, I guess."

In Colac, Dr Hope commended Flynn for his level of care and told him the patient should make a complete recovery.

"You look done-in from your efforts," the doctor observed.

"Yes, I am," Flynn replied. "I was wondering if you'd mind if I could stretch out in your surgery for a short rest?"

When the doctor returned a few minutes later, he found Flynn sprawled out, mouth slightly ajar and fast asleep. "He looked like a giant stick insect lying across three of my chairs," Dr Hope recalled later.

On the return journey, Flynn was unusually quiet; he was wrestling with the problem of suffering timbermen. If only the state would help! If only roads were better! If only …

After eighteen months at Beech Forest, Flynn transferred to Buchan in East Gippsland. Buchan was another pioneering community, this time dominated by hills and valleys through which the Snowy River ran in a torrent, fed continuously by the melting snows of the Australian Alps. The terrain was difficult, and so was the life of the settlers, producing poor but proud men.

Flynn used the same approach to the one he had used in the Otways. He made friends, helped where he could, and gave first-aid lectures. He also turned on "magic lantern" shows, using slides he had made at Beech Forest. He experimented with colouring these himself, being one of the first in Australia to do so. The show, entitled "How The Land Was Won", depicted the joys and problems of pioneering life. Soon his Sunday services were well attended too.

Flynn continued to hone his photographic skills in his new posting, producing further slides and another lecturette, "The Snowy River". Some of his photographs were bought and published by the *Australasian*, the *Leader* and the *Weekly Times*, which helped to defray the expense of his costly hobby.

An extraordinary opportunity arose when an excited friend, Frank Moon, burst in on Flynn at his rented cottage. "Flynn, I have just had a most fantastic experience – I want you to photograph it!" (This was an era when even good friends addressed one another using surnames.)

"Moon, I can't go back in time and photograph past experiences," Flynn replied, with a slight smile.

"Well, you can this one, in a way. I blasted into the walls of a limestone canyon a few miles from here and opened up the most incredible cave – I went down into it on a rope with only a candle for light, and found myself in huge caverns packed with stalactites like icicles, and rock curtains and giant pillars. The system is vast – every direction I took showed more branches, each a little different from the others. The dripping of water is the only sound you can hear down there. I want to return properly prepared, with more rope and lanterns. Come with me and take some photographs. These caves could make a big difference to the whole region."

"How is that?"

"Tourism. This is a poor area, but those caves are a wonder. They'll attract thousands of tourists every year."

John Flynn photographed the phenomenon using strong flashlights. The results were dramatic and gained wide publicity for the Buchan Caves. Getting to the attraction was difficult for tourists, though, and Flynn joined the Railway League, the goal of which was to lobby the government to build a railway line to Buchan. In this capacity, he was invited to a meeting with Sir Thomas Bent, the Victorian Premier. Flynn surprised himself by being totally at ease with the Premier, chatting about life in the bush. He then displayed his photographs of the caves and described their potential for tourism. Impressed, Sir Thomas subsequently oversaw the protection of the caves by law, and officially sanctioned Frank Moon to continue his exploration and mapping of them. As Moon had predicted, the Buchan Caves were destined to become a great tourist magnet and money-spinner for the region.

Private study while a home missionary had enabled Flynn to pass his preliminary examinations, opening the road to studying for the ministry at Ormond College, University of Melbourne.

It was with mixed feelings that he packed his few belongings, said his farewells to his rough-and-ready parishioners and set off for a student's life in the city.

4

THE MYSTERY OF THE CALL

Flynn began his official training for the Presbyterian ministry in 1907. At 26, he was somewhat older when he started than others on the same course.

Although bright enough, he struggled with the studies he had looked forward to for so long. The syllabus was very theoretical. While he pored over Greek and Hebrew, his mind kept straying back to the pioneers of Beech Forest and Buchan.

Flynn would have abandoned his course had he not found outlets for his restless energy and the compassion that drove him. He threw himself into helping young people on the streets of Melbourne, particularly in the inner suburb of Montague to which he had been seconded as a home missionary.

The lack of enterprise Flynn encountered among the youth concerned him. He organised various outings and practical activities for them, which they appeared to enjoy, but without him there the youngsters did little. Was there something they could do on their own, something interesting and healthy? He hit on the idea of acquiring a boat, though he knew nothing about boating, and decided to put the proposition to the manager of a shipping company, a dour Presbyterian. Friends had warned Flynn that the man had a bad temper and that he would be wasting his time.

Flynn approached the manager with some trepidation, but found him keen to help. In fact, he gave Flynn a fine boat. The trainee minister had learned a valuable lesson, that unlikely people might be willing to help if they saw that an enterprise was worthwhile. Soon the youngsters, with and without Flynn, were rowing up and down the Yarra River and its tributaries.

Flynn by now had begun to miss lectures, attending only the minimum required to sit the examinations. Meanwhile, he had developed a good relationship with the Director of Home Mission for Victoria, the Reverend Donald Cameron. This kindly man set about helping Flynn, recognising his potential and not wanting him to be lost to the Presbyterian ministry.

When Flynn became depressed about his inability to study, Cameron would divert him into talking about possible strategies for mission work in pioneering communities; he even organised promotional talks for him to give about home missions. At these, Flynn gave his magic lantern presentations of "How The Land Was Won"or "The Snowy River".

In time, Flynn saw the wisdom of Donald Cameron's strategy: it was to give a vision for the future so that he could see his studies for what they were – a means to an end and not an end in themselves. He now set about his academic work with more determination, though with no more enthusiasm than before.

At the end of the year he awaited his examination results with great anxiety. He thought he had failed, but felt he might have just passed. The latter was the case, but only by the slimmest of margins.

His second year at university was no better than the first; in fact, it was worse. Flynn decided to take two years to complete that second year, and two years of academic misery and frustration they turned out to be. He was torn now by inner conflict and indecision – his future ministry hung by the slenderest of threads. He wrote to a friend, Esther Mahood:"I spent a long, weary time and tasted a deal of bitterness one way and another."

As he began his third year, another question began to trouble him. Supposing he did pass, what part could he play in the Church? His father wanted him to take a parish and the dutiful son wanted to please him. Yet the more he saw of parish work, the less fitted to it he felt.

Perhaps he was more suited to missionary work than taking a parish in Australia? The Presbyterian Church had a mission in Korea that was desperately short of ministers. An appeal was made at the Theological Hall, and finding that everyone else hesitated, Flynn reluctantly agreed to go once he had finished his training "if you are still short of volunteers". Even as he agreed, he felt it to be the wrong decision, a discomfort which grew as the months slipped by.

"If not Korea, what then, God? Please guide me!" he called out in prayer. His cry began to be answered in 1909 when Donald Cameron passed on to him a letter sent by a Mrs Jessie Litchfield to the church newspaper, *The Messenger*.

As Flynn read, something stirred deep within him. Addressed to Mrs Kelly, wife of the editor of *The Messenger*, the letter was as follows.

West Arm, Port Darwin, 3/6/1909.

Dear Mrs Kelly,

I expect you will be surprised at this letter from a total stranger, but I was, before my marriage, a member of the Richmond Presbyterian Church. I am writing now some news of this lonely land.

I am eighty miles from a town by land, twenty by sea, three miles from the nearest white woman, two miles from the nearest white man. Chinese and blacks are my nearest neighbours ... There is a Catholic Priest, a Church of England clergyman, and lay preachers at the Methodist Church [all in Darwin vicinity] − There are no other ministers in the Northern Territory − just 500 000 square miles of country with 1500 whites, 2000 Chinese and 5000 blacks living there.

Of the whites, fully 500 of the men keep lubras [black women] or use them as they want them, and nearly all have half-caste illegitimate children whose only future in life is prostitution. There are not 50 Chinese without lubras. There is no law against this evil and there are no missionaries to teach the people right from wrong ... I know that drink, drugs and lubras are responsible for nine out of ten hospital cases, and also for seven deaths out of ten.

Why cannot the Presbyterian Church send up a missionary to the Northern Territory; an earnest, enthusiastic married man (he is better married than single), give him one hundred pounds for living expenses, a certain sum for travelling expenses, and let him make his headquarters in Darwin and have regular periods for visiting the outer places of the NT? He would do good, if he were a man who put Christ first, who worked for the good of others, and spared neither time nor money nor labour in the cause of Christ.

You may be shocked by this letter, but I have understated rather than overstated the facts.

Yours faithfully,
Jessie Litchfield

The challenge of this letter kept returning to John Flynn as he tried to study. He simply could not get it out of his thoughts for very long. Within days, his mind was made up. He wrote to his father, telling him he had decided against going to Korea – instead, he hoped to go to the Inland of Australia.

Flynn felt a strange peace after writing the letter, which he interpreted as having found the direction in which God wanted him to go. How to go about it would be his next big decision: no mission he knew of worked in the Outback. Even the federal government treated the Northern Territory as if it were a part of another nation. In fact, until recently, it had been administered through the Department of External Affairs. Neither the churches nor the government appeared to have much use for the Inland. What, then, should be his next move?

He wrote to Mrs Litchfield to learn more and they became friends by mail. Her husband was a prospector, he discovered, and she had followed him out to remote Anson Bay where he was prospecting for coal. The conditions of Mrs Litchfield's life there jolted Flynn: she lived in a bark hut with white shells for a floor and a roof strapped to two apple trees. The Aborigines in that area were hostile, so she was given a heavy German revolver as a birthday present which she carried with her outside the house. She also slept with it, fully loaded, under her pillow.

Deeply interested in bush life, Flynn hungered to know more. He read much, gathered maps, spoke to people. He had always known that Australia was like a large picture: the frame was in green, representing the fertile, inhabited fringes of the continent; but the centre was blank and red, representing the huge dry Inland – often referred to as the "Outback". Of course, there was much beauty and grandeur there, but it was a generally dry and inhospitable place – a vast area of rocky plains, contorted and eroded mountains, saltpans, sandy wastes and dust-bowls. Outside of Port Darwin, this enormous area did not have one permanent minister. Its residents were scattered and lines of communication were difficult, but it contained about fifty thousand people who thought that the churches had forgotten them, or perhaps didn't care.

A man of action, John Flynn burned to do something there and then about this situation and not wait until he had qualified. What should he try?

His research uncovered tales of great loneliness, of men who lived months, even years, without seeing another living soul and with only a dog or horse as a companion. One man's body, Flynn heard, was found in an old slab hut many months after his death, from what cause no one could say. On top of his body was the dehydrated corpse of his faithful dog. There were other tales of men doing strange things to relieve loneliness: lighting huge bonfires; firing guns into the air at random; playing a dangerous "hide-and-seek" with hostile Aborigines. Some men went beyond being "bush happy" and became insane, others committed suicide. Solitude did not affect everyone so drastically, of course, but all Inlanders needed support and human contact.

Flynn learned that the infrequent arrival of the mail, often delivered by a camel-man "postie", was a big event in the Outback and that letters and books were read many times. This triggered a new idea, a "Mail-bag League" to try to combat this isolation: city folk would write to Inlanders on a sort of "pen pal" basis and send them books and magazines.

First, he enlisted the help of friends, including his sister Rosetta who wrote a regular column in *The Messenger*. Then he promoted the idea in magazine articles, in speeches and at the conclusion of any magic lantern shows that he gave. "Books, that's what we need – bright books to brighten up the bush," he said. Next, he began collecting addresses of anyone who would participate.

Enthusiasm grew – and so did the demands on his time and meagre finances. Flynn was relieved when, a year later, the Presbyterian Women's Missionary Union undertook responsibility for the Mail-bag League from May 1910. By that time, it was bringing cheer to hundreds of Outbackers. Flynn continued to promote the work, but left the routine packaging of books and writing letters to others.

He had fired a tiny salvo against the vast problems of the Inland. All the while his fertile mind had been planning. He and Dr Cameron had spent hours agonising over the needs of itinerant shearers, men who worked up and down Australia but never stayed very long at any one location. How could the Church help those who were always on the move? Flynn had suggested a variety of strategies: "I'll go to them, on a roving mission. They always complain that the Church is after their money, so I won't take up collections, I'll give them free lectures in first aid instead."

The Reverend Cameron convinced the Home Missions Committee they should give Flynn's ideas a trial and the enthusiastic young man set out to tour the shearing sheds of Victoria and South Australia during his long vacation. He was well received wherever he went. The shearers attended his talks on Christianity, his first-aid lectures and his magic lantern presentations. Flynn, in turn, listened intently to their stories about their lives and lifestyles, thinking of new ways to help them.

It was during this mission, in November 1909, that he met the jovial, thickset Reverend Andrew Barber, who was to become a lifelong friend. Barber invited Flynn to stay with him at the manse in Hamilton. The two had much in common: Barber came from farming stock and shared Flynn's intense interest in the plight of the pioneers.

One morning a man called at the manse and handed Flynn a box filled with tracts "to give to the shearers after you have talked with them". Flynn thanked him for his thoughtfulness and he and Barber began looking through the publications to assess their suitability.

"It's just no good," Flynn concluded. "These tracts were written for the city, and mainly for those who have some knowledge of Church terminology. Listen to this one: 'Since inviting Jesus into my heart, he has become more and more precious to me.' The average shearer I have met would say, 'What's that all about, mate?' He might even spit on the ground and walk away in disgust. It's a good idea to leave something with the shearers – our friend has given us these with the best of intentions, but I can't use them."

Later, Barber brought the subject up again. "I still think we should be leaving printed material with the shearers."

"Yes, I think so too," said Flynn. "Take the story a shearer told me. He and some others had to bury a mate in the bush. They stood around the grave and looked at one another, not knowing what to say. Then one of them broke into 'Auld Lang Syne' and the others joined in. When that was finished, they sang 'For He's A Jolly Good Fellow' while they shovelled in the dirt. The shearer told me they had all felt uncomfortable and would have preferred to have done a 'proper burial'. It sounds macabre, but a simple burial service in written form would be useful for people in the bush.

"I've got another idea! A number of men have asked me to put my first-aid lectures in a booklet so they can refer back to them in time of need. It seems to me that instead of tracts, we should produce a small practical handbook for Outbackers to carry about with them in their swags or saddlebags."

"Your Mail-bag League could be advertised in it too," enthused Barber, "although 'bushies' often lose track of the days and miss the post."

"We could put in a calendar for them to tick off the days and so keep track of time."

"Financial advice would help too, like how to keep a cash account and even how to make and lodge a will."

"Like all men, they need spiritual help. Nothing too pious, though. Perhaps a few relevant Bible verses, prayers and some favourite hymns."

The two friends discussed the possibilities for hours. Back at the university, Flynn spent many more planning his "handbook for the bush", which he tentatively entitled *The Bushman's Companion*. He sought the advice of doctors, solicitors, ministers and the Inlanders themselves as to its contents.

Flynn needed an introduction that would forge a link between himself and the pioneers. One thing they had in common was a fascination with the bush, so he began to plan phrases that would capitalise on this bond: "It is not necessary to have met face to face to feel a sense of comradeship. We have a mutual love of the bush, and along with that, perhaps, a certain dread of it ..."

Was *The Bushman's Companion* a worthwhile concept? One letter in particular convinced Flynn he should see the project through: it was from Robert Mitchell, the man who had pioneered the first and only itinerant ministry to Inlanders, the "Smith of Dunesk" mission.

> I think the idea of *The Bushman's Companion* is admirable. Most of the burials here are conducted by laymen, sometimes without any service. Not long ago, I had a letter from a man asking me in what part of the Bible he could find the burial service ...

"Right, I've got to finish the handbook," Flynn decided as he put Mitchell's letter aside, "but it's taking much longer than I thought, especially the rewriting and editing. It's keeping me away from my studies. I'm heading for certain failure this time."

Writing in the third person, Flynn described how he resolved this dilemma.

> He had heard of the man who, faced with the conflict between golf and business, solved it by giving up business. So he completed writing the book during the first week of what the students called "Stew Vac" [because they were "stewing" over their studies for the impending examinations], and, during the second week, he supervised the printing ...

Though almost penniless, Flynn determined to print the book himself so that it could be given away free. He raised money through donations from friends, public lecturing and appeals his sister wrote in *The Messenger*.

The Bushman's Companion appeared at last in September 1910. An attractive little book, pocket-sized and with a durable blue linen cover, it contained 111 pages of potential benefit to all who lived in the bush. In October, Flynn put it to the test by distributing 2 000 copies to shearers. He reported gleefully that the little book "caused very serious perplexity amongst the shearers" as they were often asked to make contributions of money to various causes, but "this representative of the Presbyterian Church took no collections, and presented each shearer with a little handbook obviously worth at least twice the average individual amount dropped into a collection plate". Letters of appreciation poured in.

Many people helped with the distribution of the book. Some "bushies" carried numerous copies with them and handed them out to swaggies, miners, prospectors, stockmen and settlers of the Outback. At least one Darwin policeman also did this in the remotest corners of the Northern Territory. Other copies were sent out by mail. In these and other ways, the first printing of 6 000 was soon used up and another run of 4 000 followed.

The Bushman's Companion was Flynn's second salvo fired at a distance against the problems of the Outback. Events were moving, though, towards the launching of a direct attack.

The previous year Flynn had met a most unusual man, Reverend E. E. Baldwin, whose style of ministry deeply interested him. Baldwin was the Smith of Dunesk missionary operating out of Beltana, 353 miles north of Adelaide. The mission was named after Henrietta Smith of Dunesk, Scotland. It had operated out of Beltana for 15 years already, giving ministry to pioneers in the Outback. Baldwin explained to Flynn that he spent little time in Beltana itself, returning only to replenish supplies. Mainly he was "out bush", covering a vast area of the Outback, bigger than Flynn's home state of Victoria. Here he would spend time with anyone he met.

Sensing Flynn's empathy with the work, Baldwin said, "I am close to retirement and need someone to replace me in 1911, by which time you will have qualified."

"There is no certainty that I shall ever qualify," Flynn rejoined, with a wry smile.

Baldwin actively pursued Flynn as his successor in a series of letters written from Beltana.

> The ideal Smith of Dunesk man is long, thin, speaks slowly, and is very droll. In all these respects you should make a worthy successor ... He also dabbles in photography, and possesses a magic lantern. Here again you would fill the bill ... The more I think of it, the more convinced I am that the vacancy here is being created for you to fill.

Beltana, in the Flinders Ranges, was as close to the heart of Australia as Flynn was likely to get at that time. Nevertheless, he hesitated. His desire was to minister to the whole vast Inland, not that tiny fraction that could be reached by horse from Beltana. As he questioned Baldwin more closely, though, he uncovered some exciting possibilities – official limits had never been drawn for the Smith of Dunesk field! "In theory," he wrote to his father, "I suppose the field includes Port Darwin." Perhaps he could use the auspices of the Smith of Dunesk appointment to investigate the Inland as a whole?

He also read what he could find about the mission. A previous missionary, Frank Rolland, was discouraging. He had written in *The Banner*: "The odds against religion in this district are so heavy that unless God works miracles as great as making deaf men hear and dead men live, this mission to the Far North is hopeless and ridiculous."

Thomas Flynn also tried to discourage his son from taking up the "impossible" position at Beltana. He wrote to him:

> I want you to know that you have a chance of assistant at North Melbourne and hope you may get the position. As to going up to the Centre of Australia and hiding yourself there for two years, I hope that won't come off. What is your sister to do? And what would become of you if you took ill? In that new country, a young fellow unused to the climate and life would be almost certain to take the typhoid fever as hundreds did in the west. Let someone else take the mission – a man of more years than yourself ... You could only get a setback of two years and get into rough ways and out of touch with the world.

John Flynn did not want to disappoint his father, but knew that he had to go to the Outback, to which God's mysterious magnetism was attracting him. Otherwise, he felt, his life would never amount to anything. He wrote in reply:

> As to the future, God only knows what it holds in store for us. My going to the bush must seem to you inconsiderate, and I shrink from it terribly at times. But I dare not turn back ... thank you for all the love and care of the long years now behind ... let me take this opportunity of heartily thanking you for your pains and sacrifices on our behalf.

This was not to say that Flynn relished the challenges that lay ahead. He also wrote to his father: "Sometimes I wish I could turn my back on it all and just be an ordinary parson in a little Victorian town ..." He was already a driven man, though, and "ordinary" would never be an adjective that could be linked to him.

The month before his final examinations began Flynn committed himself, providing he passed, to a two-year posting to the Smith of Dunesk mission at Beltana. But he was already dreaming and planning ahead, beyond that tiny place to the Inland proper. He discussed his plans with his sister. "Zetta, what would the Presbyterian Church need before it started a mission to the thousands of pioneers in the 'Never Never'?"

"I don't know. I've never thought about it."

"They would need to have some facts and figures about the people and the conditions out there. They would need to know what they were up against, to be able to plan strategies. In short, a survey is needed. Baldwin agrees with me on this, and so does Cameron."

"A survey like that would take ages and cost a great deal. Surely you are not wanting to do it yourself?"

"I could shorten the time required by collecting information while I'm at Beltana. That wouldn't be enough in itself; an official survey would still be needed later on."

"Where would you find the money for that? I suppose you want me to launch another appeal for you, through my column in *The Messenger*?"

"I confess the idea had crossed my mind."

"John, I have just finished raising money for *The Bushman's Companion*. I don't think the readers will welcome another appeal from you so soon."

"Zetta, the appeal doesn't have to come from me – it is from the Inland and from the caring Church."

"I don't catch your drift."

"Anyone can write letters to *The Messenger*. You could write yourself and get your friends to as well. Once the public gets behind the scheme it'll develop its own momentum."

"What will the letters be about?"

"About conditions in the Outback and the need for a survey. That 'Quarter-mile of Pennies' concept you used to raise money for hospitals in Korea worked well. How about a 'Quarter-mile of

Threepenny Pieces' appeal? That would raise almost £350, which is what I estimate the survey will cost."

"I can see you have been doing your homework!"

Rosetta was persuaded to agree to the scheme. The letter writing was left to friends who acted as "agitators". Gradually the tactic worked, and support slowly mounted.

By the very slimmest of margins, and to everyone's relief, Flynn passed his final examinations. "They let down the sliprails for me to slide through" was how he described his achievement.

John Flynn was ordained at the Presbyterian Church in Flinders Street, Adelaide, in January 1911. He was now 30 years of age. A few days later, he and Reverend Baldwin stepped onto a northbound train. A strange exhilaration gripped him while on that train. At last he was steaming towards the vast heartland of Australia, which had been drawing him powerfully with its mysterious call. What would he find? Whatever happened, it was going to be an adventure.

5

FINDING A WAY

>This country is peculiar to a Victorian. No grass for 50 miles
>to the south and none to the north ... All around here is rubble
>on the surface and all over is undulating ... The manse is a
>stone cottage ... Mr Baldwin, my predecessor, came up with
>me and will show me over as much as we can cover in four
>days ... I did not come for an easy billet and will not find it.

So Flynn wrote to his father on arrival at Beltana. He found that
the stone manse was gloomy, dirty and dusty. It had air holes in place
of windows, and loose planks on the compacted dirt formed its
entrance. The wooden beams and timber crates used as furniture had
been attacked by white ants.

Noticing Flynn's surprise, Baldwin said by way of consolation,
"The manse is rough and ready, but no matter. You will spend little
time in it, and when you do return it will appear rather grand
compared to some places you will have slept in. Come, I want to
show you something in which you will spend far more time than the
house."

He took Flynn to a shed in which was housed a hooded buggy,
which had been used continuously since 1894 when Robert
Mitchell had started the mission.

"Mitchell travelled 3 000 miles a year in that buggy and another
3 000 by horse or rail. He tried to visit everyone within range at least
once a year. Frank Rolland and I have copied his method although
we have found his standards impossible. On many trips he took along
his daughter, Agnes, who played the old organ he carted with him."

"An organ! How did he fit that in?" asked Flynn in surprise.

"He would lash bags all over the sides of the buggy until it looked
like a loaded camel, so I'm told. That organ of his was a great
drawcard and he would not leave it behind. Most bushmen love

music and would ride in from camps miles away just to hear that girl play. Do you play an instrument, or sing?"

"No. Well, I sing, but that would disperse a crowd, not draw them in."

"No matter. The bush will hear that you have a magic lantern and that you give away books. Take your first-aid kit and a pair of forceps with you, to pull teeth with. I taught myself to pull teeth after watching men in a camp using a pair of fencing pliers to yank them out. I figured anything I could do instead would be an improvement."

"The men out here are pretty tough, I take it?"

"Those who stay out here are, most of them. Then again, some have come here to escape from cities, or want to live alone, so you get a variety of types."

Once Baldwin had returned to the city, Flynn planned his first trip. He would travel north for 250 miles to Oodnadatta, where the railway line ended. Supplies from there into the "Red Centre" of Australia were carried by camel teams.

First he stocked up at the general store. It was choked with goods for every local need: cooking utensils, clothing, tools and other items danced above his head on ropes where they had been strung up to conserve space. Here he met the storekeeper and a younger man, William Coultas, who was to become a good friend. They had a long yarn before Flynn got down to the business of purchasing.

Flynn was gratified at the warm welcome he encountered wherever he went. "Glad to meet you, Padre. We old bushmen have very kind thoughts towards Mr Mitchell and Mr Rolland, and also Mr Baldwin, who has just left. Pull off your packs and come and have a cup of tea." "Lesson number one," Flynn thought to himself. "Any mission I plan for the Inland must be started by padres who are liked and respected. Then those who follow, and the message they bear, will be given easy passage."

Although he had not intended holding services during his exploratory journeys, Flynn was sometimes invited to do so. At Leigh Creek, miners swept the fine red dust, which crept in under the doors, through keyholes and between window frames, off their mess-room floor. A fair number gathered there to hear "what the new parson is about". Flynn spoke on mateship, the importance of having a friend you could depend upon in the bush, and how millions of men had found that Jesus Christ provided this kind of mateship. While he was talking, he noticed an emaciated-looking man with a scraggly beard standing at the back. This man made a series of facetious comments until two others rounded on him and told him to shut up, whereupon the bearded one left.

At the end of the service, one of the men spoke to Flynn. "Sorry about Alf Davis disturbing you there, Padre. He has an opium problem, poor blighter. Buys it from an Afghan teamster, or so we think. It's killing him, that and the booze. He works out at Fabian Mine and is a good worker until he gets paid."

Flynn felt a sweep of compassion for Alf Davis. What could he do to help? He wondered whether he would ever see him again. Lack of continuity was always going to be a problem in an itinerant ministry, but would the population around Leigh Creek ever warrant a resident minister?

He pondered the situation again as he rode along next day. Back in the cities it was said that "the Inland will one day be the granary of Australia", but the gibber plains covered with millions of angular rocks looked more like a moonscape than a serious proposition for growing crops. Probably the Outback would always remain thinly populated. How, then, could the Church best help men like Alf Davis?

Flynn was still thinking about this when he pulled up under a patch of desert oaks to allow his horses to "have a blow" in a pool of shade. He drew a little thermometer out of his pocket and tested the shade temperature: it was 119 degrees Fahrenheit.

A stockman riding nearby came over to chat in the friendly fashion of the wide-open spaces. He was a thin man with a very sunburnt, lined face. One glance at Flynn's three-piece suit, watch and gold chain dangling from a pocket and he said, "You must be Reverend Flynn. I heard on the mulga wire you would be on the road. My name's Bluey Johnson. Cripes, you must be hot in that get-up!"

"Pleased to meet you, Mr Johnson. Yes, I am hot, but it is worse for my horses, I fear." Flynn did not dress smartly in the bush because he wanted to be recognised easily: he did it because the Bible described ministers as ambassadors of God's Kingdom. In his view, ambassadors should be smartly dressed.

Bluey Johnson's face crinkled up in mild surprise as he studied Flynn's horses. "Your horses may be hot, but they look in fine condition to me," he commented. Flynn was pleased by this comment. He knew that pioneers judged a man first of all by his horses, so he combed Robin and Dodger each morning before setting out. Pioneers told scathing jokes about "the parson's horse", which was another reason he took special care of Robin and Dodger.

After some small talk, Flynn began asking searching questions. "Before I came here, I was told the Inland could be a grain belt one day. What do you think of that idea?"

"Not much, to tell you the honest truth. The soils are not good enough. Most of the water underneath the ground has soda and salt in it, but even with sweet water the soils are too light or too rocky for good farming. It's not even dependable for livestock. When I first came out, I worked on Beltana Station, but it was overstocked and the ground feed was stripped. It didn't recover. This past seven years it has lain idle, seven hundred square miles of it, with no stock on it." Bluey twisted on his horse and waved his arm expansively towards their immediate vicinity. "A good saltbush area like this one can carry only thirty sheep to the square mile, but we Australians are used to runs near the coast which carry hundreds per square mile — so we put too many sheep on."

"What is the future of the Outback, then? Will there be cities one day?"

"Unless they find diamonds or gold or something, it will stay much the same as the years go by. At least, I think so. You see, drought is another thing, it comes here regular as clockwork. We have a few good seasons, managers forget drought will come, and they put too many beasts onto the land. The droughts here can be terrible, Mr Flynn. In truth, I find it hard to believe in a loving God while I watch stock dying from lack of rain."

"God didn't put stock here, Mr Johnson. Man did that, and put too many, as you have just told me. God put 'roos here. This land is fine for 'roos."

This conversation left Flynn with much to think about as he continued towards Oodnadatta. If the stockman was correct, cities would not develop here, and Church buildings would be few. How, then, could the benefits of Church life be extended to the pioneers?

There was one person Flynn particularly wanted to meet on his travels. In Oodnadatta lived someone described to him by Robert Mitchell as "a tiny but dynamic lady of great talent. She is a deaconess, triple certificated nurse, 'dentist', dispenser, Sunday school teacher, counsellor and preacher. The pioneers call her the 'little White Angel of the North'. To me, she is a heroine." These glowing terms referred to Sister Latto Bett, who served as a nurse in the Smith of Dunesk Mission.

Flynn saw little of Sister Bett during his first visit to Oodnadatta, because she was too busy. Without a clinic from which to operate, she nursed people in their own homes. She also went up and down the railway line so patients could visit her at stopping points. In one emergency, she had ridden eight hours on a springless railway trolley, ramrod-straight with no support for her back, in full uniform, under a blazing sun.

"Is your biggest need not for a hospital?" Flynn asked her, when they finally had the opportunity to talk.

"Yes, definitely. Did you know that my predecessor, Nurse Main, began to collect money to build a hospital? She collected over £200, but I have not had time to continue fundraising."

Flynn was alerted by this information. He felt on the verge of an important concept. Should he build a hospital at Oodnadatta? Should a missionary be involved in building hospitals rather than churches?

Next day, he wandered the streets of the town, chatting to everyone he could, asking them about the need for a hospital. The first man he spoke to offered to show Flynn the spot near the railway line to which a man with a crippled spine had dragged himself. It had taken him two days of torture to get there, but he knew he must catch the fortnightly train to Adelaide to get help. As the train approached he arched his injured back enough to wave desperately, hoping to catch someone's attention. A passenger saw him and waved back in greeting and the train went steadily past. "But they found him in time," Flynn was told. "The man was very lucky. His waterbag was bone dry, his tuckerbag was full of ants. It took a year in hospital in Adelaide to get him right again."

Other tales of suffering convinced John Flynn how badly Oodnadatta needed a hospital. That evening Sister Bett found him in an excited state. He explained, "I have been floating in a sea of half-formed ideas since arriving in Beltana, waiting for some mysterious impulse to direct me one way or another. I like to operate like that. This afternoon it happened, now I can see all the threads coming together."

"What are you talking about, Mr Flynn?"

"Look at it this way. It has been easy for me to follow in the steps of Mitchell, Rolland and Baldwin, because they are so respected. Men are fickle, though. What if the next few missionaries were to make a mess of things? That could make it very hard for those who follow. We need Christianity to become associated with some great work rather than with mere men. We need a permanent monument to Christianity, a visible monument, one that bush people will appreciate and talk about, one that they will come to."

"Do you mean a cathedral?"

"No. A cathedral would be a white elephant, at least until the men understand more about God's Kingdom. The day may come when one would be appropriate, and a non-denominational one at that, but such a day is far off."

"What monument do you mean, then?"

"This morning a man told me how he and a friend trotted four hundred miles to Oodnadatta carrying a sick friend in a camp sheet slung between the two horses. Imagine the effort that required, and despite it all their friend still died. I doubt if the same two men would ride four miles to attend a church, let alone four hundred. They would have taken their friend four hundred miles to a Christian hospital, though, and they would have blessed us for it. Pioneers like those men would respect a Christian hospital and the work done there more than a church building."

"I can see that they would come to a Christian hospital, but can a hospital do the job of a church?"

"Yes, by showing the Outbackers that we care enough to build it. It will become associated with Christianity in their minds, that visible monument I was speaking about. We could also make it much more than a centre of healing for their bodies. You already teach Sunday school. You could hold those classes at the hospital, for example. Do you see what I am getting at?"

"I think I do. We could have a small library and hold social events like musical evenings. It could slowly become a kind of community centre in which Christian care and ministry would take place."

"That's it! Not just a hospital, but a Christian community centre, supplying health for the body, education for the mind, love for the lonely soul and Christianity for the spirit. We'll call it a 'nursing home' rather than a hospital, because it needs to be seen as a place of caring for the whole person, not for the body alone."

"It will take a lot of money, Mr Flynn."

Flynn's blue-grey eyes became distant and dreamy. After a pause, he said, "One of my favourite verses of Scripture is that 'Faith is the substance of things hoped for, the certainty of things not yet seen'. Therefore, the hospital will happen, providing I play my part. Something in me tells me it will."

On his return to Beltana in high spirits, Flynn unfolded his plan to William Coultas.

"Already his vision had expanded," Coultas recalled. "He was planning an ambulance, either motorised or buggy, to ferry patients from outlying areas to the hospital at Oodnadatta. While he spoke, it all seemed possible. He had a way of making you want to help him. I became one of his supporters."

How could Flynn raise the considerable funds needed to make his vision a reality? He wrote immediately to Rosetta and her friends to mobilise them to canvass for money for the hospital. As he patrolled his huge parish, waiting impatiently for the response, he noticed all around him signs of death. Graves of men, women, children and babies were everywhere: rain-flattened, wind-scoured mounds under desert oak, gum and coolabah, alongside dry creek beds and by billabongs. Invariably he would climb down from his horse or buggy to look at them, pace around them and think. Often he was gripped by such intense compassion that tears ran down his cheeks. He found this reaction bewildering – and embarrassing.

It was the same when the police sergeant, returning from a patrol, showed Flynn a pitiable photograph. All he could see at first was a pile of rags. Peering into a rent in one of the rags, he discerned the bare thighbone of a man. His tragic story? No one knew. Flynn had to turn aside to hide his emotions.

While he waited for funds, Flynn drew maps of Central Australia in the sand of his camps, locating where people lived, brooding over the long distances and rugged country that separated them. What could be done to help them? As the weeks passed, his ideas hardened into a definite strategy:

> If we can establish a successful hospital at Oodnadatta, we may, in time, be able to extend that model throughout the Inland. I estimate that such cottage hospitals should be no further than 300 miles apart, and even that will be too far in many cases.

The whole concept was all the more incredible considering he had yet to build his first hospital.

Back in Beltana, Flynn contacted his sister and asked her to redouble her efforts to raise funds. By now he was so convinced the money would come that he sat down and drew up plans for the projected building, incorporating ideas discussed with Sister Bett.

When it came, Rosetta's reply was not encouraging – money had only been trickling in. Flynn's faith was not shaken. He remained certain the funds would arrive from somewhere.

And an anonymous gift of £400 for the nursing home did come "out of the blue"! An enormous sum of money in those days, it was enough for Flynn to go ahead and erect the hospital.

First he took his rough plans to Port Augusta and Adelaide, to have them professionally drawn up. Flynn watched like a hawk, keen to learn as much as he could: he wanted to be able to draw up proper plans for other cottage hospitals himself later on.

Should he try to build the first himself? Materials were short and would have to be transported in by rail. In the end, he decided the most prudent course would be to employ the well-known Tom Trottman of Port Augusta to assemble the whole building at the coast; it could then be transported to Oodnadatta for erection.

During construction, Flynn acted as "clerk of works", learning much. In addition, he put to use skills that he had observed at Buchan in order to build a selection of useful furnishings for the hospital: a table, cupboard, wardrobe, bookcase, wash-stand and towel rack. (He considered them to be a temporary measure, but they were still in service 30 years later.)

Sister Bett was delighted with the nursing home. She told Flynn, "It is the smartest building in the area, and pioneers and friends from the cities are sending in gifts to make it cosy. Yesterday, three separate parcels were left at the door: one contained blankets, another some curtains and the third two lamps. The locals are taking our hospital to their hearts."

"Good," replied Flynn. "I've arranged for a plentiful supply of water and some seeds," he went on. "I'm hoping you can start a garden, even a lawn, to show the locals that such things are possible even in the Outback."

"What a wonderful idea! The shabbiness of the buildings and yards here was one of the first things to catch my attention when I came. Inlanders appear to take no pride in their surroundings."

"It's because most say they intend to leave next year or there-abouts," Flynn explained. "There is no feeling of permanence here. We must work to change these attitudes. Once people know medical help is here to stay, more women will be prepared to come out here to live. The women will take more pride in their homes and sur-roundings than the men do, and a social revolution will have begun!"

Sister Bett laughed. "Mr Flynn, you are a great dreamer," she said, then softened her statement by adding, "but I hope that your dreams come true."

A tall, slightly stooped man toured the nursing home with Flynn on 9 December 1911, the day before the official opening. He was Robert Mitchell, the famous pioneer missionary of the region, now in his sixties. Tears came to his eyes when he inspected what had been accomplished. He saw a fine ward, tiled for easy cleaning, with crisp, white linen on the six beds. He marvelled at the well-stocked dispensary, and admired the sitting room, bathroom, bedroom, kit-chen, scullery, wash-house, and outside "isolation tent" for patients with infectious diseases. A wide verandah surrounded the building and patches of green were already to be seen in the garden.

"This hospital is a beacon of hope, a silent ambassador for Christ in this community," was Mitchell's emotional verdict. The visitor was guest of honour at the official opening of 'Rolland House' the following evening. Some of the invited guests had travelled great distances from the cities to attend the ceremony. Nearly every local resident was there too.

As 8 p.m. approached, the weather became sweltering and ominous. Huge black clouds rolled over and the temperature built up to 110 degrees Fahrenheit despite the lateness of the hour. Everything around became silent in anticipation. Then gusty winds arrived, whipping up dust clouds. Lightning began, great sheets and forks of it, continually illuminating the scene, and compensating in part for the failure of the electric lights.

There was excitement among the crowd. Could this mean the breaking of the drought, or was it just another "dry storm" of wind and dust? Some drops fell, big fat ones sounding like hail on the tin roof. An involuntary cheer went up from sections of the gathering. Everyone hurried to cram together under the generous verandah as the rain began to pelt down in earnest.

At precisely 8 p.m. Robert Mitchell, spasmodically illuminated by the continuing flashes as if in a heavenly spotlight, took the key from John Flynn. He opened the front door, then turned to address the applauding crowd, shouting to make himself heard above the din of the storm. Fortunately, he had a deep, booming voice.

"In the name of Jesus of Nazareth, the great healer and redeemer of man, and in the name of the Presbyterian Church of South Australia, I declare this medical hostel open … This building is dedicated to suffering humanity and to Him who took our infirmities and bore our sicknesses.

"Nurse Bett is Sister-in-Charge of the hostel. Here she will do her best for all who seek her services … without preference for nationality or creed. Her business is not to tamper with the beliefs of her patients, but to surround them with a womanly Christian influence."

Some others gave short speeches while the wind drove showers into the verandah, soaking the crowd. The rain was warm and welcome. Flynn heard one old bushman say, "This is God's way of giving Sister Bett sweet water for her tea, filling those thousand-gallon rainwater tanks for her. He don't want his angel drinking our bore water because it contains too much soda!"

To have built a hospital within his first year as a missionary was an astonishing achievement for anyone. During this period Flynn was already dreaming beyond Oodnadatta to greater challenges in the scorching desert wastelands.

As he explained to William. Coultas, "Lack of maps is a major stumbling block to my plans. I rode out to Tarcoola recently and all I had to go on was a rough map that a prospector had drawn for me with a stick. I became unsure whether I was still heading in the right direction, but I saw no other white man in five days. If I'd lost my way, I might have perished from thirst."

"It's the same everywhere in the 'Never Never'," said Coultas. "There are no reliable maps. What can you do about it?"

"Nothing in the short term, but I'm collecting data everywhere I go. I hope to make maps for the Inland myself one day, because I can't imagine anyone else doing it."

"Besides having no maps, what else is a major problem?" asked his friend.

"The great distances a missionary will have to travel. I need to take a long trip on a camel, to find out how good they are. I must also experience sandy desert, not just the stony type."

"You want camels and sand? I'll set those up for you. There are plenty of both around here."

Coultas introduced Flynn to a water conservation officer, who invited him to come on a patrol. Flynn subsequently spent seven days on a camel, and was not impressed. He found them cantankerous beasts, and frustrating because they travelled so slowly, averaging only four or five miles per hour. How could his mission to the Inland succeed if this was the transport over thousands of miles? Motor buggies were causing excitement worldwide: might they not perform better in the desert than camels? Perhaps one with iron tyres? The concept excited him.

A short time later Coultas was surprised to find Flynn building what looked like a large shed next to the manse. "This is no ordinary shed," Flynn told him. "It's built to house the first motor buggy to be used for mission work in the Inland."

"You told me that there isn't a motor vehicle that's suitable."

"It will be invented, though. By faith, I can see it here already."

Coultas laughed good-naturedly, then told Flynn, "I have arranged, if you're still keen, for you to accompany one of our best-known bushmen into the sandy desert regions. He's Lou Reese; you may have heard about him already. Lou's an identity in the Inland, which he knows better than most."

Flynn jumped at this chance to journey along the Birdsville Track. The trip would take him into stretches of true sandy desert, with giant sand-dunes that ran like ancient ribs across the country-side, as if great beasts lay buried just below the surface of the sand. This was the scenery generally conjured up by the word "desert", while in fact most of the Australian desert was not sandy but rocky or hard-clay terrain. Much of this "desert" carried flocks or herds, though very sparsely distributed.

As they went, Flynn and Reese carried the mail for the homesteads en route, which guaranteed them a welcome. Flynn wrote enthusiastically of their reception: "It was the Australian hospitality you read about." Along the way he carefully analysed the problems of the pioneers of the Birdsville Track, in order to plan a ministry to them. He found the few housewives he met to be "heavily pressed by the difficult circumstances of life". For one thing, the fine sand and heat combined to seize up watches, clocks and other mechanical items. Pioneer men were either too busy or too unskilled to repair such items, resulting in frustration for their womenfolk.

"Flynn was the fastest interpreter of needs I ever met," a close friend said of him. "Within an hour of entering a home, he could tell you the difficulties and personal problems the people had, and would already be planning ways to help them. He was uncanny in this regard." For items made defunct by the elements, the padre had with him a small can of oil and some tools, and he would gather together in the kitchen whatever needed repairing. When everyone else had gone to sleep, he would begin his painstaking repairs. Lou Reese recalls finding Flynn still at work early one morning, peering through his spectacles at the tiny components of a watch, dusting them down very gently with a feather he kept for this purpose. This propensity for repairing household items in Outback homes became a lifelong habit. He was seldom unsuccessful at what he undertook.

What really appalled Flynn was the struggle mothers had in educating their own children. "Mr Flynn, could you tell me what this school book means when it says to draw a daisy? I have never seen a daisy, nor have my kids. Most of this book is too hard!"

To give the mothers a break, Flynn gave reading or writing lessons to the students; he also made arrangements for pen-pals and correspondence lessons for them. "To make the Inland properly habitable, though," he concluded, "we must devise better ways to help the mother educate her children."

The men of the Birdsville Track were colourful and fiercely independent. Despite this, he noticed most were lonely. Two bushy-bearded men who ran a store at Mirra Mitta were a case in point. The store was 25 miles from Mungerannie and there were no permanent residents any closer. Despite their lack of customers, the pair manned the store every day. Flynn was surprised to find their stock included luxury and expensive items, including silk stockings. Who would buy silk stockings in the hot, dry, sandy desert? Flynn concluded that the store was mainly a ploy to attract passers-by, so that the storekeepers could have a yarn with travellers and break their aching loneliness. He arranged to send them books and magazines.

Flynn had wanted to find out the problems caused by sandy conditions, and this he did. Wheeled vehicles sank to their axles in soft sand time and again, then groaned and creaked as they were dug and pulled free. The motorised buggy he dreamed about would most likely bog down too!

Sand, he soon discovered, was more than a nuisance to transportation, it was a cause of personal discomfort from which there was no escape. It invaded everywhere. The padre crunched it in his damper and ate it raw; he found it inside his tight-shut lips and slept with it inside his well-strapped bag. He watched it billowing like a pennant from the peak of a sandhill and also saw it slithering like little snakes across the road. He felt it sting as it came on the wind in horizontal streams. He even experienced a tinge of fear as a giant funnel of sand danced across the desert towards them, but fortunately veered away.

"Damnable stuff, sand," Reese said between tight lips as they yanked their packs out from it one morning, the sand having banked up against them during the night.

"You wouldn't need to bury a man here," Flynn joked. "You would lay him on top of the sand, say a quick service and then run before you got stuck down with him."

"Too right," agreed Reese. "I remember speaking to one battler who nearly got buried in the sand. It was up to his knees and he was waving his hands as if he was swimming, imagining the sand dunes to be waves of water. A boundary rider happened along and saved his life."

"What'd happened?"

"His camel had broken free of its hobbles one night and had taken off. The sand had blown up and the old boy lost the camel pad (track) he was following. Once his water gave out, he began to die of thirst. I questioned him closely to see what he'd experienced. After all, dying of thirst is a possibility we all face out here, so the more we know about it the better."

Flynn pricked up his ears. This was the sort of information he needed for his future missionaries. "What did he describe?"

"Similar to others I have spoken to. Thirst; raging, hellish thirst, then a feeling that he was in water up to his knees. Whenever he stooped to drink it, the water ran away into the sand, only to return when he stood up again. Later, the ache of thirst left him and he suffered no more. He began to hear a beautiful music, finer than any he had heard previously. Then he hallucinated: the dunes were ocean waves among which he was swimming. He pulled his clothes off so he could swim better. He was quite naked when the boundary rider found him. Ever since, he's been listening for music like that he heard while he was close to dying, but hasn't heard anything near as beautiful."

Flynn reflected on the irony in this story. That old battler would have been like most in this tortured country; struggling for a crust and finding life a pretty rough spin most of the time. Perhaps the grandest experience he ever had was that music on the point of death! It was going to be hard to launch a mission to help men like him.

At Pandie Pandie, just 11 miles from the Queensland border, Flynn and Reese were told that the Diamantina River had come down in flood and was impassable! The rains had fallen many miles upstream, causing the waterway to break its banks in the desert. "I'd still like to go and have a look," Flynn said.

They crossed the border fence between South Australia and Queensland; in some sections, sand had piled so high against it that the top strands had disappeared. A few miles further the travellers were stopped by a huge expanse of water. The Diamantina did not flood often, but was quite impassable when it did.

As Flynn sat looking at where the tracks disappeared into the water, he heard a strident call aloft. Looked up, he saw a pair of birds, cockatoos he thought, flying without hesitation over the flooded land.

"I envy those birds," he said to Reese. "I wonder whether those flying machines the Americans are making might not one day allow us to fly over the Inland too. Just imagine the freedom to travel that would give us: there would be no sand to bog us down, no floods to stop us."

Reese gave him a funny look in response, a look Flynn was destined to see on many faces over the years. Flying machines were dangerous toys, nobody took them seriously.

On his return to Beltana, Flynn dashed off another issue of *The Outback Battler*, a quarterly journal he had started. More like a newspaper than a magazine, it ran only to several pages; the cost was just one penny to purchase and Flynn gave away most copies free. The publication carried articles about the bush, snippets of advice and wisdom, and details about the Smith of Dunesk mission. Flynn also wrote in *The Outback Battler* to raise issues he felt needed addressing. For example, he was frustrated by the lack of drive he had seen in many Outbackers; as he put it in one of his letters:

> The Inlanders themselves are the Inland's greatest resource. They are hardy, self-reliant and a repository of traditional Australian virtues such as "mateship" and individualism. Despite these qualities, I see a great many being listless and unmotivated. Most do not see a purpose to life and lack vision.

How could the problems of the bush be solved if its inhabitants were lackadaisical and defeatist? What could he do about it? He hoped through *The Outback Battler* to influence the children of the bush, the adults of the future, to encourage them to adopt a positive approach to life. In the magazine he was, of course, expressing his own philosophy.

> I want to tell you something very important. What is it? Just this. A man is what the boy is willing to be made, and a woman is what the girl is willing to be made. You think that we are what other things make us, but other things cannot mould us really: we mould ourselves ... You must learn to be like boats. A boat is a thing which always goes the way it wants to go. If the wind agrees to help it the boat accepts help with thanks, and gets there quickly. If the wind decides not to help, but to send the boat back in the opposite way, the result is just the same, for every well-made boat is able to place its sails in such a way that winds trying to blow it back make it slide forward [instead]. It has to "tack", or wriggle in a zig-zag line, and move slowly, but it gets there all the same.
>
> SO BE BOATS.

Was Flynn's positive, interventionist approach bearing any fruit? He was encouraged, when he visited Oodnadatta, to find that the new lawn at the nursing home was being used by the locals for the game of croquet! It was still the only lawn in the town, but nearby houses had tidied up their yards. The whole area was looking more cheerful.

Sister Bett had placed wooden benches on the verandah and every morning taught 30 local children there. "We need two nurses here, Mr Flynn," she told him, "not because of the workload alone, but because when there is an emergency, the children still come, but find no one here to teach them." Flynn replied that in future two staff would be his aim.

But if his decision had been for nursing homes rather than church buildings for the Outback, how could ceremonies like marriages and baptisms be conducted? He solved the dilemma in a novel, Flynnian way. Initially, he talked to those requesting such services, telling them that their home, however humble, would be as the finest cathedral to God during the ceremony. Then he would don a minister's robe and collar. Next, he would conduct the ceremony as if he were indeed in a cathedral, with the same reverence and sense of awe. "If people can see that their homes can become churches in the eyes of God, then we have solved the problem of needing to build churches in the Inland," he concluded.

Despite these gains, Flynn became terribly restless. He wrote again to Rosetta, urging her to accelerate her fund-raising. When the call came for him to survey the Inland, as he was sure it would, the funds would need to be ready.

His travelling began again. At his next service at Leigh Creek, he was surprised to see the emaciated figure of Alf Davis. Alf was the miner who had rudely walked out of Flynn's previous service there.

Once again, Davis stood at the back and passed noisy and disruptive comments. Flynn ignored these, but silently prayed for him.

For his sermon, Flynn told stories of Outback rescue, drawing the parallel that all men need to be rescued from the results of mistakes and sins. He told the story of the old battler swimming in the sand, and likened the rescuing boundary rider to Christ, who is able to save anyone from disaster and death, not just an earthly death of the body but an eternal death of the soul.

At the close of the service, a subdued Alf Davis indicated to Flynn that he would like to talk with him privately. He told of a harrowing life of bad women, heavy drinking and opium addiction. He had escaped from trouble and family censure in Brisbane by running away to the Centre, only to find he could not escape from the guilt he felt. When he learned that his mother lay dying, he had been too ashamed to return to see her: even when she died he would not return, hoping that his family would presume him dead also. Many times he had tried to break free of his addictions and start a new life, but had found them more powerful than his willpower.

"The Christ I serve is more powerful than your sins and problems, and can rescue you from them," Flynn reassured him.

"Do you believe that?"

"I am sure of it, I wouldn't be here otherwise. Would you like to pray and ask Him to forgive your sins and come into your life and rescue you?"

"Yes, please."

Flynn prayed for him. Davis then said his own faltering prayer aloud.

The look of peace on Davis's face when they parted the next day was encouraging. Flynn had seen "conversions" before, based on emotions, that had not lasted, and for these he had no time. However, he had also seen lives totally transformed by deep, spiritual changes. He judged Alf Davis to be one such instance.

Flynn felt lighter of heart as he bounced around in the buggy on leaving Leigh Creek. Davis had answered a nagging question as to whether an itinerant ministry could really help people with personal needs. It would not be as effective as a resident ministry, but it could still do a valuable job. He needed to know that, because his plans for the "Never Never" could not include the provision of resident ministries, at least in the short term. The settlements were too small and scattered for that. Perhaps welfare centres and mission stations would supplement the nomadic ministers one day, but such a day was far off.

As Flynn travelled, he pondered the enormous problems that faced his plans for a ministry to the Inland. He did not yet have solutions, but he was overflowing with ideas – sufficient to make a start. The buggy happened to be passing between two rocky outcrops as he came to this conclusion. On impulse he called out aloud, "Great Father, I'm ready to start now. Please help!" He smiled at the resounding echo that returned.

Would the echo be the only response to his call?

6

MISSION IMPOSSIBLE

John Flynn read the letter with mounting excitement – an invitation to survey the conditions in the Northern Territory and prepare a report for the Federal Assembly of the Presbyterian Church.

It was already April 1912, and the Assembly was meeting in Sydney in five months' time. A commission such as this would have been impossible to undertake from scratch, but Flynn had been collecting information for several years. The bulk of his report would have to be constructed from what he knew already.

In addition to his existing data, he would need to gather new information at lightning speed. This would necessitate a quick tour of the north: a ten-day trip by sea from Brisbane to Darwin was the answer to getting him there.

"Thank you for your efforts," he wrote to Rosetta. "I now need to call on the money you have raised so faithfully."

Surprisingly, now that the invitation he wanted had come, Flynn's mood became sober. Exactly what was he up against? He spread a map of Australia out on the floor and knelt down with a ruler, scribbling his rough measurements onto a scrap of paper. He converted these into miles using the mapping scale and multiplied it out. TWO MILLION SQUARE MILES! "No, that must be wrong," he thought, and checked his calculations. They were correct.

What did two million square miles of Outback mean? He scratched through his geography books and discovered that the combined area of England, Scotland, Ireland and Wales – the British Isles – was only 121 000 square miles. Eight British Isles would fit into two million square miles. In all that vast area there was not one permanent Christian minister to the pioneers, and within five months he had to produce a detailed report on what amounted to half of Australia, and suggest plausible remedies for its problems!

This was not the first time that the difficulties of his calling had impressed themselves upon Flynn. As he wrote in *The Messenger*:

My emotions have never quite found their relation to my work. I cannot decide whether to look upon it as serious or ridiculous, possible or impossible, credible or a crying shame.

Less than three months remained of the five when John Flynn stepped off the SS *Taiyuan* in Darwin. He was excited: he'd arranged to meet Mrs Jessie Litchfield, whose letter in 1909 had first stirred him to do something about the Inland.

He and Mrs Litchfield spent many hours talking. Among the information she gave him were details of local medical problems. During recent outbreaks of malaria at Umbrawarra, for example, men had died like flies simply for lack of medical attention.

"I have heard of your nursing home at Oodnadatta. We need homes like it in all the remote areas," she concluded.

"I agree, but who will pay for them and who will staff them?"

"A way must be found."

Flynn was challenged by his informant's descriptions of widespread immorality. She outlined the sexual exploitation of Aboriginal women by lonely Outback men, resulting in children who belonged in neither community. One example involved a station which was openly "breeding" such children to work there! She also related how men in pubs would go outside and whistle for Aboriginal women to come and act as prostitutes.

"I don't know what you could do to change the situation," Mrs Litchfield told Flynn.

"Since reading similar things in your original letter, I have been pondering what might be done. Moralising would do no good – a social revolution is what is needed. I believe that we must make family life possible and respectable in the Outback. The presence of white women and children would, I believe, result in the changes we are looking for."

Flynn next visited a variety of centres in the north. He took many photographs and spoke to everyone he met: prospectors at Pine Creek; graziers and stockmen at Katherine; residents of hamlets; politicians and government officials in Darwin; Catholic missionaries on Bathurst Island.

Time sped past. It was 24 August before Flynn embarked on the SS *Eastern* for his homeward journey. Only a few weeks remained in which to compile his report. Facts, figures and ideas swirled through his head, and he took to pacing the deck, thinking and praying. His report had the potential of launching a ministry to the Inland, but much would depend on how he presented it. If he painted too bleak a picture, the Presbyterian Church would back away; if the solutions he suggested were too ambitious, they would discount them. Most of all, though, he had to convince the Presbyterians to act. He had to motivate the wealthy churches in the cities to recognise their responsibility to the pioneers. It would be both a difficult and a delicate task.

How should he begin? How could he capture attention? Church reports being on the whole stuffy documents, he decided to incorporate a number of his own photographs and maps to save on words and stir imaginations.

He then had to find a way to defend his emphasis on the practical. Many churchmen would consider his approach to be "unspiritual", unless he could convince them otherwise. He decided to quote Dr Wilfred Grenfell, a medical missionary, who commanded great respect among Presbyterians. "Grenfell of Labrador" had set up a chain of hospitals to minister to the Eskimos, Indians and whites of that land. He had written articles and books, from which Flynn quoted:

> When you set out to commend your gospel to men who do
> not particularly want it, there is only one way to go about it –
> to do something for them that they will be sure to understand.

This practical approach would have another advantage: it would remove preconceptions in the mind of the pioneers, whose image was of an ineffectual clergy interested mainly in taking money from them.

His presentation and approach now decided, Flynn found the body of the report began to fall into place. The sentences started to flow. What was proposed was a nomadic ministry of patrol padres to become the business end of an evangelistic work. By their loving Christian example, he suggested, "it is possible for a few men – an apparently ridiculous band of 12 or 20 – to influence the thought and life of half of Australia". Based on Sister Bett's striking success at

Oodnadatta, Flynn suggested another nurse-deaconess be sent to Alice Springs, despite it being a small field. "*Small*," he warned, "is a dangerous word to use in regard to religious undertakings."

He gave a vital reason for the Church becoming involved in medical work:

> The first thing to do in any effort to uplift the tone of bush life is to give women a sense of security; in other words, to make child-bearing comparatively safe at the outposts. Then brave men will not hesitate to lead partners further back, and the presence of women and white children in greater numbers will sweeten the whole life.

In Flynn's opinion a separate mission would be needed to minister to the Aborigines because their problems were very specialised and different from those of the pioneers. (His own calling from God was to the pioneers.)

These schemes were clearly going to cost a lot of money. The Presbyterian Church, with its roots in Scotland, was traditionally "canny" about money. He needed to suggest a practical means of raising funds, otherwise the Assembly would throw his plans out. How about a "Bush Brigade" of 5000 volunteer supporters, each donating just one pound annually? In return, they could be informed of progress through a free quarterly magazine about the Inland.

Now to goad the Assembly into action! Flynn observed:

> 5000 pounds does not appear so ambitious a request for more than half Australia, especially when the church in the other half spends 250,000 pounds per year on themselves!

He concluded the report with one last prod.

> The failure of the Church, as a whole, to reach our outposts is our shame. I am convinced that never can "Health" be manifested fully in our home congregations until "Faithfulness" marks our frontier policy.

> Difficulties of a serious nature will arise in shoals in every fertile mind. To each one a reply can only be made in words already familiar:

> "Do not pray for tasks
> Equal to your powers;
> Pray for powers
> Equal to your tasks."

Although the gist of the report was now complete, Flynn found he had run out of time to finish it properly, with photographs and tables of data, before the deadline! He could not bear to postpone its tabling as that would delay his planned mission for several years.

Depressed and unsure what to do, he went to see Reverend John Ferguson, Convener of the Federal Home Mission Committee and minister of the big St Stephen's Church in Sydney. Ferguson was in charge of arranging the "white book" of reports which would go before the General Assembly.

"I'm sorry," Flynn apologised, "but I have failed to finish the report on time, despite working right through some nights. It's been more difficult than I thought. The deadline you gave was tomorrow. Is there any chance of extending it?"

"I would like to, Mr Flynn, but it is out of my hands. The printers have told me they will be struggling to complete the "white book" in time for the Assembly as it is. What's causing the delay?"

"What I am proposing is so new, it has to be right first time. Any flaws and it will be rejected without having been properly considered."

"I'm sympathetic, but my hands are tied. Give it to me to have a look at, just in its rough form. Perhaps we can include a synopsis to which you can speak?"

The thought of a synopsis of his carefully planned work did not appeal. Flynn handed over his rough draft and left. Surely he could not get so close, yet fail?

Ferguson called him in next morning to the vestry of St Stephen's. "Mr Flynn," he said, "I read your report in one sitting last night. It certainly is revolutionary, not just in what you propose, but in your presentation. We cannot shorten it or it would lose its impact. I think it should be a separate document, not stuck in with all the others."

Flynn's heart leapt. Here was hope!

"In that case, what are we to do?"

"I have a plan. I meet with my committee this evening and I'll discuss it with them."

Ferguson read out extracts of the report that evening and showed his committee the photographs. He told them, "This is not a mere document, it is a living message, an urgent call, a noble vision of Christian enterprise." His ringing endorsement helped convince the committee that the report should be printed as a separate document, photographs and all, to be posted out in advance to the members of the General Assembly.

The cost of this would be covered by £70, which had been sent from England, quite spontaneously, for "bush work in Australia". Until now there had been no call on this money.

An excited Flynn rapidly finished the report, then handed it to Ferguson. Two hundred copies were printed on the best paper, in clear type, with 16 pages of illustrations. They would stand out handsomely from the rest of the dry documents. The whole job was rushed through in the space of a week, but even so there was not enough time to post copies to members in advance. All that could be done was to distribute copies at the close of the opening night of the Assembly. The Home Mission report was to be given at eleven the following morning, leaving delegates only the first evening to preview it.

Many in the Assembly on that morning of 26 September 1912 had glanced through Flynn's report the previous night and were attentive to what he had to say. They waited patiently while he set up a map for them and arranged papers at the rostrum.

Ready at last, Flynn adjusted his spectacles and looked out at a sea of faces. He paused, a trifle nervously, before he began. Those close enough to scrutinise the speaker saw a lean man with thinning brown hair and an aristocratic appearance. This image was fostered partly by his smart clothing and partly by his long, thin features, especially a gently curving nose on which balanced round-rimmed spectacles. His mouth was firm and definite, suggesting a man of determination and decision.

Flynn's style of presentation was pleasing and gentle. His voice was measured, almost clipped, and he peppered the talk with good humour. Points were illustrated with anecdotes that were not mentioned in the report, but which gripped the listeners. He also paused now and then to refer to the large map. By the time he wound up, he had the delegates in the palm of his hand.

The report was adopted "with acclaim" and authorised for "immediate action". Flynn could not have dreamed of a better response! He found himself appointed "Field Superintendent" and commissioned to put its proposals into action. He was 31 years old.

Flynn's new unit became known in general parlance as the "Bush Department" of the Presbyterian Church. Its field spread across several states, forcing him to think and plan on a national scale right from the start. To the visionary, this chance to take in the whole sweep of the nation was most exciting. For Australia, it was to prove of incalculable value.

The Reverend John Ferguson insisted on bold action to launch Flynn's new mission. Under his leadership, the Home Mission Committee issued 5 000 copies of Flynn's Assembly report to churches. Ten subscription forms for the Bush Brigade were included in the appendix. Ferguson's prompt action did much to find early financial supporters.

The new mission was launched publicly in Scots Church, Collins Street, Melbourne. Frank Rolland spoke, followed by John Flynn. Enthusiasm ran high and found a valuable new potential recruit. As Flynn descended the steps after addressing the crowd, he found a young man in his path.

"My name is Bruce Plowman," he introduced himself. "I was deeply stirred by what you were saying. May I take a few minutes of your time?"

"Yes, of course. Pleased to meet you, Mr Plowman." The two men shook hands.

"As you were speaking, I could see myself out there helping the pioneers. It was a boyhood dream of mine to be a missionary in my own country. Tonight that dream has become a possibility."

"It is a worthy dream you have, Mr Plowman. Are you ordained, then?"

"No, I'm afraid not."

"We would need an ordained man to pioneer our mission, if that was how you were thinking. The Mission Board would not appoint a man who was not ordained."

"I am not without experience. I spent a year as a home missionary, as you did yourself. I have also served as a youth leader and Sunday school teacher. Look, the job will be a hard one and I keep myself fit enough. I am so sure that I should do it that I offer to take the position in an honorary capacity. All I would need would be my expenses and recognition as a minister."

"That is extremely generous of you. Do you have any experience of the Inland?"

"No, but I was raised on a farm and I know country people. I can also ride and handle horses as well as most. I would be blazing the trail for ordained ministers to follow."

Flynn looked hard at Bruce Plowman. He liked his strong, square jaw and his obvious manliness, but his own words in the Assembly report returned to unsettle him: "I am assuming that your Board would not contemplate the employment, in such fields as here discussed, of any but fully trained men." He was in a quandary because in other respects Plowman seemed the right sort of applicant to be a "patrol padre", as Flynn began to term the proposed nomadic ministers.

Plowman noticed Flynn's hesitation. He added, "I offer five years of my life to establish your mission. I would return after that and pick up the threads of my own life again."

"Thank you for your interest," Flynn said at last. "Please consider training for the ministry as you are just the type of man we need. Unfortunately, we will need to wait until then." Plowman asked Flynn to take his name and address "in case there is a change in policy", and Flynn was happy to do so.

Despite the euphoria over the new mission, Flynn realised the immensity of what lay ahead. He was young and needed advice and counsel, but who could give it? None of his church friends could, as they knew little about the Inland. He then remembered Mrs Jeannie Gunn, famous authoress of *We of the Never Never*, who had helped him plan an unfinished *Bushwoman's Companion*. She was a Christian woman of rare insight, especially regarding the Inland and its problems.

Flynn visited Mrs Gunn at her sister's home in Ida Street, Melbourne, as soon as he could creep away.

"Jeannie, the Reverend John Flynn is here to see you," her sister Elizabeth announced grandly as she ushered him through.

Mrs Gunn put down her knitting and stood up with a smile of welcome. "Mr Flynn, how nice to see you! I have heard about your report to the General Assembly and how enthusiastically they accepted it. You must be very pleased. May I add my own congratulations?"

"Thank you. Yes, I am pleased, only I am not sure I have got it quite right. That's why I have come to see you, to hear what your thoughts are. If you had been given a free hand to plan a mission to the Inland, what would you have concentrated on?"

"Well! Let's sit down while I think a little. Would you like some tea?"

"No thanks, I cannot stay long, I'm afraid."

There was a silence while Mrs Gunn thought and Flynn waited expectantly.

She picked up her knitting needle in her right hand and held up her left hand, displaying three fingers, spread apart. She tapped each finger in turn with her knitting needle as she spoke.

"I would do three things. Number one, the Maluka [her husband, Aeneas] should not have been buried in the Outback. There are too many unnecessary graves out there, Mr Flynn. There are a hundred stations who have a workman, wife or child buried near the homestead who should be alive today. If there had been medical help available, my own husband would still be with me. I went to the 'Never Never' a bride and returned a widow. I am only one of many. Some kind of medical missionary work would be my number one priority. The Christ you represent healed people, so you'll need to take healing into the Inland. Women out there grow old before their time and it's not only the harsh life that does it, it's fear – fear for themselves and their families, nagging fear of sickness or accident.

"Secondly," she tapped her middle finger, "I would try to knit the people together like the strands in my knitting, by social work. For example, a man and his wife rode seven hours to see me, she holding her baby in her arms, all because she had not spoken to another woman in over a year and could no longer stand it. I don't know how you could achieve social work out there, though, Mr Flynn; the vast distances could defeat you.

"Thirdly, I would give them the good old gospel, straight spiritual work. Men in the bush are like men everywhere, they need God."

She then closed the three fingers into one unit. "When you have found how to combine the medical, the social and the spiritual into one ministry, you will have closed your grip around the heart of the Inland. It will be in your hands."

Flynn and Mrs Gunn exchanged social pleasantries for a while, then she offered him further counsel: "One tiny thing more, if I may be so bold. Whoever you choose to be your first Outback minister must succeed, and be a very visible success. Your plans for the 'Never Never' centre about your nomadic ministers. Your mission will be rejected by both the Church and the Inlanders if your first man fails."

Flynn left Jeannie Gunn feeling more settled. Her "three goals for ministry" accorded very much with his own thinking.

The immediate task was to appoint his first patrol padre. Flynn had too many duties as Superintendent to return to Beltana, so his appointee would need to stand in for him there for a few months until the two-year contract was completed. That same man would then move to Oodnadatta and launch the first Christian ministry patrols into the "Red Centre" of Australia.

Over the next few days, Flynn spent much time asking God to lead him to the right man: an adventurous man, a practical man but with a sense of humour, a man's man, a spiritual man, good with horses and camels, tough, compassionate and brave ... and much else besides.

No one came to mind. No one volunteered either, despite the rousing talks he gave to various groups. That is, no one other than that young man with the square jaw who had offered his services at Scots Street Church. The more Flynn prayed, the more Plowman's face and staring eyes came back to him. "I wonder if God intends it to be Bruce Plowman after all?" he pondered. This question kept returning, so he set up a meeting between the young man and the Home Mission Board.

The interview was searching. Both Flynn and Plowman knew it was not going very well.

"How long do you envisage serving in the Inland?"

"As long as will be needed to establish the ministry there which, at a guess, could take as long as five years."

"I believe that you are engaged to be married. There would be little opportunity for you to return to see your fiancée during those five years."

"We have discussed this. We are prepared to postpone our marriage until the mission to the Inland is properly established."

Plowman's fervour and determination were obvious assets. However, he was not a minister. How could the Presbyterian Church send out a man to be their first representative in a new mission if he were not even ordained?

William Wood had sat quietly throughout the session. To everyone's surprise he suddenly asked a most unusual question. "How many senses are there, Mr Plowman?" A brief, bemused silence greeted his intrusion.

Plowman answered, "I have six senses, sir."

"Oh? And what is the sixth?"

"Horse sense."

The tension seemed to break at this: and there were smiles all around at his reply. Against Church policy and all the odds, Robert Bruce Plowman was unanimously appointed as Flynn's first missionary to the Inland.

"Why have you appointed such a young, inexperienced man to be your first patrol padre?" Andrew Barber, Flynn's old friend, asked him later.

Flynn fixed him with his ingenuous blue-grey eyes. "Because he's the right man," he replied. There was a tiny smile playing at the corners of Flynn's mouth as he said this.

"He'd jolly well better be, because everyone will be watching him. Your whole credibility will depend on his success."

"I didn't notice you or any of my other ordained friends volunteering for the position," Flynn chided gently, and Barber laughed.

Dr Fred McKay, Flynn's close friend and historian, is still bemused by the Board's unexpected decision. He comments:

> I find it hard to believe that at a General Assembly gathering, when ministers would be present from all over Australia, there

was no ordained minister who volunteered to become the first patrol padre. My only explanation has been that God was at work in a strange way and that Bruce Plowman, who couldn't wear a clerical collar, was none-the-less the right man.

Flynn had hoped to spend a reasonable length of time with Bruce Plowman at Beltana, to introduce him to the work there. He shortened this to only four days when he realised how slowly funds were coming forward for the mission: he would need to promote the cause vigorously in the cities for a good while yet.

When he met with Plowman to brief him about his new life, he asked, "Do you smoke a pipe?"

"No."

"Get one then and learn to. It will help you to get along with the bush folk. It's a tradition out there to have a pipe and a yarn together. They will relax better with you if you smoke." Flynn gave this rather strange advice in 1912, an era when smoking was not considered unhealthy by most and was sometimes even recommended by doctors as good for "the nerves" and "keeping diseases away".

"Great hopes rest on your performance in this work, Mr Plowman. I'm sure you are aware of that."

"Yes, I am. I have no illusions about what I face. With God's help, I won't let you down."

7

GETTING STARTED

John Flynn went to Beltana ahead of Bruce Plowman, to organise the changeover. The new recruit followed soon after, by train. He struck up a conversation with a fellow-traveller, who had originally come from north of Alice Springs.

"What were you doing in Adelaide? Visiting friends?" Plowman asked.

"No. I went because Nurse Bett put me on the train. She's an angel, that one. She saved my life: the doctor in Adelaide told me she did."

"Oh really? What'd happened?" Plowman pricked up his ears; he would be working with Nurse Bett.

The man leaned forward, turned his head slightly and pointed to a cream-coloured scar the size of a man's fist above his right ear. "Guess how I got that one?" he demanded proudly.

"It's big, right enough. Could a horse have kicked you?"

"You're right, young feller. I fell and was kicked by my own horse. When I came to, I had a headache you wouldn't wish on your mother-in-law. I stumbled about and luckily managed to track my horse or I would've perished. He walked me into 'the Alice' [Alice Springs] where friends tore up a shirt, none too clean, and bandaged my head with it.

"There being no medical help in the Alice, I had to ride to Oodnadatta. It took nine days and my head felt like it was being hit with hammers from the inside when I got there. That Nurse Bett just put me onto a hospital bed with no ifs, buts or maybes, and started to take off my bandage. I had not allowed anyone to get near that bandage, but how could I show a tiny woman that I was scared?" He paused to chuckle at the memory.

"Go on."

"She was very gentle, like a butterfly, soaking it off inch by inch, but cripes it still hurt! 'You've got blood poisoning,' she said once she had it off, 'and your skull has been cracked. After I deal with the blood poisoning, you will have to go down to Adelaide for an operation.' I had a bad few days then, funny dreams and stuff, but whenever I woke up she seemed to be there looking after me. That woman is a marvel, I tell you."

Plowman settled back in his seat, encouraged by what he had been told. Whatever sacrifices might be called for, he was going to be involved in something worthwhile.

John Flynn met him at Beltana railway station. As they struggled along the road under the weight of the luggage, heading towards the manse, they topped a slight rise and paused to look at the unprepossessing township.

"Do you like what you see?" Flynn asked.

"I don't, frankly," said Plowman. "Did anyone plan Beltana, or did it just happen? Look at the shabby housing and those scruffy yards."

Flynn smiled, liking the young man's candour. He said, "That's because you are seeing what is there now. You must look with vision at the Outback, Mr Plowman. You are seeing drab houses, but I see modern homes with gardens and children playing in them. There, over there beyond the pub, I see a big white hospital with up-to-date equipment. It is a major reason for the children I see playing in those gardens – after it was built, women felt confident to start families out here. And down there, alongside the creek, is our school. It is another reason for the many children."

"And where is the church? I can't see that yet." Was there a hint of sarcasm in Plowman's voice?

"That is planned and they will start building it soon. Do you know what that church building will mean to our mission, Mr Plowman?"

"No. What?"

"It means we move on. We are an itinerant ministry, we go out to those who are still pioneers. There will always be plenty of them, in our two million square miles."

After a good meal at the local hotel, the men returned to the manse to talk. They lit their pipes and sat outside on the open verandah, watching the sun go down. The colours of sunset seemed more startling in Beltana than in Adelaide. The distant Flinders Ranges glowed as if illuminated from the inside by a coppery light.

Flynn began elaborating on his visions for the Inland, to inculcate them in his protégé. Soon he noticed the young man rubbing his eyes.

"You must be tired," Flynn observed solicitously.

"Yes, I'm tuckered out. I'll need to turn in shortly."

"Do you mind if I continue talking while you prepare for bed?"

"Not at all. I'm fascinated by your plans and stories."

Flynn sat at the bottom of the bed, still talking, as Plowman drifted off to sleep. When he awoke later, Flynn was still talking as if he hadn't noticed! Plowman dropped off again, a slight smile on his lips, and this time he slept through until the crowing of chickens, the barking of a dog and the "hee-haw" of a donkey all occurred at once. The sun was already streaming through the window of his room. Flynn, he noticed, was sound asleep and remained so for a further two hours. A night bird, Plowman decided.

Flynn took Plowman to inspect Mitchell's buggy. "I found it a great introduction to bush folk just to be in this buggy, because Mitchell had been so loved and respected. I did a rough count from the log books: this vehicle has covered about 70 000 miles in its 18 years, much of it on rough bush tracks or no tracks at all, and it has never required the services of a coachbuilder or wheelwright. Naturally, we have done some running repairs ourselves, though not very often. They don't make them today like they used to."

The time came for Flynn to depart. "What do you see now when you look at the Outback?" he asked impishly.

Plowman smiled before replying, "I see good roads and railways to telescope distance. There are cars and motorised ambulances hurrying through the desert, saving lives. Irrigated crops wave in the breeze and travelling libraries service remote towns and homesteads. Women's groups help isolated mothers and there is one unified church working to evangelise and serve the people. How have I done?"

"Splendidly!" They both laughed.

Flynn returned south to an unexpected suggestion from his Board. "Mr Flynn, support is coming in more slowly than we had hoped. We believe that there are people of means who would

support us willingly, if they knew about our plans. As Superintendent, might you see that as a special responsibility of yours,
perhaps, to seek them out and speak to them?"

Consequently, John Flynn began to buttonhole all those he
thought might be interested and helpful. He was gifted at
communicating his ideas and had a rare talent for making friends. In
recognition of the increasing contribution those close to him were
making, Flynn coined a phrase that became one of his trademarks:
"A man is his friends".

Flynn's ability to befriend almost anyone within minutes of
meeting them was extraordinary, almost mystical. How did he
manage it? Dr Fred McKay speaks of Flynn's charisma and "special
social skills". For example:

> He was quite at home in any company, rich or poor. I have
> seen him completely at ease sitting with cattlemen on a hotel
> verandah, sipping a glass of beer, one only, to show his oneness
> with them. He was equally comfortable in the company of
> women or children. He loved women's groups and would
> quickly win their devotion and help.

There was one group of people, however, with whom Flynn did
not always enjoy a good relationship: that was his own controlling
Board, the Home Mission Board. To be fair, it was not easy for
members to work with this young man of impatient vision. Often
they were cautious about his concepts and reined in some of his
more ambitious plans. Flynn found that very hard to cope with
when he was struggling to get his new mission started.

The situation was typified by the Board voting to name the new
mission the "Australian Inland Mission" (AIM) against Flynn's wishes.
He would have preferred the title "Frontier Services" because it
sounded less paternalistic and more in keeping with his intentions. The
word "mission" was associated in most people's minds with putting
up buildings, not with an itinerating ministry to build up people
instead. Furthermore, the word "Inland" hardly seemed appropriate
when the Board was responsible for half of Australia's coastline as well.

Wishing to avoid open conflict, Flynn accepted the Board's
decision, though his personal visiting card carried the title "Frontier
Services". He designed official letterheads and pamphlets with the

required heading of "Australian Inland Mission", but placed his own logo "For Christ and Continent" above it and a very prominent "Frontier Services" below it. This "compromise" fooled no one: friction and confrontation lay ahead.

Left to his own devices, oblivious to Flynn's struggles, Plowman set about preparing for his first bush journey. He knew nothing about tracking, cooking bush tucker, finding water, steering by the stars or sun, shoeing horses, dealing with Aborigines, recognising quicksand – or countless other pitfalls. However, as he explained it: "Providence was looking after this new chum." Fortunately, so were kindly Outbackers.

The station manager at Myrtle Springs was very busy with his multiple responsibilities, yet he took the time to teach Plowman how to shoe a horse properly and gave him snippets of valuable advice. With his sharp mind, and following Flynn's dictum to "always listen carefully to the pioneers", he learned many things quickly.

"Be helpful wherever you can," Flynn had instructed Plowman. That meant he had to be prepared to try almost anything asked of him. His first social challenge seemed simple enough, to cut the local police trooper's hair. He protested, but Trooper McLeod insisted, saying he would need to learn because there were no barbers in the bush.

"You're a brave man to trust a new chum. How do you want it then?"

"Take it all off."

It should have been easy, but it wasn't. Perhaps the scissors were too blunt, but it was like trying to cut through steel springs with a pair of pliers. Within a short time, though, Plowman had become an adequate "bush barber".

Soon he was out ministering to the lonely pioneers. As promised, his pipe was a great introduction. "One sight of a pipe makes smokers kin," he was told by men as they fished out their own pipes, knives and tobacco.

Flynn was pleased with Plowman's early reports from Beltana. As a natural publicist, he wanted everyone to know that the young man had started well. He decided to publish an edition of *The Outback Battler* in February 1913 in which Plowman would feature strongly.

Mr Plowman has shown no inclination to spare himself. He writes that "I have already travelled over 700 miles in the two months I have been here, and have visited the places most urgently in need of visiting ... horses are flesh and not spirit, and when the temperature registers nearly 120 in the shade, journeys across the burning plains must be curtailed."

Flynn used this edition for an even more vital purpose, to inform the Inland precisely how the new mission intended to operate. The twin pillars on which the AIM would be built, he promised, were "love" and "faith". The whole mission was to be motivated entirely by these two qualities.

By "love" he meant not a soppy, selfish sentimentality: rather, a "tough love" that was unselfish, practical and committed to serving the pioneers.

We will need a very large measure of love. That sacred word is used with hesitation, but no other is adequate. Strong love alone can bridge the long distances; strong love alone can prove effective where men meet but once or twice a year. ... strong love alone can suffice, because everything not strong must be rejected by pioneers.

We will need strong faith, for faith is tested where platitudes cease to echo, and where with relentless regularity Nature assumes her harshest mood ...

The movement is founded on the fact that there is One who takes a personal interest in the lives of all men.

No one can understand John Flynn unless they understand the energies that drove the man – his "love" and "faith". Fred McKay puts it like this: "Flynn was driven by a love, a compassion, which welled up inside him. It made him unstoppable in the things he wanted to do ..."

What he was sending Plowman into, once the youngster started travelling north from Oodnadatta, bothered Flynn. What unexpected problems might he find? As Flynn himself had never gone into Central Australia, despite having total responsibility for it, he decided he must take a look at the "Red Centre". He travelled with the mailman, who enjoyed reading books atop his swaying camel. The camel knew the way well and simply plodded on.

Flynn's joy at escaping from the pressures of recent months is evident from his descriptions.

> No birds are near, for water is far away. But we have brought our music with us – a regular swish in the canteens, which keeps harmony with the muffled drum [of camels' feet], for the camel is a master bandsman, drumming with ugly feet on the surface of Australia …

> The fourth camel is loaded with quart pot, water bag, swag, blankets, and, crowning all in an attitude hardly coiled up or anything exactly orthodox, the scribe [Flynn]. He is not reading. The present is too good to be wasted that way.

It was on the back of his camel that John Flynn first entered Alice Springs. Here was the symbolic heart of Australia, which many people described as "the dead heart". He intended to win it over and give it life.

The town was smaller than he had imagined: a few scattered homes around a dusty hotel, two stores and a police station. Gloriously isolated, its closest neighbouring towns were 400 miles south and 800 miles north.

In his 1912 report, Flynn had suggested the AIM send a nurse-deaconess to Alice Springs. Before this happened, though, he needed to know what local residents thought of the idea. He spoke to them and to some visiting bore sinkers and teamsters, and received a mixed reaction. Most were enthusiastic, but some expressed the sentiment he had heard many times before: "It sounds a good idea, Padre, but this is no place for a woman."

"Then we must change that. In the long run, country not fit for women is not fit for men either," Flynn would reply. He wrote in his report:

> There are two great evils arising out of this dread [of disease or injury]. Bushmen laugh at risks for themselves, but they mostly stick to their motto "The bush is no place for a woman". Hence their temperaments suffer. They are great boys, most of them: but when men are deprived of the society of women and children they inevitably miss something in tenderness and brightness. It isn't fair! And there is an irreparable loss to the

nation when our most virile, most enduring, most resourceful, most intuitive men remain celibate. Their qualities perish with them, and their race is as if they had not been.

What did Alice Springs do in medical emergencies? Flynn inquired. "We use the telegraph when a man is sick," a storekeeper told him. "We call up a doctor in Adelaide. Usually he prescribes some medicine or other, which we take by imagination; there's no pharmacy hereabouts. For sure, a cottage hospital built here and with its own dispensary would save lives."

Flynn roamed the ancient MacDonnell Ranges as part of his orientation, marvelling at their vivid colourings – blues, whites, reds, oranges and purples. Mount Gillen, a few miles out of Alice Springs, in particular caught his attention and he took a number of photographs of it. "I had a strange sensation when walking in the MacDonnells," he said later, "as if I belonged there."

At the Board meeting following his return, Flynn spread the photographs of his Alice Springs journey across the table, together with some crude maps he had drawn and many scraps of paper on which he had scribbled information: bore delivery rates, stock routes, rainfall data and hundreds of other observations he had made or found out.

After giving members time to look through it all, Flynn told them, "Almost nothing is published about the true nature of the Inland, gentlemen. Our children in schools are not taught about it as there is no reliable information to teach them from. I believe we should play our part in putting that right. I propose we publish a magazine of quality about the Inland and about our work in it, a magazine supplying useful information and advice to Inlanders and good enough to be sold in our cities and used in our public libraries and universities."

The Board baulked at this suggestion. They were satisfied with *The Outback Battler*, with its homely, cheap, newspaper-style presentation. Flynn's vision was a new concept and far in advance of anything they had thought of. Understandably, they were cautious.

"How many pages do you envisage and how often would it appear?" Flynn was asked.

"Length would vary according to available material, but from what I have already gathered, I expect it to be around 50 pages and to appear quarterly," Flynn replied.

There were exclamations of surprise. "Fifty pages! Whatever would you fill it with?"

"Social concerns like the need for schools, hospitals and a new mail service; economic concerns like markets, meat-works, government subsidies and new railways. Much of it could simply provide information about the Inland: pearling in Broome, travel methods, mining techniques used and so on. This would all be in addition to the type of material covered now in *The Outback Battler*. The bush needs a worthy champion, and that is what we would supply. In addition, it would help in the development of a community spirit in the bush, where at present we have thousands of individuals."

"But that is not the Church's work, Mr Flynn."

"Why not? It is part of loving people, which is our stated policy."

"What sort of cost would be involved? We should be cutting costs as funds are coming in much more slowly than expected, except in Victoria. Launching an expensive project now would be foolhardy."

"On the contrary, it would give us a wider audience and increase donations," claimed Flynn. "There would also be proceeds from sales to bookshops and newsagents."

"Why should the man in the street buy a magazine we publish?"

"It would be superior to other magazines in format and presentation. For example, I plan to use photographs liberally. I'm sure you noticed how all of you went first to the photographs of my trip and took an interest in them. I'll try to capture the man in the street in a similar way."

Flynn was disappointed but not devastated when his proposal was rejected. He determined to keep raising the need in different ways at Board meetings until it was accepted. This he did, generating antagonism from dissenting Board members in the process. Somewhat grudgingly, they agreed in August 1913 to the quality magazine he wanted – *The Inlander*. He would have to produce it himself, single-handedly, despite an already overcrowded program. This meant that some nights Flynn worked right through in order to bring out the first copy before Christmas.

Meanwhile, during a promotional tour of Brisbane, Flynn had received a letter from Alf Davis, the opium addict he had first helped at Leigh Creek. He had often wondered whether the man's conversion had been real and the changes in his lifestyle permanent. He read, in part:

> I fought my battles out myself for years, thinking I had sufficient strength, in my frail body, to conquer myself! But how soon I found out how weak I was! Thank God I can say today I am free. My sins are things of the past. Opium's power over me is dead!
>
> How did I do it? Well, that is easy to answer. I came to realise that there was only One who could help me. I found that One, and by prayer and trust He conquered, and I won ... I *will* see my brothers and sisters again, look them in the face and shake their hands, knowing that I can do so as an honourable man ...

Davis concluded by asking Flynn to send him a Bible, which he did. A few months later came a letter of thanks from Davis, saying how valuable he was finding the Bible. He ended by saying:

> Here I am at 33, just beginning to live, just beginning to find the true joy of life, the life my Father above sent me on earth to live. Believe me when I say, dear brother, that I pray always your words may do for hundreds what they have done for me, for to you I owe the thanks ...

While reading this letter, Jeannie Gunn's words came back to Flynn: "Men in the bush are like men everywhere. They need God." At its best, then, the itinerant ministry could help men to find God. Alf Davis's transformed life proved that.

Amazingly, the first issue of *The Inlander* came off the press in December 1913 as planned. The pressure of Flynn's frenetic lifestyle is evident in his introduction:

> The Superintendent is always glad to receive letters of inquiry, but correspondents should remember that answers may be long delayed, and occasionally letters are lost through disorganisation, owing to constant travel.

Nothing quite like *The Inlander* for journalistic quality had appeared in Australia before. Flynn's photography and fluent writing made the magazine easy to read and interesting. Complimentary letters flowed in, many from teachers and university lecturers, appreciative of the careful statistics and other information Flynn presented which were not available elsewhere.

Would *The Inlander* make money? Its initiator hoped so, but immediate sales were below his expectations. However, he argued strongly to the Board that it required more time to become known. The Board was hesitant, but agreed to continue publication, at least for the time being. (In fact, circulation increased rapidly, reaching 6 000 within the first year. Later, the Education Department of New South Wales recognised its quality and authority by including it as part of its syllabus material.)

Flynn was pleased with *The Inlander*, but his success in this and a number of other projects had come at a great price. He complained to his father in December: "I must work with a committee which doesn't understand half the time, and sometimes I have to bluntly overbear men who from timidity, or ignorance, would wreck the concern."

Flynn was very uncomfortable taking such a hard line, preferring to convince rather than to bully. He sensed he was creating a residue of ill-feeling in some Board members, but also believed passionately that if the mission did not go forward it would die away completely. He encapsulated this concept in a rather strange expression: "We must do more – or less."

"What have you been doing to antagonise your Board, Flynn?" asked his good friend, Andrew Barber. "I hear murmurings that you are an unsuitable Superintendent and could be voted out at the next General Assembly. That meets in less than a year. You had better do something fast about the dissatisfaction."

In this climate of criticism, all eyes turned to Central Patrol as the keystone of Flynn's strategy for the Inland.

Aboriginal "wurlie" near Durrie station

Flynn's Inland in the 1930s and 40s

Drover's camp

"Life was often tough in this harsh land".

The homestead, Durrie station (Note Windlite generator)

Mrs Aiston's isolated store at Mulka. She lived alone except for her cat.

Where we shop

Mail bogged again

Alec Rabig's Whippet in the sand.

Flynn's Push Towards a Brighter Bush

Jim Stevens in Western Australia (1913)

Patrol Padres—Sunburnt friends who helped

Alf Traeger with the very first pedal transceiver (1929)

Birdsville Hospital (1937)

Cottage Hospitals staffed by "Outback Angels"

A wireless network to defeat the tyranny of distance

Mercy flight taking Mr Elliott to Mt Isa hospital

Flying Doctors—Only the best need apply

Bush Communicator

"He would just yarn, and you would think how impossible his ideas were. But then your soul would catch on fire and before long you would be helping him."

Flynn in Action

Off to Hermannsburg (1926)

The famous Dodge Four—wireless history was about to be made. Note the "extendable aerial" lashed to the side.

Bloods Creek

Already immaculate, Flynn breaks camp

Flynn in Action

Making friends and finding supporters in the cities

Shaving "on the wallaby"

"He was always smartly dressed in a land where no one else was."

Special Helpers

Qantas's support was vital

Jean Flynn—A wonderful secretary became a marvellous, supportive wife

Wishing Meg and Fred McKay well. The were off to serve the inland in 1939

Faces of a Visionary

AGED 33—"Combining faith with action alone can achieve our dreams"

AGED 61—Jean Flynn's favourite photograph of John, who was energetic and enthusiastic as ever

AGED 70—"You know, all my dreams have been fulfilled"

Passing the Mantle

The Frontier News

PUBLISHED BY THE AUSTRALIAN INLAND MISSION of the Presbyterian Church of Australia
5TH MAY 1952

JOHN FLYNN
MEMORIAL ISSUE

FRONTIER NEWS
memorial issue

Fred McKay picks up the reins

Rev. Fred McKay, Superintendent

FROM THE NEW SUPERINTENDENT

In producing this issue of the "Frontier News" the endeavour has been made to keep alive the spirit which was so characteristic of the young John Flynn.

But even he would not want me to apologise for the individuality which, if I am true to myself, must inevitably show itself.

Dr. Flynn warned me of the shoals ahead of our old ship. So I am not expecting a steady course.

But if we think in terms of centuries and continents—and Christ—we surely must experience something of the joy that comes to optimistic adventurers.

I have no misgivings about the crisis which is at present facing the A.I.M. Some aspects of our financial position are positively frightening.

One of our real problems is that the church and the public generally do not know the true facts; and false prophets tell wild tales.

I want you to do me the justice of believing me when I say that the A.I.M. is in dire financial straits.

We have exhausted our reserves—and already stern measures are being suggested by trusted advisers.

If retrenchment is forced upon us, then we shall face it with courage and wisdom.

Meantime, we are going forward.

We have reorganised our Headquarters administration and costs have been cut down severely.

All members of the team in the field are working with a will.

And I believe that once people are aware of our problems, they will stand with us.

Pessimism and panic have no place in a missionary platform.

In this bold undertaking in the name of the Presbyterian Church of Australia ,we shall go on—with faith in God—and with faith in our fellow men.

"Remembering his old boss and dear friend"–Fred McKay at Flynn's graveside; Gillen, 1953. (Before the new millennium, the original stone would be replaced.)

8

TEST CASE

Bruce Plowman moved to Oodnadatta in February 1914. Once there, he began equipping himself for long desert patrols to areas never visited before by a Christian minister.

Flynn was acutely aware that Plowman had only succeeded at Beltana, where others had succeeded before him. If Plowman failed in Central Australia, Flynn believed the AIM as a whole would fail. He had given the younger man some simple instructions: "Your patrol is greater in area than the British Isles, but it has only around 400 pioneers in it. Try to visit every one of them, if you can. You will need to use camels on your long patrols. Buy some, find out what to do, and do it."

Plowman's first task, then, was to put together a team of camels. For this he sought the help of Harry Jepp, a local storekeeper.

Jepp advised him, "Never trust a camel. Never. They're not like horses. A camel will plod along and be as docile as you please for years, until you think it is your friend. Then, in a flash, when you are off guard, it will try to drown you at a waterhole or crush you against the side of a hill."

He helped Plowman choose a string of five camels, so called because of the string joining them nose-to-tail. A peg was put through the camel's sensitive nose and a line attached. Tugging on this line was the only way to control such a cantankerous beast.

All camels snarl on occasion and growl, but Ameer and Robin seldom stopped from the moment Plowman bought them. Robin sometimes tried to roll on him and Ameer snapped at him with his powerful jaws. To these two Plowman added the massive white Doctor, which could carry up to a ton, and two faster riding camels, Cabool (which later tried to drown him) and Shah. His cattle dog, Streak, and a pile of gear completed his preparations. Later on, he employed a young part-Aborigine, Dick Gillen, as a "camel-boy". Dick helped him load up, unload, "hobble" the camels' legs with weights so they would graze at night without wandering too far, then catch them next morning. A fine young man, willing and loyal, he and Plowman became firm friends.

The pace at which his camels travelled was Plowman's first frustration. They were, he wrote,

> slow and sure – ninety per cent slow. Camels are born tired, and like most such beings have great endurance. They only average about three miles per hour, and when you have two thousand miles to travel, that is a frustrating rate. However, in hot weather, and it is often 120 degrees in the shade (only there is no shade, just hot stones and sand) the camels can travel three days without water, six in cooler conditions.

In such extremes of heat, Plowman dispensed with attempts to dress smartly and looked instead like the bushmen he set out to serve: wide-brimmed hat, khaki shirt, long trousers, tough leather boots. As before, he "mucked in" with whatever he found men doing, and was soon mustering, branding, slaughtering and droving with the Centralians.

Was his young protégé a success or not? Would the Centralians accept Christian ministry after so many years of neglect? Flynn waited impatiently for news.

Good news came in a letter from a young girl, Elsa Johannsen, from "Deep Well Station, Near Alice Springs":

> Mr Plowman gave a doll to my little sister Gertrude out of the box ... Mr Plowman baptised my little baby brother on Sunday afternoon and afterwards photographed us ... Today Mr Plowman married Mary and Billy. They are both half-caste people and they work for us ... Mr MacKay, the police trooper at Alice Well, sent me two pussies. They were in a box on the camel [Plowman's] and had to ride for fifty miles ... Mother gives me school lessons at home, because we are fifty miles away from the school. When Mr Plowman was here, he gave me some lessons and I liked it very much ... I will be nine years in June.

Flynn published a copy of this letter in *The Inlander*, commenting proudly:

> It shows the itinerant ministry at its best: bringing presents to isolated children, conducting Christian sacraments like baptism and marriage, serving the people, helping in the education of children. Mr Plowman is proving to be an ambassador for Christ.

Not everyone was quite so enthusiastic. Questions were asked when Plowman furnished statistics of his patrols, like the one to Tennant Creek:

> 6 weeks; 770 miles; 33 men; no women; such is our task ... we must just go on until the remotest Inlanders know that they are a part of our life, and their lives a part of ours.

"Six weeks to see only 33 people! It is possible to visit 33 lonely people in a single day in Melbourne, without all the expense and danger of Central Australia. How effective is Plowman really?" Flynn was asked at a Board meeting.

"It's not just the people visited," Flynn explained. "Out there, every man's business is known. A man passes on a camel, for instance. He notes Plowman's appearance and that of his riding camel, the four others, and Dick Gillen. The two white men have only passed the time of day as far as speech is concerned, but is that all? Never! The observer thinks, 'That man has staked his life – a big slice of it for certain, the whole of it if a nasty accident happens – on the old story of God's love to man. Many who have sent him out have staked their hard-earned savings that he might have camels and gear. Perhaps there is something to this Christianity after all, for them to make such an effort.' It is a thought this man will share with others around the camp fire. Plowman may have visited only 33 men on his patrol, but his efforts will have influenced many others. At stake is the attitude to Christianity of the whole of Central Australia: at present it is negative, but Plowman is busy changing that. You could never have a wide effect like that by visiting 33 people in Melbourne."

Flynn was not exaggerating about the chances of Plowman having a nasty accident. Working from mud maps, the young man nearly lost his way a number of times in waterless regions; if he had, the likely outcome was death from thirst. Were that to happen, Flynn's mission would die with him. Hostile Aborigines were another threat. In Alice Springs, while running a picnic for local children and giving them rides on his camel, Plowman was warned by a helper that the tribes to the north had been involved in a number of spearings of pioneers. Plowman was due to go north himself within a day or two.

"What worries me," Plowman told the man, "is that I shan't have Dick Gillen with me. He is staying behind here while I go north. Alice Springs is his home region and he needs a break. I don't trust his replacement, George, who strikes me as a sullen type."

"Is George from the north?"

"Yes, he is."

"Then you'd better keep a wary eye on him."

Plowman started up a vigorous Sunday School in Alice Springs and arranged three local volunteers to run it. Then he took George on a patrol to the north.

It was when breaking camp one morning that he caught a stealthy movement out of the corner of his eye. Swivelling, he saw George snatch a boomerang from the front of Shah's saddle, put his left leg forward to balance and draw back his arm to hurl it in his direction. Aborigines never threw a boomerang without intent to kill!

Reacting by instinct, Plowman leapt across and smashed his fist into George's face; he fell backwards and dropped his weapon. Plowman deftly kicked it away and hit George again, this time with his left fist because the first heavy blow had dislocated his right thumb. Scrabbling around in his box he took out a revolver, and fixed it into his belt with his left hand. Then he confiscated the boomerangs George kept for self-defence against unfriendly Aborigines. Next, he wrapped George's bleeding head, using a towel for a bandage. The blood soon seeped through and George looked a sorry sight.

Once satisfied that he had the situation under control, and determined to keep it that way by riding close to George, Plowman commanded the camels to move forward. He would have to keep George under very close surveillance – his own life depended on it.

That afternoon they burst through some scrub into a clearing beside a rock pool. A group of naked Aborigines, all carrying spears or boomerangs, turned to look at them. George began talking to his fellow tribesmen in great excitement, pointing to the bloodstained towel around his head, swinging his fist and then pointing at Plowman, who rode quickly forward, gruffly commanding George to press on. The Aborigine, now very fearful of his "boss", obeyed at once, and they so passed the silent, threatening group.

Sensing danger, Plowman turned to look back before reaching the far side of the clearing. A young man, spear in hand, was creeping silently up behind them. Swinging Cabool around in a trice, Plowman raced back across the few yards separating them, pulling out his revolver as he did so, and pointed the revolver into a dark face whose eyes had suddenly grown very large. He shouted a warning down in pidgin, "You walk longa white fella, white fella killem dead. You knowem?" The young Aborigine, his mouth wide open, nodded vigorous assent.

Plowman wheeled Cabool and raced out of the clearing, aware that the danger had only just begun, that the group could track and hunt him that very night. He put as much country between himself and the rock pool as he could, then camped in as open a spot as he could find, tethering the camels to nearby trees for a quick getaway. It was hard on the camels, as it meant that they would not be able to graze that night.

George had been instructed to light the fire but when Plowman heard a crackling sound, he turned to see a huge blaze instead of the normal-sized fire. "A very clever way to signal your friends," he thought angrily, "and I'm stuck here because I can't move camp in the dark. Well, I shall have to make plans of my own."

He withdrew to a reasonable distance from the fire, but still in open space. With the packs and gear he built a horseshoe-shaped barrier high enough that his exact position could not be seen by someone creeping up to it. The open end of the horseshoe faced towards the fire; he made George sleep between himself and the flames. That way he was in shadow while George was highly visible to him.

Plowman lay down on his blankets, revolver in his left hand and rifle (normally used for shooting game for the pot) in his right. He had no intention of sleeping. He knew that if the Aborigines saw George lying there they would not attack, so he was determined to keep him there. George, of course, knew this and would try to escape.

Several times that night George cautiously lifted his head to check whether Plowman was asleep. Each time, Plowman lifted the rifle and pointed it at his head and George immediately dropped back flat onto his blankets.

The young minister was very relieved when daylight flooded the bush next morning. After a quick check to make sure there was no ambush waiting, he rode off safely, George in attendance.

Incidents like these took a toll on Plowman's nerves, especially when he was on patrol without Dick Gillen. He would then have to track the camels himself each day. "This is very hard work as they leave only the faintest of tracks, and on very hard ground no tracks at all," he wrote to Flynn. To lose his camels would most likely mean death.

But he found the difficulties were compensated for by the grand hospitality and mateship he experienced, and the increasing response to the meetings he held.

A sign that the pioneers liked and accepted him was the way they sometimes joked at Plowman's expense. Once, when Plowman helped at a burial, he was shocked to see the word HELL emblazoned across the coffin in large letters. "How can you be so sure?" he asked the men.

"If you'd known him, Padre, you'd wouldn't have to ask," they jested.

It took a while for him to uncover the truth. The men had knocked up the coffin from old fuel cases which carried the logo of the SHELL company. They had not required the first plank (with the "S" on it) when they had made up the coffin.

John Flynn publicised Plowman's exploits as widely as he could, expecting there would be a good response from ministers wanting to serve in the exciting AIM field. To his confusion and chagrin, there were no volunteers at all. His mission would fail if he couldn't attract staff.

Besides Bruce Plowman, there was only one other patrol padre serving in the AIM. This was Reverend Jim Stevens, who operated out of Port Hedland in Western Australia, in what was known as the

Pilbara Patrol. An officer in the Australian Light Horse in the Boer War, he patrolled in a buggy drawn by two camels, cutting a romantic figure in his pith helmet and with his erect military bearing. Stevens had begun as a member of the North West Mission of the Presbyterian Church and had been transferred over to the AIM, so he was hardly one of the "new recruits" being sought so desperately. Nevertheless, Flynn valued him as a good friend and an experienced padre.

In his search for patrol ministers, Flynn preached his heart out in churches, and at youth meetings and rallies.

In Tasmania, he spoke for hours one night to a young student, Kingsley Partridge, who had expressed an interest in the work. As they tallked, they marched up and down the street in order to keep warm. Excitedly, Flynn shared his visions with Partridge, who limped along on a bad ankle behind the master, ignoring the pain because of the fire that burned in him as Flynn spoke. Partridge went on to complete a Master of Arts degree and win a scholarship overseas, but he never forgot the dreams that Flynn had spoken of. Later in life, this encounter would draw him towards work in the AIM.

Flynn was successful at last in finding a recruit, and Reverend Frank Brady joined the work. In late 1913, he and his wife took up the ministry at Broome in Western Australia. Broome was a pearling centre teeming with two thousand itinerant aliens. Brady established a regular Sunday service in the town and went on long patrols into the rugged Kimberley Ranges and associated regions.

Stevens' predecessor, Reverend Payn Lewis, had left the field because of the danger and strain of the work. Stevens and Brady also found their lifestyles very difficult. For example, where it existed, their accommodation was rented and of poor quality. Flynn was aware of this lack and wanted to put up buildings for the AIM on the basis that "rent paid is strength lost. Furthermore, comfort to a certain level is desirable in that it establishes conditions favouring highest human efficiency" – and in the Inland that meant reducing heat, dust, flies and the blinding glare. Although he recognised these needs, Flynn did not as yet have the resources to meet them and his staff continued to struggle along in inadequate living conditions.

Patrol work was very taxing. Stevens described his situation thus:

> It is difficult to understand this indifference in view of the events here recently – two murders, one death by drowning (a pearl diver), and one death from thirst, the last on a track whereon I had rather a "close call" myself a few months back. This trip took me to the edge of the desert, beyond the last fence, and to the farthest-out settlers. One brave-hearted woman had lived out on the desert for four years and had only seen one other white woman during that time, and that when she had visited a neighbouring station to record her vote. Wild blacks are numerous, and her home is in the dreariest of dreary sand and spinifex country ... The need of the people and the call from the regions beyond become more urgent every day. I cannot move through the countryside fast enough.

Flynn visited Jim Stevens in June 1914, and went out on a patrol with him. On their return, Stevens raised a looming issue. "Mr Flynn, it would seem that the clouds of war are gathering once again and that Australia may soon be in the thick of it. Were that to happen, I would feel it my duty to volunteer."

Flynn was silent a few moments. "I respect your patriotism," he said, "but don't you think your work here too important simply to leave it? We'd be unlikely to replace you. There's a manpower crisis as it is."

"I've thought a lot about the problem of finding a replacement, but I'm convinced I should go," reiterated Stevens. "Have you considered the implications for the AIM if war does break out?"

"Not deeply, but my gut feeling is that the AIM will not survive a major war. However, I intend to carry on somehow. Look, go if you must; you have my blessing, especially if you join the Chaplains or the Medical Corps. I somehow feel they are the most appropriate for a man of God."

The approaching war affected Flynn's few remaining staff as well. Two of these were at Oodnadatta.

When Bruce Plowman was not on his 2500-mile patrol, which occupied six strenuous months, he had no place to call home, where he could relax. Based at Sister Bett's nursing home, he became her "Mr Fixit", helping with chores and teaching some of the daily classes.

"I intend to volunteer to serve in the war, should it come," Sister Bett first informed him in 1913. "What are your intentions, Mr Plowman?"

Bruce put his hammer and nails down to think a few moments before he replied. "I'm not sure yet what I'll do. You'll be sorely missed locally, not just for the nursing but for your social work here as well. The local people all seem to like you and trust you."

"Here I can help a few people each week. In the war, it'll be hundreds."

While Plowman wrestled with the question of whether to volunteer, he visited the people in the Oodnadatta region. He was surprised to find Mrs Mac, at Alindum Well, with another babe in arms – had he not baptised her eighth very recently? How could this be? He soon discovered that the new baby was not her own, but the child of her friend, Clara, who had died in childbirth. Without a murmur, Mrs Mac had taken on the infant until the bereaved husband, Dick, could make other arrangements. Plowman regarded this action as heroic, considering the struggle she was having to feed and clothe her own eight children under tough pioneering conditions. When he said as much, the good woman blushed and was covered in confusion.

After giving Mrs Mac's children some school lessons, he set off 45 miles over rough tracks to visit Dick. He wondered how Dick was coping with his other four children now that he had lost his wife.

Dick's homestead was a crude settler's affair of tents and bough-sheds constructed from split logs lashed together and roofed with a rough thatch of sticks, leaves and grass. Despite these difficult conditions, the loving father had managed to keep the children clean, fed, healthy and clothed – even if the clothing was rudimentary and patched.

The padre found Dick distraught with grief, but unbowed. His first concern was for his children, whose future he wanted to discuss with Plowman. They planned that Dick should sell the property and invest the proceeds for the children, while the father continued to earn his living in the bush. Meanwhile, Dick's sister would take the youngsters and give them a city education. Would Plowman be prepared to arrange their transport down to Adelaide? The padre replied that he would be glad to do all he could.

Dick was still listless and depressed; he clearly needed to get something off his chest. Eventually, he broached the subject: would the padre come and look at Clara's grave with him?

Dick shared his burden, haltingly and with difficulty, as the two men walked towards the sandhill where she was buried. "There were only me and the kiddies on the property when Clara died … She was a big woman and I tried but couldn't lift her body into the buggy to take it to where I had dug her grave. The kids were too small to help. Not having any wood to make a coffin, I wrapped her in a blanket.

"Eventually I placed her on a dry bullock-hide because it would be easier for that to slide over the ground. I hitched the hide to a horse and dragged it over to the grave … " Here Dick's voice became unsteady. He continued, "I had to put her into the grave myself." After a further pause, he revealed, "I could not fill in the grave because the police at Oodnadatta had to be notified first, so I covered it with a large sheet of corrugated iron. It took a fortnight for the trooper to come. He signed the death certificate. Only then could I fill in the grave."

There was nothing Plowman could do but listen to this moving and distressing account. Dick, however, seemed to gain great comfort from his presence.

Back at the homestead, Plowman gave the children their lessons, using the opportunity to try to prepare them a little for what life would be like in the big city. But even he didn't realise just how little they knew.

This became apparent when the children had to wait several days in Oodnadatta for the train south. Sister Bett immediately set about mothering them, organising baths, clothes, food and some little extras to make them feel loved.

The eldest girl, aged 11, was by herself in Sister Bett's sittingroom one day when a sudden draught blew the door shut. The noise startled the child, who panicked and tried to find a way out. The windows were covered with wire screens that could not be moved so she pulled and tugged at the door handle, which would not budge. Finally, terrified, she started screaming.

Sister Bett heard the noise and ran to yank the door open. Seeing the stark terror on the child's face, she looked around for a snake or some other cause. She could see nothing. Through chokes and sobs, the child told her that she was upset because she'd been trapped inside the room.

"Oh, you poor lamb!" Sister Bett said, gathering the girl into her arms and patting her back reassuringly. Then she gently released her and showed her how to turn a door handle, something the child had never seen in her tent-and-shed homestead. What enormous adjustments lay ahead for the four!

As Plowman pondered the help he had been able to give to Dick and to others like him, he made the decision not to volunteer for the war; he could do more good right where he was. Besides, he had promised five years of his life to establish Central Patrol and he did not intend to renege on that undertaking.

Plowman's visible success and his decision to remain at his post were heartening to Flynn in an otherwise discouraging year. Manpower for the AIM was at crisis point and funds were rapidly drying up because of the impending war. Furthermore, Flynn's post as Superintendent was due to be reviewed in September 1914, two years after his original appointment. He knew that the survival of the AIM and his own position in it were by no means certain, and would be the subject of lengthy debates at the General Assembly.

9

A TIME TO HEAL

Did the AIM have a future? This was the question John Flynn had to address in his report to the General Assembly. He would have to get the delegates to look beyond what had been achieved to date, because, in fact, little had. Tortuous hours were spent preparing the crucial document, which ran to over fifty pages and contained much impressive data.

The logical program for Flynn to propose would have been to curtail expansion because war had been declared the previous month, August 1914. This was the course the Board had been urging him to follow, to "cut the suit according to your cloth, Mr Flynn". He paced his hotel room at the Metropole, Sydney, thinking and smoking pipe after pipe. The needs of the pioneers were too great for conservative proposals; he would not sell them short.

His pragmatic friend Andrew Barber called in to see him. Barber and Flynn kept in close contact and would meet whenever their paths crossed. "You must plan for a lengthy war, Flynn," he advised. "I don't believe it will be over in a few months as many predict."

"How do you see the war affecting the mission?"

"Wars gobble spare money, so you will struggle financially. Recruitment will be another casualty. You have had hardly any success getting men and women to serve in the AIM in peacetime. From now on, most candidates will be caught up in the conflict. Have you thought about that?"

Flynn drew silently on his pipe a few moments. He replied, "I have, and it strikes me that while men have enormous pressure placed on them to go to war, the situation for women is different. Perhaps we could survive by developing the nursing arm of our work? For example, Jim Stevens is off to war. I thought his patrol would remain empty, but now I foresee a nursing home starting up there. When he returns, he will find that the AIM is far from forgotten because of the goodwill our nurses will have generated. I refuse to suggest a lessening of our work to the General Assembly; instead I'm going to suggest an expansion!"

"I'm not sure that's wise," cautioned Barber. "I hear that some men are going to speak against the 'extravagance' of the AIM as it is. Now that war has been declared, they'll have a strong argument. What makes you think the General Assembly will accept a visionary approach at such an uncertain time?"

John Flynn sucked his pipe thoughtfully before replying, his shoulders hunched and his forehead puckered. He looked frail and vulnerable. "I cannot back off now," he said at last. "When I worked out the principles on which the AIM was going to be based, I identified 'faith' and 'love' as fundamental. Neither appears to be logical, but both always succeed. Therefore, by faith, I must plan as if the war will not prevent us going forward. Wars always have an end, don't they?"

Flynn spoke from the heart when he stood and presented these ideas to the General Assembly. The survival of the AIM was in the balance so he was unusually forceful, probing for the core of each listener. A short excerpt gives the flavour of his speech that day.

> What has been accomplished during the last two years? In particular – not much. In general – quite a deal ... After all our enthusiastic Assembly declarations, publication of elaborate reports and magazines, formation of committees, campaigns in church meetings and public demonstrations, deluges of circulars; after all our patriotic Church talk, and writings of the needs of workers in Inland areas – we have increased the number of Church workers in the Inland by two men only!

He referred to the financial situation, how less than half their target of £5 000 a year had been raised: "Also not, on the face of it, a very brilliant performance. But we must look beneath the surface of things. Doing this, we immediately find evidence of much to be deeply grateful for, much to justify hope." He explained that his "hope" centred around the organisational structures that had been put in place and which had started to function, and *The Inlander*, which was proving very popular.

Flynn then switched gear and began to sketch his vision for the future. He boldly outlined to the Assembly how he intended to expand the role of nurses.

> To see that hospitals and nursing facilities are provided within a hundred miles of every spot in Australia where women and children reside; not hesitating to err on the reckless side. Are we justified in sending out a nurse at great expense when there are "so few" people?

He answered this question with another:

> Should one woman [a pioneer], who is bold enough to accompany her husband far beyond the habitations of other women, who sacrifices all the ordinary privileges of community life, be allowed to pay the price of suffering or death, or watch her children pay it instead, for the privilege?

> And, if that is the case today, can our Church – knowing the facts – can our Church, receiving a total revenue of more than a quarter of a million pounds per year, look on inactive and yet retain self-respect?

Flynn paused to allow his words to take effect. The Assembly was totally silent, absorbed in the powerful challenge flung at it. The speaker used the pause to scrabble among papers on the rostrum, emerging with a recent letter from an AIM nurse which he read it to his listeners. The tenor of the address changed now, becoming emotive, tugging at the heartstrings.

> The baby from Alice Springs was one year and nine months old. It was the most shocking thing that I have seen. The jaw had been either fractured or dislocated. Its whole head and face was black, and the mouth fixed wide open; the eyes right out of the head, and the child unconscious ... It is a good case for Alice Springs [to have a hospital], as, if there had been a nurse near, it could never have got into that condition.

He stopped for effect, then thrust for the heart:

> I do appeal to this Assembly to become impatient enough to say "bother expense!" where the welfare of isolated women and children is concerned. By the blackened face of that poor

child, and the agonised heart of its weary mother, for it must have taken EIGHT DAYS for the parents to reach the hospital, I urge you to roll back the shame of years by doing generously what the nation has been too indifferent even to discuss seriously!

The critical point had now been reached when Flynn had to present his detailed plans for the future. Unless the General Assembly had been thoroughly convinced by what he had said to this juncture, they would never support the expansion he was about to unfold. He felt unusually tense.

In summary, what he proposed was that the patrol regions be doubled from five to ten, that 18 ordained ministers and four deaconess-nurses be employed, that two new hospitals or other buildings be erected every year for at least the next ten years. These ambitious plans would require more than four times the money their best efforts had managed to raise to date, and this in wartime! He also suggested that a part-time secretary be employed at his office in Sydney to help him with his mountain of paperwork.

Flynn went on to discuss possible financial strategies, but admitted that "only a revolution in home mission thinking, feeling, and giving will make possible the establishment of an adequate Inland mission."

What if the war, or drought, should impose additional burdens on the AIM? He did not sidestep the issue completely. "The AIM has no reserve funds and no property of consequence," he informed the Assembly. It was therefore a problem to which he had no solution, one which "I must leave to other and wiser minds".

What of the murmurings that he should be ousted as Super-intendent? Flynn knew that his report alone was sufficient fuel for him to be labelled as "irresponsible". How might he forestall moves against him? He now did a most unusual and uncharacteristic thing: he listed the work he had done since assuming the office of Superintendent two years earlier. His personal input was awesome, straining belief. The question was not asked but was inferred – could anyone else do more? More importantly, was there another in that hall who would like to take on Flynn's role? Who else would forgo a house and spend most of his life on the road, accommodated in travellers' clubs?

Flynn stood awkwardly and alone on the podium at the completion of what he had to say, peering anxiously from behind round-framed spectacles. Two years previously, his report had been greeted with acclaim. This one was met with silence.

There were many there that day who doubted the AIM would survive the two years until the next General Assembly, but who felt that Flynn's leadership gave it its best chance. Besides, who else would want to take on the mammoth problems he faced? So, despite its cool reception and the murmurings, somehow the report was passed. Flynn was reappointed Superintendent for another two years.

With the trauma of the General Assembly over, he threw himself afresh into AIM work. Against all expectations, the recruitment crisis began to ease. The losses of Jim Stevens and Sister Bett were compensated for by outstanding replacements. Furthermore, a new patrol was begun in Queensland in 1915 by Reverend Frank Heriot, who worked out of Cloncurry.

Keen as he was to press on with his plans to extend the nursing arm of the AIM, Flynn found his productivity choked by routine paperwork. He had to write more than 50 letters a week, send out receipts and materials to members of the Bush Brigade, write articles for the print media, write and edit *The Inlander*, prepare and send out multitudinous organisational details, and the tasks were growing daily. When he was away from Sydney the paperwork grew even more, causing tensions with the Board.

Flynn lost weight under the burden and, already thin, became haggard. He never took a break. Clearly, he needed help, a personal secretary, but other needs took priority.

He was thinking about this problem while ministering at an Easter Christian Camp in 1915, dreading his return to his office. He felt tired, not bounding with energy like the young people around him playing ball games. If only he could absorb some of their energy and youthful enthusiasm.

Suddenly it struck him. That was the answer to his exhaustion: other people's strength. Why hadn't he thought of it before? Certain Christian supporters might be prepared to give a few hours a week on a voluntary basis to help with office work. Book Teams had operated on that basis for years for the Mail-bag League, providing sterling service. Some months they sent off in excess of a ton of printed material.

The first Office Team or OT was trialled in Sydney and proved to be a great success. It was soon followed by similar teams in other cities. In due course the services expanded to supply household goods and hospital linen to AIM nurses and provide dress patterns and materials to pioneer women. Office Teams created a "family bond" with people in the bush, while back home they transformed the functional AIM offices into comfortable, homely centres to which people gravitated: Church people, inquirers, AIM staff on leave. The term "AIM Family" began to be used.

Flynn liked the concept of a loving AIM Family and employed it widely in his writings. How better to promote family life in the bush than for the AIM to be identified as an "extended family" itself?

He was appreciative of the fact that the OTs were staffed by unselfish voluntary workers. He often told them how valuable they were and where he could he showed his gratitude in little ways: free theatre tickets, cakes for tea, small personal gifts. Best of all, their work freed Flynn to pursue his vision for the Inland. Happier and healthier, he began looking actively for places to build cottage hospitals.

Port Hedland had first approached Flynn with a request for an AIM nursing home in 1913, "like your one at Oodnadatta". The need was great, and first Reverend Jim Stevens and then his replacement, Reverend Jim Shaw, raised funds towards this end. Flynn advertised widely to try to attract a suitable nurse to pioneer the hospital, but more than 20 nurses and trainees who had originally expressed interest had since left for service in the killing fields of Europe. Eventually Marion Haines, a fine prospect, committed herself to go, but needed to complete her training in midwifery first. The calls from Port Hedland became more urgent. Couldn't Flynn find someone sooner? He tried, to no avail. Then Sister Linda Rutherford showed interest, agreeing to fill the gap until Marion Haines could replace her. She began her work in February 1915, in a leased cottage overlooking the beach, where she was extremely busy.

Then came the news Sister Rutherford had been dreading: her terminally ill father had died. She couldn't attend the funeral because it would have taken too many days for her to return home. Her consolation came in restoring to life one critically ill old man who reminded her of him. In fact, the nurse had a run of successes with seriously ill patients, which helped to ease her pain. So did some of the appreciative comments she received: one Aborigine said, "You best woman around these parts, you make better quick," and an old man told her, "I'm at home here. It's the first home I've been in since my mother died."

In due course Nurse Haines replaced Sister Rutherford. When John Flynn visited the Port Hedland hospital, he was delighted to observe the many roles this talented newcomer filled:

> as a dentist to extract teeth, as an ambulance officer, a welfare worker, minister, friend, confidant, doctor, social worker and teacher. These extras make Christ visible to the community. For many, the only religion they see is our sister and her love.

His second cottage hospital a stunning success, where to next? Flynn was obsessed by his vision of an AIM nursing home right in the heart of Australia, in Alice Springs. Every month he was reminded of the need by some report or other. He spoke of his dream to Sister Jean Finlayson, now the nurse at Oodnadatta. Enthused, she offered to go and pioneer the work at Alice Springs.

As soon as a replacement was organised for her, Jean Finlayson set out. She had plenty of opportunity to think about her impetuous decision as she swayed atop a camel for the last 200 miles. No cottage hospital awaited her, nor even a house in which to live.

Sister Finlayson was to work under the most primitive of conditions in the Alice, living in a tent and seeing patients in a cubicle. She taught Sunday school from her one chair behind her only table. But despite her heroic efforts, Flynn's move to the centre was premature: after her year's service, Jean Finlayson left and there was no one to replace her. The men and women of the region continued to lack medical attention. Flynn withdrew to lick his wounds.

Money became desperately short for the AIM during the First World War, but Flynn refused to curtail his plans. He spent much energy dashing hither and thither across Australia in fundraising ventures – and not only for the AIM. It is proof of his great compassion that he raised even more money for the Red Cross during the Great War than he did for the AIM.

Desperate needs kept surfacing in the Inland, and each time Flynn tried to do something about them. For instance, Jim Gibson, the new AIM patrol padre at Pine Creek in the Northern Territory, had ridden up to the bustling tin town of Maranboy in 1916 only to find all was eerily quiet. What had silenced the creaking windlasses, the clink of hammer on stone, the shouting of the miners? His only clue was a rash of fresh graves dotting the hillside.

Gibson found the first paperbark hut empty, but the second contained a man on a metal bed that rattled as the man shook with fever. Malaria! Rushing from hut to hut, the padre discovered Maranboy to be in the grip of a death-dealing epidemic.

"I'll get Flynn to send a nurse here to help," he told the remaining miners, "providing you supply a building to act as a hospital. The AIM will pay her salary and all expenses. She would not get here in time to help in the present epidemic, but she will be here for later ones. Your mates should not have suffered without medical help and died."

Mr Stutterd, the battery manager, had just lost his little daughter in a failed dash to reach the doctor in far-off Pine Creek. He gave his blessing to the concept.

The men were also supportive of Gibson's plan and a hat passed around soon overflowed with donations. Gibson hastened to the nearest telegraph station and sent an emergency message to Flynn. Rapid consultations followed between Flynn and the Northern Territory government, which agreed to build a cottage hospital to Flynn's design and equip it, on condition that the AIM would provide staff to run it.

Flynn cast around for a nurse and companion prepared to venture 3000 miles from home to an isolated part of the "Never Never", to live and serve among a rough mining community of over 100 men and only two other white women. It was a settlement that received supplies by donkey team only every five months or so.

Two young women with adventurous spirits volunteered: Sister Hepburn and her companion May Gillespie. Flynn was aware that he needed to impart the thrust of his vision to Sister Hepburn before she left for the rigours of her post. On her youthful shoulders rested the reputation and future traditions of the AIM Nursing Service in that region. So he told her one of his own experiences, hoping that she would catch the deeper implications.

"One time while on patrol in the Beltana district, I was asked to come to a sick well-sinker. I found a man in his forties on a dirty bed in a tin shed. I could do him no good: he had a high temperature, his heart was fluttering and, from what his mates told me, I surmised his appendix had burst. My examination also suggested gonorrhoea. His mates had left messages at various points along the line for the railway doctor to come, so I tried to be of some comfort while we settled down to wait.

"As I watched him fighting for each breath, it struck me what a wreck that man had become: I saw lice in his thin hair, blackened teeth in a mouth that seldom if ever received a visit from a toothbrush, his body and clothing stank and his skin was covered with tiny scratches that had gone septic. The only food he had was salt beef and old damper, no vegetables. His body had been so degraded he could not have lived many more years, though he was only middle-aged.

"Looking down at him, the solution came to me as clear as day: many more women were needed in the Outback to change the lifestyles of men like the well-sinker. Women would raise the standard of hygiene, diet, conversation and moral practice – they would be like a light shining out into the darkness. I let my imagination roam a little and visualised the same man with a wife and children by a proud little home, healthy and happy. 'Good women make good men,' I decided, and it is a principle I have been convinced of ever since. So I am asking you to shine out into the darkness of Maranboy, teach the men about hygiene and having a healthy diet, set them standards by your conversation and conduct."

"I shall try to," said Sister Hepburn. "Whatever happened to the well-sinker?"

"The doctor was delayed by the condition of the roads. He arrived in time to sign the death certificate."

After an exhausting journey, the two women arrived at Maranboy where they found a bright, fresh, well-equipped hospital they described to Flynn as "A-one". It was a two-storey building with a fine view over the tinfields.

Another fierce malaria epidemic struck soon after the women arrived. Nineteen seriously ill patients were treated in the hospital itself and dozens of others were tended in their bough-sheds in the tinfields.

The battle raged for days. Sleep was something the staff could only snatch for a few minutes at a time. Slowly their efforts brought the epidemic under control, and as a result of it not one new grave had to be dug. The contrast with the deaths caused by the previous outbreak was so striking that the Maranboy community at once placed the new arrivals on a pedestal.

This respect helped raise the social and moral standards in the area, just as Flynn had hoped. Where they were able to, men began to scrub up and wear clean, starched clothes when going to the hospital for treatment. More importantly, they listened to Sister Hepburn when she moved about their camps and gave advice on how to prevent disease, teaching them that "prevention is better than cure". The women also encouraged men to borrow books from the AIM library at the hospital and organised a few very successful social events, featuring entertainments such as any large gathering of Australian bushmen can produce.

Sister Hepburn had taken Flynn's wider commission to heart and had started nothing less than a social revolution. The *Northern Territory Times* picked up on this and ran a flattering article, concluding: "With no fear of sickness the womenfolk are going to Maranboy, and there is no greater need nor hope for the [tin]field than in this process ..."

Flynn quoted this impartial observation by an independent newspaper in *The Inlander*. It proved that his "battle for a brighter bush" was being won.

Later, when Sister Hepburn and Miss Gillespie were about to be replaced, the local residents presented them with gifts and a written testimonial:

> Since your advent the conditions, socially and otherwise, have shown an unmistakable improvement, and your professional services have this year averted a catastrophe. You leave this way-

back centre with the good wishes of every resident, not only locally, but in the surrounding district. Your stay has made for good, and in regretting your departure we sincerely wish you God speed.

Shortly after, Flynn received a letter from his old friend Jeannie Gunn. She it was who had encouraged him to make "healing" one of his three important goals. It so happened that the station where her much-loved husband, Aeneas, had died of fever in 1903 was only 50 miles from the new Maranboy hospital. Had the hospital been there, she believed the Maluka would not have died. She wrote:

This is the best – perhaps the only – true advance the poor old Territory has made in the last five or six years. What a hospital and nurse will mean out there, only those who have known utter helplessness when a beloved life is at stake can ever quite realise.

Flynn was much encouraged by this show of support. However, another envelope was on its way whose contents would cause him great soul searching.

10

CASUALTIES

The envelope Flynn received appeared to be empty, but when he shook it a white feather floated out and settled on his desk. A white feather was an accusation of cowardice for not volunteering to go to war. It was considered to be the greatest of insults.

"Is that what people are thinking," Flynn wondered, "that I am hiding behind my clerical collar? What influence can I have for Christ if people think I am a coward?"

While he wrestled with this question over the following months, his sister Rosetta was subjected to abusive letters: partly because her brother had not volunteered and partly because their Irish ancestry made some people question their loyalty to Australia.

Flynn knew that by volunteering for active service he would rebut such allegations. However, he was also certain the AIM would cease to operate without his leadership. Surely his call from God to the Inland took precedence over his call to duty for his country? The debate raged within him without resolution.

Eventually, Flynn spoke to his good friend Frank Rolland when the latter enlisted as a chaplain to the forces. What did he advise?

After a few seconds' thought, Rolland said, "Every man must make up his own mind on the issue. The way I see it is that ministers are a little like fathers. Wherever our children are most in trouble, we should go. Many of the men I have ministered to have gone, so I believe I should too. Your situation is different, though, Flynn. The AIM is your child; you've fathered it and it is too young to survive alone."

Flynn received a second white feather the following year. He took it to the window and dropped it out. A breeze caught it and it drifted away, glinting in the sun. He later expressed his attitude to volunteering in a letter thus: "I should like to join Frank Rolland [at the front], but I have a trench here that needs holding for Australia's sake."

What was Flynn's attitude to war? Generally, he detested it and believed that there existed superior ways for nations to solve their differences: "God does not call His creatures to discord. His world is big enough for the harmony of all nations ..."

Although armed conflict was anathema to him, Flynn began to borrow from the imagery of warfare in his writings, both to capture attention and to show that it was not only armed conflict that separated people and caused suffering – Australians' neglect of the Inland produced the same results. Military terms such as "warfare with nature", "the battle for the bush", "national heroes", "dauntless courage", "our infantry", "the front at Oodnadatta", "necessary munitions" peppered his AIM propaganda.

Despite employing these phrases, Flynn always pointed ahead to the peace that must follow, encouraging Australians to plan for the future. Early in 1917 he made an appeal to soldiers to return to be nation builders, to "volunteer" for service in the Inland, quoting the poet C.J. Dennis:

> When all the stoush is over, Mick, there's
> 'eaps of work to do
> And in the peacetime scraps to come,
> We'll still be needing you.

As the AIM field expanded despite the war, so did the problems. For instance, Flynn received a letter of strong criticism from a disgruntled doctor who had been co-operating with the AIM nurse at Oodnadatta (this was atypical as he received many letters of praise). The doctor had been offended by her "arrogant manner" – he was the doctor, but the nurse often behaved like one herself in the decisions she made. Consequently, he had withdrawn his co-operation, except in emergencies. He gave suggestions as to how AIM nurses and doctors might relate better in the future.

His letter was several pages; Flynn's reply was succinct:

1. Our institution has been, some time ago, excommunicated by you.
2. That fact is only now communicated to us by you.

3. You invite us, after the event, to discuss the situation.

It seems to us that the present situation, as created by yourself, has left nothing open for discussion.

Flynn's sharp intellect had gone to the heart of the matter here: no doctor should withdraw professional services for personal reasons. Indeed his Hippocratic oath did not allow for such behaviour.

Some people considered Flynn to be a simple man because he was humble and lived simply – food and material things held no interest for him – but his dealings with people were astute. Often he would appear not to be paying much attention to a conversation, but when he did speak he would surprise everyone by his grasp of the issues.

Another difficulty, more serious, lay in the work of patrol padres. Early warning signals could be picked up in a letter Reverend Jim Gibson wrote from his Pine Creek patrol in 1915: "At the close [of the patrol] I found that I also had had quite enough! Suffered more from nerves than anything else. The strain of the days in the trackless country which has a slender water supply is severe."

Gibson resigned in 1917, as much from nerves as anything else, and left behind an empty patrol. Statements by Frank Brady and Jim Shaw indicated that they too found Outback patrols to be very stressful. Even the redoubtable Bruce Plowman wrote to the AIM Board to suggest ways to lessen the strains he was feeling. He included a request for a residence away from the nursing home at Oodnadatta, so that he could be undisturbed when back from a patrol and have time alone to unwind.

Surprisingly, Flynn was slow to respond to these danger signals, perhaps because stress did not affect him to the extent that it did other people. He was always under a myriad of pressures, but never spared himself. He explained, "I have to work long hours, the AIM is growing out of its boots." The strain did take its toll on him, but he had a sanguine personality. "John Flynn will never die of a heart attack," Andrew Barber once remarked caustically, adding, "but I might, trying to keep him on time with his schedule." Similar frustrations were felt by most of his co-workers.

On a deeper level, time itself played an odd role in Flynn's life: he was a seer about the future, but struggled to come to terms with the present. In a strange way, this otherworldliness, this ability to live in the future, protected him from the stress of present problems. However, it meant he did not always appreciate what others were going through.

In 1917, after five years of magnificent ministry, Bruce Plowman suffered a nervous breakdown – a combination of stress and the poisoning of his tough body by infected teeth.

Flynn was devastated. He insisted he be allowed, personally, to go out and fetch Plowman home. He would then replace him for a period of service in Central Patrol, until a suitable recruit could be found. His Board refused to permit this because he was too valuable an asset to be spared for patrol work. Flynn cast around desperately for someone else: not just anyone could minister in the rigours of Central Patrol. It would have to be another Bruce Plowman.

No minister even vaguely qualified presented himself. But after an AIM rally in Phillip Street, Sydney, a fit young man stayed behind to chat to Flynn. It was Kingsley Partridge, who four years earlier in Tasmania, in 1913, had hobbled up and down until two o'clock in the morning discussing the mission with Flynn. Partridge had achieved remarkably well at university since then, winning a scholarship to Scotland to further his studies, yet the fire that Flynn had ignited still flickered.

As Flynn looked at Partridge, he realised this was his man for Central Patrol. He told him about the need and asked him to fill the position.

Partridge refused. What about his plans to go to Scotland and his bright academic future? Flynn persisted. The longer they spoke, the more the young man felt he should accept, at least for a short while.

Kingsley Partridge, later known as "Skipper", had a baptism of fire into the arduous nature of the work in Central Patrol. Flynn described this in the Presbyterian of May 1918.

> Mr Partridge has had a varied experience on a trip west of Oodnadatta. He had spent the day on one of the stations about seventy miles out of Oodnadatta, and just as he was preparing to leave, a man took ill.

> Our minister at once took charge of the case, and as there was a motor on the place it was sent off in haste to bring Sister Hore [of the AIM] from the township. But the nurse arrived too late, for the illness proved as fatal as swift.

The problem then was to make a coffin; and there Mr Partridge acted as assistant to the amateur carpenter of the station.

After that he assisted to dig the grave, and conducted the service subsequently.

What an instance of entering into the life of the people on the frontier!

A few days later it was found that a man had been lost, so Mr Partridge joined Constable Welsh in the search. They travelled from Friday morning till Sunday at daylight. The sufferer was found, just in time. He had been two days without water and five without food. He was placed in the hospital [at Oodnadatta] under the care of Sister Hore, and is making satisfactory progress.

The report ended on a sad note.

It is with deep sorrow that we announce the bereavement just come to Sister Hore, of Oodnadatta. Her brother has died of wounds at the front. The sympathy and remembrance of our circle goes out to one thus saddened while far from home.

The carnage at the front was robbing AIM workers of loved ones. The AIM Family supported each member in their loss.

Then came a heavy blow for Flynn – the loss of a personal friend, Reverend Jim Stevens, who had been patrol padre at Port Hedland and had intended to return. He was killed in action and buried in the soft soil of England, far from the baked ground of the Inland he had loved and served so well.

Testing episodes continued the while for young Kingsley Partridge. A miner at Hatch's Creek recorded one of these.

Brown, a Queensland miner, complained of having strained himself whilst assisting to timber a shaft. He became feverish next day and had pains in his right arm and his left leg, which he attributed to muscular rheumatism. In the course of ten days, other ailments suggested themselves to him and he began to fancy he was suffering from pretty well nearly every ill that flesh is heir to. He became very despondent and had much difficulty in moving about.

Mr Tom Hanlon, mine owner (for whom Brown was sub-manager), saw that he had every possible attention, and by Mr Hanlon's instructions there was always someone at hand to give him food, drink and any assistance he wanted.

On Sunday morning, September 8th, Brown came to the door of the building in which he slept and stood there in his pyjamas for a few seconds. He was seen to retire from the doorway and about half a minute afterwards a shot was heard in the building.

The shot startled the men, who were at breakfast, and some of them ran up to see what was wrong.

They found Brown lying on the ground with a large wound in his forehead and brains protruding, and blood and brains on the ground at his head. A six-chambered revolver was lying beside him, with an empty shell in the chamber last discharged and two live cartridges in other chambers. He was alive then, but unconscious.

He was carried outside, and all that could be done for him by laymen was done. He died about an hour afterwards without having regained consciousness.

The Reverend K.F. Partridge, of the Australian Inland Mission, was in the locality, and he was sent for, but Brown was dead before he arrived. Later in the day a committee of six residents who were not present when the fatality occurred, met as a jury to take evidence.

Mr Partridge conducted the inquiry and took evidence ... which conclusively showed that the deceased came to his death by his own hand ... The committee added a resolution, as all concerned were far removed from a police centre [300 miles], "that in the interests of public health Brown's body should be interred forthwith."

As weeks would have to elapse before an official inquiry could take place, that last resolution was acted on. A coffin was made, a grave was dug, and the remains of poor Richard Brown were laid to rest. The Reverend K.F. Partridge read the burial service most impressively ...

Partridge wrote to Flynn that Brown had taken the old bushman's way out when faced with being a nuisance to his mates. Flynn was disturbed to hear of the miner's suffering and death. He wanted desperately to do more to help, but what? He probed below the surface, seeking deeper understanding. He laid his thinking bare in *The Inlander*.

> Will the reader kindly note that Brown was ill for TEN DAYS. Within the first two days, his mates knew that things were too serious for them to cope adequately with the situation, but what could they do? The nearest telegraph station was nearly 150 miles to the south-west, at Barrow Creek; and from there the nearest township, tiny Alice Springs, was a similar distance, but the amateur doctor there knew comparatively little. The next township, Oodnadatta, lay 320 miles further south: but the Oodnadatta doctor is really an official of the Railway Department. His specific duty is to care for railway men between there and Marree, i.e. 250 miles southwards.
>
> Even if the message had been carried per man and beast to Barrow Creek, and repeated by wire to Oodnadatta: even had the doctor been found at home, and succeeded in getting the Department's consent to abandon his contracted task till goodness knows when in the future: even then, what?
>
> This: the doctor would have been lucky to arrive in less than twenty days. For, in the Inland, there are no livery stables keeping horses ready, and corn-fed, for quick rushes over weary stages of unmade track ... So they had to resign themselves and their patient to the old, old bush method which often fails: they decided to "CHANCE IT".

"It is the large distances," Flynn concluded, "that are killing the Inland."

While Partridge was facing the challenges of Central Patrol and Flynn was agonising over the problem of distance, Bruce Plowman was slowly recuperating. *The Inlander* of 1918 reported:

> All our readers join in wishing Mr and Mrs Bruce Plowman every joy and prosperity in their united life. Mr Plowman is now in charge of an important industrial Young Men's Christian Association Hut in Queenstown, Tasmania.

However, Plowman had not fully recovered, and the arthritis which began on Central Patrol dogged him for years. His daughter, Jean, remembers him spending weeks in bed or dragging himself about in great pain. As therapy, his doctor suggested he try writing – though the pen proved hard to grasp and kept slipping from his stiff fingers. The dogged determination he had displayed as a patrol padre stood him in good stead: he penned three volumes covering his Outback experiences: *The Man from Oodnadatta, Camel Pads* and *Boundary Rider.*

Happily, Plowman recovered sufficiently to be able to walk about without a stick, and to achieve later success in the insurance industry. In 1962, in a letter to Reverend Fred McKay, he wrote, "although I had a nervous breakdown during my last patrol … I count it a great privilege being allowed to do the work and would do it once again if that were possible."

Painfully slow transport, Flynn decided, must be defeated, so he experimented with motor cars. Frank Heriot of Cloncurry Patrol received the first car used for patrol work in the AIM. Other patrols received motor cars too, easing some of the difficulties faced by patrol padres. Cars proved to be better than horses and camels, on balance, but were too slow – and in a land of gibbers and sandhills, most uncertain.

If cars were only an improvement but not an answer to the transport needs of the Inland, was there anything else that might be tried? On the Birdsville Track in 1912, the words had come into Flynn's mind: "The wings of death are swifter than camels or horses"; and he had wondered idly whether aeroplanes might not one day prove swifter even than the "wings of death". When he shared this idea with others they were highly sceptical, as aeroplanes were still in the experimental stage, "mere playthings, dangerous toys". However, the Great War had accelerated their development. Might they yet help to answer the need for fast transport in the Inland? Flynn needed someone with expert knowledge to advise him, otherwise what he said would be discounted once more – just "funny Flynn off in the clouds again".

A young officer in the Australian Air Force was about to give him the assistance he needed.

11

WINGS OF MERCY

In November 1917, on the way to Europe on the troopship *Nestor*, young Clifford Peel penned a thoughtful letter to John Flynn. Peel, a second lieutenant in the Australian Flying Corps, had read an article by Flynn in *The Inlander* about the difficulties of transport in the Outback. An intelligent medical student who had put aside his studies to volunteer, Peel's experience of aeroplanes convinced him that they could be used to telescope the vast distances of the Outback.

When Andrew Barber stopped by to see him, Flynn waved the letter triumphantly and told him, "This is our manifesto! This letter will open the way for us to provide air transport for our pioneers. It is written by an airman, so people will pay attention to what it says."

"What's it say, that you are so taken with it?"

"Listen, I'll read some to you:

> The first question to be asked is sure to be, "Is it safe?" To the Australian lay mind, the thought of flying is accompanied by many weird ideas of danger. True, there are dangers, which in the Inland will be accompanied by the possibility of being stranded in the desert without food or water. Yet even with this disadvantage, the only reply to such a query is a decided affirmative ... if we study the records available, and deduct accidents that occurred while the pilot was "stunting" over enemy territory, we will find that the number of miles flown per misadventure is very large.

There it is – flying is a lot safer than we all thought!"

"I'm surprised. Mind you, I'm not so sure we'll find it that easy to get old 'Saltbush Bill' into the stomach of a roaring flying machine. Aren't aeroplanes frightfully expensive?"

"Peel deals with that, in some depth. Listen:

To run a train, motor car, lorry or other vehicle, roads must first be made and kept in repair; the air needs no such preparation. The capital expenditure in Europe (according to an eminent English authority) before a motor car can be run is six thousand pounds per mile, for a train twenty four thousand pounds per mile, and for an aeroplane only about six hundred pounds per mile.

Isn't that fantastic, how cheap it is in comparison?"

"There would be other running costs, like repairs and maintenance."

"He goes into that and computes a final cost of only about eight pence per mile, which must compare favourably with motor cars. There's the initial outlay for the aeroplanes and bases to add to that, of course. He estimates we could set up three bases and four planes for only £10 000, which is not an impossible sum."

"Ten thousand pounds! Isn't that several times your present annual budget?" queried Barber.

"Yes, but we don't need to start with several bases and aircraft: even one would allow us to service a vast area very quickly. Listen to his figures for an aeroplane: 'From Oodnadatta, Alice Springs is about a three-and-a-half hour trip. Overland it takes NINE DAYS – long ones too.' Just think of the saving of lives this would represent! Peel says: 'It takes little imagination to see the advantage of this to the mail service, government officials, and business men; while to the frontier settlers it will be an undreamt-of boon as regards household supplies, medical attention, and business.' Frankly, his figures electrify me. Aeroplanes could break the isolation that is the curse of our pioneers at a stroke. He touches on another exciting possibility, a missionary doctor flying anywhere he was needed. I can picture aeroplanes swooping down from the sky and saving the lives of isolated pioneers!"

Flynn wrote an enthusiastic reply to Peel, asking him to keep an eye open "for a few likely Sky Pilots for our staff". He added that he had put aside a few notes of his own, made some time before, as to the possibilities. He would combine his ideas with Peel's information to come up with a strategy.

Flynn published Peel's letter in *The Inlander* under the title "A Young Australian's Vision". Sadly, by the time it was published, Peel had been shot down and killed on a reconnaissance flight photographing gun emplacements along the St Quentin Canal in France. He would never become that missionary doctor he had hoped to be. His letter, though, had convinced Flynn of the need to put the aeroplane into the Inland's skies as soon as possible.

The first step was to get his Board to agree. Flynn approached them enthusiastically.

"Mr Flynn, the war is not yet over. It is still taking its toll on our resources. It seems incredible, to me, that you are putting forward a new dream at this juncture. Our first task, when peace returns, must be to rebuild our shattered patrols," was one response.

"Yes, and from what we read, these flying machines are very expensive," was another.

"Up to a point," Flynn replied, "but after the initial outlay, they are cheap to run. The main point is not the expense, but that lives will be saved and isolation overcome. How can men and women be measured in currency? Doctors need wings so that they can fly across the lonely miles, wings so that they need never arrive too late. Believe me, gentlemen, as far as the Inland is concerned, it is either aeroplanes – or coffins. I do not exaggerate when I say that."

A silence greeted this sombre statement. Bemused Board members looked at one another, not sure how seriously to take Flynn.

"Should we cut back on our nurses and patrol padres to finance this new scheme, then?"

"No. The nurses and patrol padres will always be vital; they are the infantry in our war against isolation and hardship. Aeroplanes will supply the cavalry attack to defeat the enemy where the infantry cannot reach in time. As cavalry, they won't be needed very often and I predict our fuel bills will be low. The chief thing is stationing help within call, which will give security and enhance family life in the bush."

Flynn found that his Board was interested, but would not be swayed into an early experiment involving aeroplanes. He would need to keep working on them while exploring other avenues.

Something significant and unsolicited occurred to help his cause. A prominent Singaporean banker, Alma Baker, sent Flynn £100 after reading Clifford Peel's letter in *The Inlander*. Baker made some penetrating observations which Flynn quoted later:

None but the men, women and children who live in the "Never Never" can appreciate the great blessing and boon an aerial medical service would be to them. The people of the "Never Never" help to keep the big commercial centres together, and those who live in the big cities and towns of Australia must recognise this.

What should Flynn do with Baker's gift of one hundred pounds? His Board let him put it into a separate account with a reserve on it, "for Aerial Medical Services", in case one day an experiment needed to be undertaken. He began to feed the account towards that day.

The conviction that aeroplanes could minister to the needs of the Inland was growing. Who else would share this vision? Flynn targeted the defence forces, as they already had aeroplanes and doctors and pilots. He supposed the returning personnel and aircraft would be employed to protect Australia's

Northern gateway, to secure our safety from attack through our vast north coast. If there is to be an attack against Australia in the future, it will surely be through the north, probably by air … If Australia can use the flying machine to kill men, it can use the aeroplane to cherish lives. The late "eagles of war" can become "doves of peace" …

Flynn warmed to this theme. Why shouldn't the Air Force, he wrote, use its doctors stationed in the north, and its planes, pilots and radios, to respond to emergencies in the region?

The Australian has no interest in Dummy-drill. For him to develop zeal there must be an immediate purpose in every employment: what better purpose than to cheer the dispersed pioneers? What better practice for perfecting our communications against the time when they will mean life for our nation, than in providing, meantime, a service that will assuredly spell life for many an individual here and now?

The Defence Department had no plans for a permanent aerial defence system in the north and ridiculed Flynn's visionary suggestions. This was a blow because they alone had the resources, there and then, to put his dream into practice. But although Flynn was disappointed, he would not be diverted from his goal.

He decided to harness public opinion through a sustained media campaign. Examples of arguments he used included: In Texas, a doctor had flown by aeroplane to visit outlying patients; in India, 1 500 British soldiers were airlifted to hospitals in Delhi; two "sons of the saltbush", Ross and Keith Smith, flew from England to Australia in 1919 and were lauded as heroes. Their achievement demonstrated the range and reliability of aircraft.

In 1918, Flynn produced a remarkable map of Australia. It showed how a network of sixteen "sky doctor" bases could give protection over all of the Inland. Copies of the map were hung in AIM offices and a variation was published later in *The Inlander*. Flynn wrote about these bases:

> Sixteen only for the continent would make no difference in the nation's annual expenditure – yet would make all the difference in the world for the brave people in the bush ...
>
> IF WE ONCE DREAM IT, THE REST IS EASY.

The main problem was just that; others did not share his dream. Reactions ranged from scepticism to straight-out ridicule.

Andrew Barber gave a perplexed Flynn insight into why this was. "People are scared of aeroplanes. They think flying is dangerous. Aircraft are noisy little boxes that creak and groan and bounce around in the air. They put goggles on you and strap you in before they let you fly: how could anyone think it was safe? Look, I put your ideas to my doctor to get his reaction. He told me the fear of flying would do most patients more harm than good. By the look on his face when he said this, he won't be applying to become your first 'sky doctor'."

"Mmmm. I believe you've hit on something there," Flynn said. "The flying most Australians see is stuntmen at country shows who *want* everyone to believe it is dangerous."

"Yes, that's the problem. You will have to change people's image of flying before they will take your 'sky doctors' seriously."

"How can I do that? How can I change the perception of a whole nation?" Flynn asked. He drummed his long, bony fingers on his desk while he considered this challenge. He concluded at last, "I think it is time to cash in on the good relationship I have built up with certain newspapers over the years. I'll ask them to run an information campaign about my 'sky doctors'."

The newspapers loved the idea – it was romantic, adventurous and in the public interest. Even prominent papers like the *Sydney Daily Telegraph* and the *Bulletin* wrote articles strongly in favour of "air doctors".

The *West Australian Age* supported Flynn's vision directly:

> The Australian Inland Mission now contemplates a ring of aerial doctors around the continent where flying radii would reach to even the most remote settlers ... It is not impossible. Could we but look into the mysteries that Father Time has tentatively in store for us, especially in his inventory of scientific wonders, we would chide ourselves for our hesitating lack of present belief ...

Flynn's media campaign was extraordinarily successful. Even politicians began to take notice because of his astute emphasis on nation building. Some sought Flynn out, to talk to him about his dream.

Excited by this political interest, Flynn decided to approach the different state governments. After all, they had the resources to put "aerial doctors" into the skies. He wrote to his father from Perth in 1920:

> The idea has caught on well, and it is probable that the Western Australian Premier will approach the Federal Government and suggest an experiment to test the possibility. I had lunch with the Premier and Speaker and several members today.

Flynn sent a copy of *The Inlander* to the Prime Minister of Australia, the Hon. W.M. "Billy" Hughes, who happened to be a flying enthusiast. He received a thrilling reply. The Prime Minister had read the magazine "from cover to cover during early morning hours", and was highly supportive of the ideas Flynn was promoting.

Hughes followed this with a speech to Parliament in November 1921, in which he elegantly expressed the case for aviation.

> I hope that honourable members will thoroughly appreciate what the conquest of the air means to a great island continent like Australia. If we had been asked before the development of aviation what was the greatest benefit that could be conferred

upon a handful of people in a sparsely settled and immense area, we should have replied "the annihilation of distance".

A month later he received another letter from Billy Hughes, one that almost took his breath away. The letter announced a government subsidy to AIM nursing homes of £2 for every £1 raised by local citizens, up to a value of £2 000! The Prime Minister also made a tentative commitment to help to "make an aeroplane available in the district".

Here was real progress. Flynn felt as though a great weight had lifted from his shoulders. For years he had carried the financial burden for the AIM almost single-handedly. He would still have to be very involved in raising support, but it would be much easier because of the government's subsidy.

Wanting all of the AIM Family to be likewise encouraged, Flynn sent a copy of Hughes' letter to each member. He included a letter of his own with the following enthusiastic comment:

> The action of the Commonwealth Government in making such generous provision for subsidising nursing homes in the Northern Territory is by far the greatest encouragement the AIM has yet received ...

Flynn could not leave it there; he had to share his hopes and dreams of what this could mean for the future:

> It is more than probable that these fine subsidies to nursing work will prove the forerunners of very generous offers towards experiments, followed by permanent subsidies in event of success, in flying doctors.

The implication was that a flying doctor experiment had to be initiated. There was no one else, so he would have to plan it himself. The challenge was awesome. How could he, a mere minister, succeed in a field right outside his experience? And where would he find the finance to start?

Flynn turned to wealthy industrialists for support, using the argument: "The Outback supplies the raw materials of industry, so industry has a responsibility to help in the development of the Outback in turn. This will provide benefits that are mutual."

Most businessmen listened politely to John Flynn but did nothing to help. One man, though, appeared to be genuinely interested. Perhaps this was because he had followed Flynn's progress since they met when Flynn was hunting rabbits as a youth. This man was Hugh Victor McKay, the wealthy manufacturer of Sunshine Harvesters. Flynn visited him several times to discuss the concept of flying doctors swooping out of the sky to pick up suffering pioneers. McKay was no passive listener at these meetings and made many astute and creative suggestions. He even looked into the possibility of investing in aeroplane companies to speed the development of aviation and thereby generate suitable conditions for flying doctors.

A genuine understanding developed between Flynn and the age-ing industrialist. Flynn felt confident that McKay would stand behind him financially "once the action really starts".

However, the action was yet to begin. Flynn needed detailed information before he could plan his experiment. Who might advise him on aircraft? None of his colleagues knew much, this being such a new field. He needed expert help. He asked around. Good reports were given him about two young airmen, Hudson Fysh and Ginty McGinness, who had returned from the war as aces and had set up a fledgling commercial airline in the north. Like Flynn, they were struggling to make a doubting public take them seriously. They flew to small towns to give "joy flights" and held public meetings to inform people as to the possibilities. Certain wealthier individuals chartered them for personal flights, or for transport, but it was a precarious living. They named their company "Queensland and Northern Territory Aerial Services", shortened to "QANTAS" and later to "Qantas".

Flynn contacted Fysh. Might QANTAS give him the help and advice he so badly needed if he were to set up a flying doctor experiment? Fysh, hoping for financial spin-offs, was immediately interested.

Hudson Fysh and John Flynn had their first meeting in Sydney towards the end of 1921. Flynn arrived with a bundle of maps under his arm, which he plonked on the table. He launched into a barrage of questions on technical matters that were concerning him. Was there an aeroplane that could carry a stretcher, a doctor and a couple of patients? Were there suitable sites for bases in Northern Queensland? What about the west? What means of communication could be used at a base? What would be best – to purchase an aeroplane or to hire one? ... and so on, for several hours.

Fysh was impressed by Flynn's quick intellect and grasp of the problems, and also by his obvious determination. He made a snap decision to help him: Flynn just might succeed and his cause was worth supporting.

This first meeting was followed by many briefing and advisory sessions between Flynn and Fysh, despite there being no financial benefit to QANTAS in the immediate future.

Fysh then made several flights that demonstrated the feasibility of Flynn's ideas. He flew Dr Hope Michoûd, a member of the QANTAS Board, to some emergency cases. Encouraged, Fysh was eager to get the flying doctor started, but Flynn put the brakes on because he wanted a plane that could evacuate stretcher cases. Dr Michoûd, for example, had had to hoist one patient into the rescue plane using a block and tackle. The patient then had to sit upright in an open cockpit during the flight to hospital.

"What I need," Flynn told Hudson Fysh, "is an aeroplane with a large cabin for the doctor and patient, not two cockpits as at present. I know that it would increase the length of the aeroplane, and its bulk, but they are designing more and more powerful engines, aren't they?"

"Father Flynn," Fysh replied, using his jocular title, "you have marvellous ideas, but you know nothing of aerodynamics."

"Yes, but what happens if a man is injured in the middle of nowhere – how do we get him to hospital? We need to do more than take a doctor to him; we need to evacuate him safely and properly, on a stretcher."

Fysh smiled patiently. "What you want hasn't been invented yet. Aviation is exploding, but it's still in its infancy. It'll take time for what you want to become available."

"I don't want to wait that long," said Flynn. "There are too many lives at stake, I receive reports of tragedies every week. Won't you mention my ideas to any aircraft manufacturers with whom you deal?"

Fysh sighed. "Yes, I'll mention them," he promised.

True to his word, Fysh took Flynn's ideas to de Havilland, the famous aeroplane designers and manufacturers in England. Fysh told them, "Don't laugh. There is a person back in Australia who won't take "no" for an answer. If you don't come up with what he wants, someone else will. Besides, an aircraft with a large closed-in cabin would interest QANTAS for passenger and mail transport. It makes good sense to me."

The lack of a suitable aircraft did not deter Flynn from pursuing his dream. Much groundwork could still be done in advance. For example, pilots over the Inland required maps far superior to those then available, which were hopelessly inaccurate. Flynn decided to produce a new generation of maps that could be used by them, and by others too.

He found a key ally in his mapping in "Uncle" Norman Orr, a retired draughtsman who gave his services freely. Together they sorted through thousands of details Flynn had been gathering for years and produced a new breed of map. Accurate and detailed, it became the standard for use in the Outback.

Hudson Fysh found the new maps invaluable for his pilots' use and wrote to Flynn:

> I must compliment you on your enterprise in getting out such a fine production, particularly because it gives our back-country the prominence it so urgently deserves, and is the first map to show the great aerial routes. In many ways, we consider your Inland hospital scheme and your flying doctor scheme sister endeavours to our own. They both have the same big object in view − the opening up of Australia's "back-yard".

In his thinking, then, Fysh was linking QANTAS and Flynn's ideas as "sister endeavours". This pleased Flynn, convinced as he was that QANTAS would one day supply the aeroplanes for his dreams. That day drew closer when in 1924 Fysh wrote that at last an aeroplane was available that would satisfy Flynn's requirements for a flying ambulance. It was a DH50A and QANTAS had ordered their first from England. With a closed-in cabin and a lifting door to enable a stretcher to be loaded in, it would be Australia's first aeroplane built specifically for civil work.

In January 1925, QANTAS received approval from de Havilland to build DH50As themselves at Longreach, under royalty. Soon there would be a whole fleet available for a flying doctor to use.

Flynn used this news to try to rekindle flagging enthusiasm for his flying doctor dream. To his great disappointment, his Board opposed an early experiment. They pointed out that financial and logistical support was lacking; for example, there were too few landing grounds in the Outback as yet, nor did the pioneers have an effective means of calling up a flying doctor for help. As early as 1917, Flynn had suggested wireless might fill this communications gap, but by 1925 suitable wireless sets were not yet available.

"I shall continue making my preparations," he told his personal secretary, Jean Baird, after receiving the Board's disappointing decision. "Then everything will be ready for the experiment one day. Whatever else happens, we *will* put flying doctors into the Inland skies."

It was seven tedious years since Flynn had first published his concept of "sky doctors". How many more years of struggle lay ahead? What more could he do?

12

FIGHTING ON THE GROUND

While John Flynn was doggedly chasing his flying doctor dream, he continued to develop the AIM "on the ground". He saw it as one grand strategy to solve the problems of the Inland. Until the flying doctors were ministering and until he had a wireless network in place for pioneers to call for help, the whole burden had to fall on the willing shoulders of his "infantry" of nurses and patrol padres. They carried the burden magnificently, but continued to struggle under the hardships of service in the Outback.

Despite Flynn's efforts to alleviate some of the stresses, patrol life continued to exact a heavy toll. Frank Brady served in Broome for five years, then left the field for a few years, returning in May 1925. That same October he died after completing a gruelling 1 700-mile patrol, his overtaxed body falling prey to malaria. His brave wife held the fort at Broome for a further year because a replacement could not be found sooner.

Flynn wanted to double up patrol padres to lessen the burden on each, but could not attract a sufficient number of new recruits. "We need bush padres to travel everywhere in nowhere," Flynn pleaded in the media, but few ministers showed interest: they looked at the challenges and backed away. In a rare outburst, Flynn commented wryly that too many young ministers "would rather rush to support the strong and the wealthy" than join the AIM. "We are trying to bridge the gaps in our frontiers, but need more patrol padres to build those bridges," he wrote despairingly. All the while, he had the frustration of knowing that those gaps would not be a fraction as wide if his plans for aircraft and wireless were implemented. Sadly, fewer and fewer people seemed to take his dreams seriously any more.

His nurses also experienced stress in the Outback, though of a different sort from the patrol padres. The change in conditions from city to Inland was so great, some of them suffered "bush shock", one being rendered speechless for three days.

In the city, the nurses had experienced good food, regular working hours and a doctor at hand to make those vital life-and-death decisions. Transport was convenient, living conditions were comfortable and adequate equipment was readily available. At her new post in the Inland, the nurse's diet might become salt beef and dry bread. She might work 20 hours out of 24, and then days of frustrating inactivity could follow. In the absence of a doctor, she would have to make all decisions herself, some of which would make her heart stand still. Regarding transport, she would take advantage of any she could, including riding a horse, sometimes in the dark, at times perhaps clinging to its tail as it swam over a swollen creek. For equipment she would make do, even cutting splints from a nearby tree or using borrowed pliers to pull teeth.

When Flynn's nurses returned to the city, thank-you functions were held for them and they were helped by the AIM Family to find good positions. Many went on to senior appointments in town and country hospitals because of their varied experience; it made them ready for anything.

As the years passed, one vital question about the AIM demanded an answer: was Flynn's infantry having any success in reaching the pioneers in regard to religion? Many said his unusual methods were "not spiritual enough" to have an effect. Flynn refuted this, writing in *The Inlander*:

> We are intensely interested in the realities beyond the shadows. As ideal-mongers, we have been compelled to dabble in material things ... as evangelists, we interest ourselves in fishing and grazing, mining and farming, building and healing ... playing any game means dreaming, and dreaming, and dreaming after methods that may bring victory, tearing into the ruck again and yet again, contemptuous of little lost bits of garment and of skin.

Was he right? Were the pioneers learning that there were "realities beyond the shadows"? His ministers had gone to an Outback in which the majority of bushmen were antagonistic to religion. What was their attitude now? A government census gave a unique opportunity to find out – and the answer came as an emphatic positive. Flynn had changed the Inland's concept of Christianity. In fact, many bushmen in answer to the question regarding their religion, wrote down "The AIM"!

Flynn's vision of wings over the Inland continued to haunt him. Charles Kingsford Smith's rescue of a sick little girl at Carnarvon gave Flynn more fuel to toss on the fire, which he did gleefully because the famous aviator was idolised by Australians. It did no good – his pleas for action fell on deaf ears. Meanwhile, he got on with establishing further hospitals to help his Inlanders.

So called "Tragedy Corner" had long ago caught Flynn's attention. Many men and women had perished in the "corner" where Queensland, South Australia and New South Wales had common boundaries. While he lacked the resources to build a nursing home there, Flynn was desperate to do something, anything, to alleviate the suffering. The solution came to him: establish "itinerant nurses" in the same mode as his patrol padres. They would be commissioned to serve this desolate area, where even seasoned bushmen and explorers, such as Burke and Wills, had perished.

The first of these intrepid nurses, soon to be called "border sisters" or "Flynn's boundary riders" by the locals, were sisters Racking and Kinnear. They quickly became legends, travelling fearlessly in all conditions along 700 miles of dangerous track, saving many lives and preventing untold suffering. They had no home base of their own, but stayed in homesteads in the region as they travelled about. Even a bubonic influenza plague was fought and overcome, despite primitive facilities and temperatures inside the homesteads in excess of 120 degrees Fahrenheit.

Finally, Flynn prevailed on the wealthy King's Counsellor, Sir Josiah Symon of Adelaide, to make a generous donation, which enabled a fine AIM hospital to be built at Innamincka, near the famous "dig tree" of Burke and Wills. The itinerating "border sisters" consequently passed into folklore, though years later their exploits were still spoken of with reverence and awe around camp fires.

Stories of tragedies in Birdsville weighed heavily on Flynn for many years. In the far west of Queensland, the town had become known derisively as "the place where the sun goes down" and "the end of the road". So isolated that supplies came in only twice a year, on camels along the Birdsville Track from Marree, Birdsville sweltered in a dry, desert climate, although on occasion the Diamantina River flooded, covering the region with great sheets of water.

Flynn began putting money aside during the Great War to build a cottage hospital there. By the time the townspeople approached him for help, he had £585 ready for that purpose and was keen to get started. The local populace, though, had another "iron in the fire". They had earlier approached the government to station a doctor at Birdsville, and to everyone's surprise the government appeared keen to do so.

"They might be better off with two high-grade nurses than a medical wreck," Flynn said when told of Birdsville's decision to pursue the government option instead of an AIM hospital. "The problem is to secure staff who will keep sober." The Outback of the day contained a number of doctors who were professionally incompetent and undependable. As Flynn explained to Hugh Davis: "So many doctors, drug-wrecks and elbow-benders, have sunk in their profession, and the direction of their sinking has been, geographically speaking, westward."

As Flynn had predicted, years slipped by with no doctor forthcoming from the government. The area languished without medical help. Then tragedy struck. A Birdsville mother bore healthy twins, but in the absence of medical help, or even advice, both babies died three weeks after birth.

Sheepishly, Birdsville again approached Flynn for help; he swung into action at once.

Not wanting to wait until a hospital could be built, which could take years as everything would have to be carted in, Flynn rented a small, abandoned hotel in the township. Local people whitewashed it and tidied it up while Flynn searched frantically for "two angels to nurse in Birdsville". He found them in nursing sisters Grace Francis and Catherine Boyd.

Lou Reese, Flynn's friend and guide from Smith of Dunesk days, brought the two nurses on the last stage of their long journey from Brisbane. The old bushman was hugely impressed with them and said so, loud and clear. He watched them nurse several cases of illness while travelling. In one case, a four-year-old had caught typhoid. The women had saved the child's life by early diagnosis and treatment – then a dash to the Gundah Hospital. "If ever angels came on earth, I'd say these were two," Reese wrote to Flynn.

On their arrival in 1923 the nurses found conditions in Birdsville even more primitive than they had expected. Their luggage and furniture arrived two months after they did. In the interim, they used old boxes as furniture – even their dental chair was an empty box. Kitchenware needed to be borrowed until their own arrived. The locals silently observed the cheerfulness with which the nurses met all such setbacks.

The condition of the local children tugged at the hearts of the AIM sisters. Medically speaking, the children suffered from "sandy blight". This caused inflamed and discharging eyes from which permanently impaired vision could result. The ministrations of the nurses soon had the condition under control. Even then, the children seemed distant and lost somehow in that impoverished and desolate environment.

Despite their goods and chattels not having arrived yet, the nurses announced a Christmas party for every child in the district, to perk them up. A desert ash stood for a Christmas tree. Excitement mounted among the children, especially when gaily wrapped parcels appeared under the tree.

On Christmas Eve, the camel train swayed in with the nurses' luggage: "It was the queerest sight to see chairs and other portions of furniture perched so high up in the air," Sister Francis recorded. There was no time to do more than simply dump the luggage outside because there was so much preparation to do for the festivities.

Then it rained! There was a mad scramble to get the luggage inside before it was soaked. (Only two inches of rain fell in Birdsville during the two years the sisters were there – in fact, they were limited to half a bucket of water per day for their entire stay, so the wet luggage was an ironic introduction.) Once again, the towns-people noted the fortitude and good humour of the women in the face of adversity.

Sister Francis recorded what happened next:

> 64 turned up at the Christmas tree and we started at 8 p.m. It looked very nice and the wee folk were so excited about it all,

not having seen one before. When Santa made his appearance, the shouting was loud. We soon distributed the toys and gave Santa three cheers ...

When Flynn came to see how his nurses were coping, he found them in fine fettle. "One man told me he had to 'skull drag' his mate in to see us the first time," Flynn was told, "because his mate 'didn't want a woman fussing over him'. Well, he was in hospital here for over a week. When he left, he told us he would ride in 500 miles for us to look at his next injury! We took that as a compliment."

"So you should!"

"It's scary, though. They all think we can fix up everything. We are only nurses, not doctors."

Flynn paused thoughtfully before he responded. There was steel in his voice when he did. "One day there will be a doctor flying out of these skies when you most need him," he promised. That dream, though, seemed more like a mirage. Whenever he tried to advance towards it, it retreated backwards just as fast.

Another of Flynn's great dreams was to build a hospital in Alice Springs, the symbolic heart of the Inland. The land for it, two blocks in Todd Street, had been taken up by Bruce Plowman in 1914. Nurse Jean Finlayson had proved the need for a nursing home during her experimental year there and Flynn had been working towards that goal ever since, including the preparation of detailed building plans in 1918. He had even hired a builder to make a start that year. Thick stone walls had been constructed – but then the money had run out.

Years slipped past without further progress beyond this empty shell. When told that a local resident had named the shell "Flynn's Folly", John Flynn laughed and said, "Faith may be delayed, but it will succeed in the end, you'll see."

By 1925, he was convinced that he would have to play a more direct role if his two greatest dreams were ever to be fulfilled – the Alice Springs hospital and a flying-doctor service. His Board had reservations about both, and things were moving towards a crisis. He was made aware that he might be instructed to abandon, at the least, the work he was doing towards the flying-doctor dream. If that happened, he decided to refuse. They would then ask for his resignation. "In which case," he told Barber, "I'll refuse and make them throw me out. At that point I'll go to the people, if I have to. I'll not abandon my dreams. How could I? The lives of too many Inlanders are at stake."

Serious personal conflict arose with the Chairman of the Board over these issues. Something had to be done fast, before it was too late. Flynn decided to retreat into a period of "voluntary exile". Perhaps if he stayed away, things would cool down and the Board would not ask him to abandon his dreams. Where better to go than Alice Springs, to try to build the nursing home there himself? That would take many months, time enough for attitudes to change back at home base.

There was a danger in this plan. What if decisions were taken in his absence by the Board to abandon the flying-doctor dream? He would need to inform all AIM personnel what the beliefs of their Superintendent were, just in case he needed to make a direct appeal to them later for their support. He did this very cleverly in a document headed, innocuously enough, "Notes re Government Subsidies in the Northern Territory", and sent copies throughout the AIM network. The bulk of the five-page circular dealt with the need to establish a flying doctor service and never give up! It linked the concept of a flying doctor in the air, nurses on the ground and wireless sets in the hands of pioneers, calling the resulting safety network a "mantle of safety". Flynn stated optimistically that "most of our outer bush now inhabited could be covered with that "Mantle of Safety" which we desire."

He farewelled his fellow workers by letting them know his immediate intentions:

> We are also taking steps to test the practicability of wireless transmission in the hands of bushmen. Mr Towns, a returned soldier, who is a wireless operator, has very generously volunteered his assistance in some experiments, and is assembling gear in conjunction with our motor. He starts out next month to Innamincka, Birdsville and Alice Springs.

The term "mantle of safety" rapidly became common parlance amongst AIM staff. It gave them a wider vision of their role as part of a protective covering over the whole of the Inland.

Going into exile, Flynn was heading towards the most difficult, yet exciting, time of his life.

13

EXILE

John Flynn began wondering how to break the "awesome silence" of the Outback when he first went there. As early as 1912, he wrote: "The Inland is immense, silent, and for the most part dumb." He meant that pioneers had no ready means to communicate with the outside world, or indeed with each other.

The visionary began to search for ways to give the bush "its tongue". He realised at once that telegraph and telephone could not service the majority of pioneers, because the laying of cables was expensive and impractical.

On learning about wireless, Flynn was immediately alert to its potential. Here was a system that used air instead of cables – and air was free and plentiful in the Inland!

Flynn at once linked wireless to his flying-doctor dream, writing as early as June 1919:

> Winged pilots, flying doctors: but they alone cannot save. The bush is at present, for the most part, dumb. Not till it becomes vocal in all its parts can it call for the help that has suddenly become so much more mobile than of old. And is there a magic touch that can give the dumb bush its tongue? Yes there is. Wireless!

Filled with enthusiasm, he visited the armed forces and the Postmaster General's Department (PGD). Both were experimenting in the field. He discovered that wireless required a whole room full of equipment and kept experts busy just maintaining its operation. The technology, he realised, was far too complicated and delicate for pioneers to use; moreover it operated with Morse code only. In addition, it was outrageously expensive. The gap needed to be bridged between what existed and simple, robust, cheap sets.

Flynn watched each new development like a hawk. Progress in the field was far too slow for his liking. He wanted to play a more active role. Then a quirk of history played right into his hands. Many amateurs had built their own wireless sets and were experimenting, so much so that the airwaves had become cluttered. Some control was required, so the government gave the armed forces and essential services such as the police their choice of the "airwaves". At the time, long-wave and medium-wave transmission were well understood and considered reliable, so they were reserved. The enigmatic short-wavebands were left for the amateurs to scramble for. These hobbyists, forbidden to use an aerial power of more than 25 watts, were expected to die out rapidly.

Instead, they flourished. Rich in ingenuity but low on finger skills, they became known as "hams" because of their ham-fisted use of a Morse key. With limited resources, they built the cheap sort of sets that interested Flynn. Despite the low power of their aerials, some of these "hams" managed to transmit surprising distances, even overseas. Short waves were more temperamental than medium and long waves, and held more secrets, but the creativity of the hobbyists steadily unravelled them. To enable free exchange of information and ideas, these enthusiasts banded together into the Amalgamated Wireless of Australia (AWA).

When the AWA learned that Flynn wanted a small, inexpensive wireless set for use in the bush, they advertised his need. Many amateurs came forward with information and ideas. His dream eluded them all, however. It appeared to them to be unreachable.

Deciding he needed to learn about wireless (radio) himself, Flynn read books and then purchased equipment which he installed in the attic of the AIM offices in York Street, Sydney. Here he spent many hours pulling the components apart and putting them back together again. He became a proficient operator and was accepted into the membership of the AWA.

His dreams were fired by what he was learning. In 1921 he wrote to the *Sydney Morning Herald*:

> Frontier missionaries with portable wireless sets, drawing power from the engine of the motor [car] by a simple adjustment of the machinery ... would continually be obliging bush

folk who needed to send wires [telegraphic messages] … actual [air doctor] emergency calls would be comparatively few UNTIL the elimination of dread led to the establishment of more families far out.

Flynn then sought help from men prominent in the field of radio in Australia, men such as Harry Kauper, David Wyles and Ernest Fisk. Once again, his gift for making friends proved invaluable. All these men gave him hours of patient advice. But the years passed without Flynn getting closer to the radio set he wanted. He decided he would have to do the experimentation himself, but was always too busy.

When it seemed in 1925 that he would be "exiled" from his Board, Flynn decided this was the ideal opportunity to start the wireless experimentation.

Needing technical advice, he went to see David Wyles, who had developed his own wireless skills during the war and knew how vital a radio message could be for saving a life. Wyles worked for Philips Lamps and was an elder in the Presbyterian Church.

"Mr Wyles, what do you see as my main problems?"

"Expense, first of all. For a set to be any good out there, it would cost many hundreds of pounds, but that would be only a small portion of your costs. You would need to set up large base stations for the small sets to communicate with.

"Another problem would be electricity for the wireless sets. Few homes in the bush generate their own, so batteries would have to be used. Batteries would not perform well in the extreme heat."

Wyles paused for thought, then continued. "However, your biggest challenge would be to invent a set simple and cheap enough for your pioneers. The world is many years away from such an invention. What do you think about that?"

Flynn did not reply directly. He asked a question of his own instead: "Would the Inlanders need to send and receive in Morse code? Can't they simply talk into a transmitter as we do when using a telephone? Some amateurs are starting to do this. They call it 'voice telephony'."

"Yes, but not over the sort of distances you are considering for the Outback. For a given power output, Morse code gets much further. I can see your concern, though. Many of the pioneers will have had little formal education, so sending and receiving in a complicated code will be, well, extremely difficult for them. They would have to train and pass an examination before a licence would be issued to them by the PGD in any case. I can't see very many settlers and cattlemen going to all that trouble, can you? Mr Flynn, I respect what you want to do, but have you considered that it might not actually be possible?"

Flynn retreated to lighting his pipe and taking a deep draw before replying. It was a ploy he used when he wanted a moment or two to think. Then he said, "I want to start inventing that set myself as soon as possible. Then I want to test it under bush conditions on my way out to Alice Springs. Do you know of anyone who might be interested in helping me?"

"Are you serious about inventing it yourself?"

"Yes. Absolutely."

"Then I do know someone who might help you. I'll approach him and let you know."

Flynn soon received a letter from Wyles with the good news that a radio expert, George Towns, had offered his services in an honorary capacity for six months, after which he would have to return to Sydney. Wyles described Towns in these words:

> He will certainly help solve some wireless troubles. He is an old friend of mine – aged about 40, over six feet and in proportion, ex-bushwhacker, miner and prospector, also ex-wireless operator. He is loyal, clean living, exceptionally well balanced mentally and with an outstanding personality. His grandfather was Captain Towns of NSW historical fame, which makes Wentworth an ancestor. Apart from his wireless help, you would find him a good companion.

Sadly, though, Towns was still suffering from war wounds received while he was a wireless operator with the New Zealand forces.

Flynn had already ordered a Dodge Buckboard to be constructed in Adelaide for his use in the Inland. He and Towns would "baptise" it by taking experimental radio gear into the Inland in it. Flynn would remain in Alice Springs, to build the nursing home there.

The two men had much in common and made good companions. Once in Adelaide, they approached Harry Kauper for advice. Kauper was chief engineer of the recently formed Australian Broadcasting Commission. His position meant that he was as up-to-date in wireless knowledge as anyone in Australia, perhaps in the world. An inventive man with a variety of talents, Kauper had produced the gun-gear that enabled war planes to shoot through their propellers without hitting the blades. A skilful pilot himself, an engineer and a mathematician, Kauper had an ideal mix of skills with which to help Flynn.

A man who believed in speaking his own mind, Kauper immediately told Flynn, "I wouldn't attempt what you want to try. In 20 years' time, perhaps, suitable components might have been developed, but they don't exist as yet. The first Australian radio broadcasting station began only two years ago. Since then, we have started to place receiving sets in city homes. You want to establish both transmitting and receiving sets in the Inland … well … it will be like trying to … jump over the moon!"

"With no mail, no telephone and no wireless, many of our brave pioneers are about as isolated as they would be on the moon," Flynn countered.

"I dare say. Well, I am all for you having a go and will help where I can. The enterprise will cost a fortune. Have you the resources?"

"I'll get the money. If you start anything worthwhile, nothing can stop it."

Kauper proved invaluable in allowing them the use of his workshop, giving advice and lending components.

Towns and Flynn set about building different transmitters and receivers to test in the bush. They came across dozens of problems, many of which Flynn had not anticipated. The components were very bulky, not like the transistorised and miniaturised circuits that were developed later. Although composed of heavy materials such as copper, bakelite, brass and porcelain, they were surprisingly fragile – the jolting of the Dodge might easily damage the sets.

The men had to test every component, bearing in mind always the constraints of weight and fragility. Flynn looked at the growing pile of equipment with some alarm, especially the heavy batteries. He had already requested that extra leaves be put in the car springs, to strengthen them. "I hope you're not intending us to carry all those batteries in the Dodge, Mr Towns. How many of them will we need?"

"All of them, the whole lot. We will need to fit in a generator too, to charge them when they go flat. That won't be a small item either."

"A generator as well as batteries? Why can't we simply use the generator for our power and leave the batteries? We'll never fit them all in."

"Wireless requires a very steady voltage. A generator's output is too variable."

"Is there no way of running the generator to give a smooth output?" Then Flynn remembered an idea he had suggested to the newspapers in 1921. "How'd it be if we connected the generator to the motor car? I mean, if we run the Dodge at a constant speed, wouldn't that produce a steady voltage?"

Towns looked up at Flynn sharply. After a short pause, he said, "Let's give it a go."

They jacked up the Dodge so that its rear wheels could spin freely and attached a belt and pulley to the back axle. They bolted the generator to the "splashboard" – a strong metal plate used in place of the mudguard. After a few false starts because the belt slipped off, the generator ran with a constant whine. It sounded as though it might be steady enough, but it would need to be tested with a meter.

Towns and Kauper watched the needle of the voltmeter intently as Flynn ran the engine. The needle wobbled about a bit even when the car ran steadily. Fourteen miles per hour was discovered to be the optimum speed for smoothest output.

"Not quite steady enough, but very promising," was Towns' final pronouncement.

"It may be possible with another generator," said Kauper. "The better the windings, the smoother the output. We could order one to our own design."

The new generator was ordered from Sydney. Flynn and Towns spent the waiting days constructing a giant forty-foot aerial. It used four lengths of metal piping that could attach to one another. They would strap it along one side of the Dodge.

"How are we going to get it up?" Flynn asked.

"We will have to use a block and tackle to hoist it up each time we use it. I intend to build a derrick around it, so that it can stand in high winds without falling."

A large box arrived from Sydney. The men splintered the wood in their impatience to get the shiny, new generator out. They fitted it to the Dodge and Flynn climbed into the driving seat. At the signal, he drove the engine to a steady purr at 14 miles per hour.

After a few minutes, Towns held up his hand. Flynn switched off the engine and went over.

"Sorry, Mr Flynn," Kauper greeted him. "It is a lot better, but still won't do."

What now? They ordered another generator with still more windings, but again it failed to provide a steady enough voltage. The whole situation had become crushingly disappointing. Flynn expressed his frustration in a rare outburst. "I keep getting generators that don't generate!" he said, then corrected himself slightly. "Or at least they don't generate smoothly enough."

This comment seemed to spark something in Kauper's memory. "Wait a minute," he said. "There was a young fellow who came to see me a couple of months ago to show me a generator he'd made. He wanted it bench-tested. It was good, very good. It might do the trick."

The young electrician's name was Alf Traeger. Kauper told Flynn where to find him, at Hannan Brothers' Garage. Flynn shot straight off, coat-tails flapping and gold watch chain bouncing.

He found Traeger at his workbench, busily winding armatures. He was a slight lad, with tousled black hair and a shy smile. Flynn was so anxious about the generator that he did not even introduce himself but asked right away, "Have you still got that generator?"

"Which generator?" Traeger was taken aback.

"The one you bench-tested at the ABC, the one you showed Harry Kauper. Six hundred volts."

"Yes, I have."

"I would like to buy it from you."

"Oh? What do you want to use it for?"

"To provide the power for some wireless experiments in the Outback. We want to test some amateur equipment out there."

"Why?"

"The pioneers need a radio network. They live lonely and dangerous lives. How much do you want for it?"

Traeger thought quickly. He had intended asking £30 for it, but that sounded a bit much. Also, it was for a good cause, so he knocked off ten shillings.

Flynn whipped out his wallet and counted out the purchase price. In today's currency, he paid around $1 000 of his own money for the generator on the off-chance it might work! Traeger said later that he believed Flynn would have paid double, if asked.

Flynn collected the generator and went. Neither man expected to see the other again. Traeger said later to Fred McKay: "I have always believed that God guides our lives. It was God who brought Flynn to me."

Traeger's generator passed the voltage test, to Flynn and Towns' huge relief. That gave them at least one reliable power source for their experiments in the Inland.

At this point they were joined by Dr George Simpson, who had six weeks free. A tall, shy, softly spoken idealist who brimmed over with his personal faith in Christ, "Geordie" had first heard Flynn speak about the Inland as a ten-year-old in Sunday School, in Andrew Barber's church in Hamilton. He had listened, spellbound, to the padre's stories. There and then, he had decided to do whatever he could for the bush. Now, years later, he had renewed his interest. In 1925 he accepted the position of Honorary Medical Adviser to the AIM. In this capacity, he visited the cottage hospitals whenever possible, to advise the AIM nurses and update their equipment and methods. Furthermore, his imagination had been fired by Flynn's flying-doctor concept and he wanted to help.

Simpson was exceptionally adept with his hands. Had he chosen engineering rather than medicine he could have been a brilliant engineer. He realised that Flynn needed to know far more about his new Dodge, so the two men stripped the car down, Simpson explaining the function and importance of each part, and how to repair it if stranded in the bush. Then they put the Dodge together again, bolt by bolt. Flynn was destined to have many motoring problems in the bush, and was to remember with gratitude what Simpson taught him so thoroughly that week.

Meanwhile, Towns constructed a voice transmitter and a Morse code transmitter, in order to compare their performances. He also made various receivers. They were ready to leave to test them, at last. Harry Kauper promised to keep an ear for their signals, as had a number of amateurs in Sydney, Adelaide and Melbourne. The Postmaster General's Department had awarded Flynn a licence and the call sign 8AC, which would make them easy to identify.

Heavily overladen, the car's back springs sagging and squeaking in protest, the men gently eased off on their long journey.

Their first Outback experiment was to be at Beltana. They drew up at the smart "new" AIM nursing home there and were welcomed by Sister Edwards. The next day, Flynn and Towns struggled to lug their heavy equipment to the top of the highest hill nearby. Then they erected the huge aerial, a task made more difficult by the uneven terrain at the top. By nightfall, they were ready to launch their first test.

"8AC calling 5CL [Kauper in Adelaide]. 8AC calling 5CL. Do you read me, 5CL?" The bush had spoken! Was anyone listening? Towns twiddled furiously with the receiver set, but no reply came.

The lanterns kept spluttering on the windy summit, so Flynn helped by holding a torch for Towns to see by. The latter tried calling up other stations. The receivers crackled madly but gave no recognisable replies. He switched to the Morse code transmitter because of its greater range, but there were still no replies.

They returned to the hospital, dispirited but determined to begin sending again before daylight, transmission range being best at night or early in the morning. But despite Towns and Flynn adjusting and readjusting their sets on the top of the hill, it was all to no avail. After a week of failure, they disassembled everything, and Towns spread the pieces out on tables in the hospital grounds. Eventually a fault was located, but the transmissions still bore no fruit.

The men could stay no longer in Beltana. Fifteen hundred miles of difficult journey lay ahead in which further tests must be made. Could transmissions be made from Sturt's Stony Desert, say by a patrol padre or by drovers taking mobs of cattle across? They decided to test this at night as they crossed the desert. Every test involved jacking up the Dodge, erecting the giant aerial, then working by spotlight while shivering from the intense cold of desert nights.

George Towns proved to be very resourceful. Some nights found him hammering out replacement parts by the yellow light of hurricane lamps, and at other times he borrowed a blacksmith's forge. Flynn wrote later:

> Of the trials that beset our start we do not speak, save to remark that we set out to investigate difficulties and found them all twice over. This was fortunate as it made us "hasten slowly" before recommending anything to anybody.

Then, one night, it happened. Intelligible signals crackled out of their receiver in reply to their transmission. The men listened intently to the dots and dashes, then turned to each other and grinned like a couple of kids. Morse code on eighty metres was reaching Adelaide! Towns switched to Melbourne and Sydney. "Hams" replied from both cities. He stood up to stretch his back and commented, "Your bush is no longer dumb, Mr Flynn, at least not to the cities."

"Well done, Mr Towns. Well done indeed."

Flynn was pleased at their success, but not overjoyed. He had known all along that powerful, expensive sets could communicate in Morse, but pioneers would not handle the intricacies of Morse easily.

On pressed Flynn and Towns, stopping at the AIM hospitals at Innamincka and Birdsville. The Birdsville Hospital was only two years old, but Flynn was delighted to read in its records that over 1500 ophthalmic treatments had been performed already. "The beauties of God's creation will not be dimmed to the eyes of these children," he wrote.

They drove to Marree, stopping at homesteads along the route. Towns had a powerful receiving set which they used to "pick up" the newly formed coastal radio stations. The pioneers were entranced to hear the music, and some even broke out into involuntary dancing. "This is serving a very useful purpose," Flynn told Towns. "It is popularising wireless. These same men and women need to see the radio as their friend, not something to be frightened of, if they are going to use it to call up a flying doctor. I want them to be excited about wireless, any aspect of it. Learning to receive and transmit will then be an interesting challenge rather than a chore."

The dusty Dodge rattled into the AIM grounds at Oodnadatta. Nine arduous weeks had passed since leaving Adelaide. The nurses rushed out to meet the car. They had hardly greeted its occupants before chattering away breathlessly:

"Mr Hall – "

"He was this university student – "

"Yes, from Melbourne University – "

"No, from Adelaide – "

"Whichever. It doesn't matter."

"He picked up your voices, you know, on his little radio. He heard you both talking – "

"From Mount Lyndhurst, twice, and from Mount Hopeless, also twice – "

"And once from Cordillo Downs."

"Dear ladies," Flynn cut in, becoming excited himself, "are you saying that Mr Hall heard our voices and not simply Morse code?"

"Yes!"

"And he was here in Oodnadatta?"

"No, he was shearing sheep on Murnpeouwie Station. He told us about it a month ago when he passed through Oodnadatta on his return to university."

"That is exciting!" Flynn said. He turned to Towns to explain, "Murnpeouwie represents reception over three hundred miles. Voice transmission may be possible after all, instead of the pioneers having to learn Morse."

Flynn discussed voice transmission with Towns later. "Did you know there are only two tiny schools between Oodnadatta and Darwin? If parents on a property send their children away to school, they often do not see them again until their years of education are over. Transport conditions out here are so difficult that no school holiday period is long enough for the children to return home and make their way back to school on time."

"That is terrible."

"Yes, it is. Some children take correspondence schooling instead of going away, but parents often cannot answer their questions. Imagine, for a moment, what voice telephony might enable as an alternative: children could receive lessons by radio from a central radio school. They could ask questions using their wireless sets and have them answered immediately by a trained teacher."

"It's a worthy dream."

Flynn and Towns pressed on to Alice Springs. Here they lived in a sweltering iron shed in which they continued their experiments. They were seeking an alternative way of running the generator instead of using the Dodge. Inlanders, by and large, could not afford motor cars, so another source of power had to be found. Every idea they tried failed.

Time ran out and Towns had to return to Sydney. Flynn wrote dryly:

> So Mr Towns returned to Sydney without the satisfaction of handling a set with some "punch". But the main fact was reached. No one with a car (and with a good bank balance) need be dumb in the bush. Yet it was all too expensive for our purpose.

Flynn put the wireless experiments behind him in order to build his dream hospital at Alice Springs. He was not a builder, and as he gazed from the plans to the old skeleton walls in Todd Street, Alice Springs, then back to his plans, the magnitude of the challenge ahead almost overwhelmed him. In typical Flynnian fashion, his design was based on his dreams, but was practical nevertheless. It targeted heat, dust, flies and glare as the four main enemies to be overcome, and included many novel features for dealing with these which had been determined in consultation with experts. The upshot was a far grander design than his other hospitals – a fitting flagship from which to fly the AIM banner in the heart of Australia.

The hospital's most unusual feature was a natural ventilation and air-cooling system so innovative that some experts said it could not work. The concept was for an underground tunnel to draw air in from outside, past staggered wet sacks on which water constantly dripped, which would clean the air of dust and cool it. "Only those who have baked in the furnace that is the Red Centre would comprehend the importance of cool, clean air to the recovery of the very sick," Flynn wrote in answer to critics.

Having hired two carpenters and a cook in Adelaide to help, he collected them from the railhead at Oodnadatta in his Dodge Buckboard, a trip of 400 miles at a top speed of 20 miles per hour on the few good sections. Most of the way he had to crawl along. No sooner had he deposited the men at Alice Springs than he had to return to

Oodnadatta to collect equipment. He lashed building materials to the sides of the Dodge, loading it until he could just fit into the driving seat.

Flynn made many tortuous journeys to Oodnadatta to collect equipment. The return trip in such a heavily laden car provided special problems each time it got bogged.

There were no suitable resources at Alice Springs to build with, so he had to be innovative. He burned local limestone to make the mortar needed, and helped cut, drag, load and unload 80 tons of ironwood tree trunks to burn in the deep lime-pits, describing the smoking pits as "too large when being charged [filled], too small when being emptied". It was onerous work, and hundreds of flies settled on his back as he sweated away like a navvy. Local stone needed to be collected and carted – more heavy work. Never very strong physically, nor robust, Flynn struggled with the heavy demands on his body as weeks of building turned into months.

Then came some urgent letters from his Board: they wanted him to return as soon as possible for important discussions. Flynn replied that the task in hand was taking longer than anticipated because of the difficult circumstances. This was a convenient excuse; he had no desire to return until the mood of the Board changed.

For one of the few times in his life, partly because he was overtaxing himself and losing weight steadily, Flynn became discouraged and verged on depression. His exile was a delaying tactic, no more. When he returned, the Board would still want him to abandon his flying-doctor plans. Whether he accepted or refused, the end result would be just the same – his dream would be shelved. "Great Father, please do something!" he called out.

Some men approached him with the information that their mate was very sick and they thought he might die. Could Mr Flynn look at him? He found it to be an emergency case, needing immediate hospitalisation.

Flynn "rushed" the patient to the AIM nursing home at Oodnadatta. His compassionate nature was touched by the additional suffering caused by the long and rough journey. "An air ambulance would skim up much faster than this," he grumbled.

Another urgent communication followed from the Chairman of the Board, requesting his return as soon as possible. There was also a letter of quiet encouragement from Jean Baird, Flynn's personal secretary. While informing him how individual Board members stood, it was sensitively written, with no implied criticism of anyone. Although she didn't actually say so, Jean Baird hinted Flynn should resist calls to return until the mood changed in Sydney and Melbourne.

Other similar letters followed from his loyal secretary, giving him great comfort. Someone understood his predicament and was trying to help. He relied completely on her astute analysis.

In May 1926, Flynn collected from Oodnadatta the first two AIM nurses for Alice Springs, Nell Small and Ina Pope. The party had reached Horseshoe Bend when they came across a man who was seriously ill. The nurses decided that the patient needed to be taken to Port Augusta for emergency treatment. Flynn turned the Dodge around and raced the 200 miles back to Oodnadatta.

The sick man's one hope was that they would catch the fortnightly train before it left for the south. Rain started, falling at first as a gentle spitting, then as torrents. Flynn prayed that they would not get bogged down in the mud that quickly became like glue. He drove right up onto the platform on arrival at Oodnadatta. The patient was fortunate – the train had not left.

The road for the return journey had turned into slush. Flynn took some marvellous photographs of his new recruits, deep in mud, amidst swarms of flies, putting down planks and matting on the track in front of the Dodge. Welcome to the Inland!

When they finally reached it, Sisters Pope and Small were surprised how grand the nursing home at Alice Springs looked. Though not yet finished, it was by far the smartest and most prominent building in the town.

Flynn set the official opening for 26 June 1926. He then laboured night and day to have it ready in time. It was now nearly a year since he had left Adelaide and he verged on physical collapse. He became his nurses' first patient, even minor scratches on his overtaxed body turning septic. Flynn was no model patient, though, taking no heed of the advice to take better care of himself.

The trimmings were not completed for the opening and only two doors were up on their hinges. But in other respects Flynn had met his own deadline.

Considering the remoteness of Alice Springs, the official party for the opening was surprisingly large. It comprised churchmen, politicians, AIM supporters and even old Robert Mitchell, who had been guest of honour when the first nursing home had been opened at Oodnadatta 14 years previously.

John Flynn faced the official opening with mixed feelings. He would savour the moment, no doubt, but soon afterwards would have to return to the Board, to serious conflict.

The last car of the official party brought his old friend Andrew Barber. Barber rushed up to Flynn and, after perfunctory greetings, drew him aside. "I have sad news for you, Flynn. Hugh Victor McKay has died."

Flynn described that awful moment later to Sam McKay, son of the great Hugh Victor:

> You will understand how my heart stood still, for you know something of the years throughout which your father, with me, studied obstacles in our path, and waited patiently for the day when the battle might wisely be joined.

Flynn was referring to H.V. McKay's support for his flying-doctor vision, on which he had been counting. McKay was the only man of resources who had taken a genuine interest in Flynn's concept. His death could spell the end of it.

Barber had not finished, though. He had further news for Flynn, tantalising news – H.V. McKay had provided some money in his will for an aerial medical service experiment.

"What's involved? Do you know?"

"I don't know the details. Apparently his wishes were only given verbally, shortly before he died. You'll have to wait until you are able to go to Melbourne and find out."

Flynn felt rather remote from the events and celebrations of the rest of that day. His mind kept returning to the concept of an "Aerial Medical Service experiment". Would the Board allow such an innovative idea? If so, where would he set up such an experiment? Who would be involved?

Questions kept flooding in. He finished up as quickly as he could in Alice Springs, anxious to return south where he could find out the answers.

14

WILL THE BUSH BE DUMB ALWAYS?

On his return to Sydney, John Flynn went first to see Jean Baird. She smiled a warm welcome, but chided him for his loss of weight.

"Well, it was difficult out there, Miss Baird. Thank you so much for your letters; I can't tell you how important they were to me. I felt very cut off, except when you wrote. Tell me, how does the land lie now?" His blue-grey eyes watched her face closely. He was always at his most brilliant when reading people, not so much from what they said as by other telltale signs.

She replied slowly, thoughtfully. "There is talk that the composition of the Board is about to change – and very much to your liking." She needed to say no more on this subject; they both understood perfectly. "What's more," she continued, "the talk of a McKay bequest has caused a flurry of excitement. He was held in high regard among Presbyterians, as an outstanding businessman and a staunch supporter of the Church. If McKay believed an experiment was worthwhile, the Board feels there might be something in it after all. I suggest you go and find out exact details of what he intended and bring those along to the next Board meeting. Any statements of his that you quote will carry great weight."

Flynn, of course, did just that. "Gentlemen," he reported to the Board, "Hugh Victor McKay was the greatest friend of my dream. He discussed its most intricate details with me. To show his confidence, he has made a provision of £2 000 for that dream, available at once, and a similar sum to be awarded yearly, if appropriate. The money is earmarked for an experiment to test the viability of an Aerial Medical Service. He was confident, and so am I, that the AIM could raise the further £4 000 that will be required."

Board members were impressed, though cautious. They gave tentative permission for Flynn to investigate further, but stipulated a higher budget by a thousand pounds. Flynn was thrilled to have the opportunity for investigation, and the extra monetary requirement did not concern him.

Next morning, though, found him rather subdued. Without a wireless network operating in the bush, a flying-doctor service would be largely futile. What about an isolated homestead that desperately needed a doctor? It might still take three days, or longer, to ride to a telegraph office and call for help.

In his moment of triumph, John Flynn felt very insecure. He contacted Andrew Barber, his close friend and confidant, who came to see him at his office. Flynn told him, "My plans for a flying doctor are in trouble. I have not yet cracked how to span the bush with radio waves."

"Can we delay the aerial experiment until we have solved the wireless problems?"

"That might take three years or more, I just don't know. Public interest is at its height now. To delay would be counterproductive, especially since we are the ones who have been yapping at everyone's heels to get started. We would look ridiculous; no one would take us seriously any more." With a wry smile, Flynn pointed at a large map of his which hung on the wall. It was headed: "Sky Doctors Eventually – Why Not Now?"

Barber said nothing. Flynn continued, "In all conscience, unless I can assure my Board that the wireless network will be started within the experimental year, I will not go ahead. It's that crucial."

"A year only? But I thought you said it could take three years, maybe longer?"

"I did. That is the crisis."

"What alternatives have you?"

"None, really. I'll have to go out bush again and get a network operating, however crudely. There is no one else to attempt it."

A brief silence followed, with both men deep in thought.

Flynn broke the silence. "My friend, I have a very special request of you."

"Oh yes, and what's that?"

"I cannot do the flying-doctor experiment and continue to organise the patrol padres, nursing homes, fundraising and so on. I need someone I can trust to take over the nuts and bolts of AIM business. How about it? I hate asking you – I know you are happy in your ministry and that I am presuming on our friendship. Many lives depend on our success, otherwise I wouldn't ask." Flynn's eyes behind his round spectacles were measured and unblinking as he looked at Barber.

For once the jovial Barber was unsmiling. He knew that John Flynn rarely asked anyone directly for anything, preferring to sell his ideas to the head and the heart until a person offered to help. For his friend to act so out of character showed the hour was critical. "What do you envisage?" he asked.

"For you to come onto the AIM staff as Patrol Organiser, a new position created until the emergency is resolved one way or another. I would like to keep you in the flying-doctor action also, so that you wouldn't miss any of the fun! An example is for you and George Simpson to report on possible bases, landing grounds and the medical needs of the Inland."

"That doesn't sound like the work of a Patrol Organiser to me, Flynn, it sounds more like your flying-doctor province."

"That's true, so I am hoping you and Simpson will serve on the organising committee for the experiment. That way you will have a foot in both camps, and I will also have the support I need. After my experiences with an obstructive Board, I want the flying-doctor committee to be hand-picked. Well, how about it?"

"Personally, I'd like to do it. I cannot give you a final decision right now; I'll need to discuss it with my family and my church first."

John Flynn then burnt his bridges. He bluntly told his Board that unless he believed that there was a good chance of putting cheap, reliable wireless sets into the hands of the Inlanders, he would not proceed with the flying-doctor experiment. "Without a wireless transmitting station at every isolated habitation, an Aero Medical Service would be 75% futile," he wrote in his evaluation. The race was on.

Thankfully, Andrew Barber accepted the position of Patrol Organiser for the AIM, freeing Flynn up. The latter spoke frantically with as many radio experts and "hams" as he could. No one in Sydney or Melbourne seemed able to help, so he dashed to Adelaide to consult with Harry Kauper.

Kauper was forthright. "Mr Flynn, you must abandon your dream of pioneers using voice transmission, at least for the present. Voice transmission, to be consistent, would require sophisticated and powerful sets. A cheaper, simpler system could be designed for Morse code."

Flynn protested, "Old 'Saltbush Bill' will have problems with that. Often he cannot read or write, except in the most rudimentary way. How could he send messages in a complex code?"

"Perhaps his wife will learn, if her family is at risk. Or perhaps someone else on the property will if lives are at stake."

Flynn sighed. He decided to retreat, temporarily. "All right, if it has to be Morse for now, it has to be. Could we make a 'mother' station so powerful that it could talk back to the bush stations by voice?"

"Yes, easily, providing you have enough money."

"One powerful 'mother' station could be within our budget. I start to see it clearly now. The 'mother' station could read the message back, in voice, to the pioneer who originally sent it in Morse. An operator at the 'mother' station would keep repeating the message until it was confirmed by the pioneer to be correct. That base operator would have some headaches and would need to be as patient as Job. Bruce Plowman told me how an old bushman insisted 'onions' was spelled 's-o-a-p' because he had once been sent some onions in an old soap box."

Kauper smiled wryly, then added, "Besides needing patience, your base operator will have to be a radio repair expert. He will have to keep the 'mother' station operating, and also no doubt repair the 'daughter' sets in the bush as the pioneers wouldn't be able to do that. Mr Flynn, the problems associated with your ideas are massive!"

Flynn's enigmatic smile played around the corners of his mouth again. He said, "I want to trial this concept of a 'mother' station that talks to 'daughters' that chirp back in code. I'll assemble some equipment as quickly as possible. Then I'll go out bush and do further experiments."

"Who will you take along to help you?"

"I would like to take George Towns again, but I'm afraid his health has deteriorated since his return. I need an electrical engineer to set up the 'mother' station, who must also know about radio, and be interested enough to come with me. Any suggestions?"

Kauper had thought about this already. He said at once, "Why not try Alf Traeger? He's the electrical engineer who made the generator you used on your last trip, remember? He's asked my advice recently about some amateur radios he has been making, and I've been most impressed with the final products. He hasn't played around with wireless for very long, but he's extraordinarily innovative."

Flynn arranged to see Alf Traeger for a meal the next day. At their dinner, he spent much time describing the flying-doctor experiment and the urgent need to solve the wireless problem. The younger man seemed interested, smiled and nodded at times, but said very little. He was obviously painfully shy. Flynn worked at drawing him out:

"Have you always been interested in wireless, Mr Traeger?"

"No. I was first interested in telephones. When I was 12, I made my own." His voice was quiet, but friendly.

"Aged 12? How did you do that?"

"With difficulty!" Traeger's brown eyes twinkled.

"Tell me about it."

Traeger was reluctant to speak about himself, but, with prodding, Flynn managed to get the story out of him.

"I was on the family farm when I read about telephones," Traeger said. "I had nothing to make one with, so I improvised. I made strong magnets by wrapping wire around old broken pitchfork prongs and passing electricity through the wire. Next, I made vibrating diaphragms for the microphones and earpieces using the tin lids off tobacco tins. I crushed some pieces of charcoal to supply the variable resistance I needed for the microphone. When it actually worked, I was hooked for life! Wireless is just a small step from telephones, so that has become another interest."

"Amazing. What did your parents think of your telephone?"

"Not much … I strung it up between the house and the shed, and it unhorsed my father when he came home that evening."

The moment came for Flynn to suggest Traeger might join him. Traeger was very interested: he was 31 years old and a little restless. He explained later: "I had no ties. I wasn't married and wanted to see the Outback. Flynn's ideas sounded intriguing. Anyway, it wasn't going to be easy to say 'no' to John Flynn!"

Flynn and Traeger worked feverishly in Adelaide to assemble equipment to test the feasibility of the "mother station" concept. As they worked, Flynn admired the ingenuity of his young aide, and the neat precision with which he assembled apparatus. Traeger was such a careful worker that he did not wear overalls.

Understanding Flynn's need for simplicity, Traeger built self-contained transmitters and receivers. The result was more compact and easier to operate than the equipment Flynn and Towns had tested the previous year. A suitable power source still eluded them, though. For the present, they would have to use batteries.

The new equipment was very expensive. Not having other resources, wanting Traeger to have everything he needed, Flynn mortgaged his next two years' salary.

It was with a mounting sense of expectancy that the two men travelled towards Alice Springs. Nor did the journey lack thrills. John Flynn's driving style ensured that! Traeger wrote:

> The padre was a fast driver and, to make matters worse, liked to drive at night. We thumped into 'roos and banged in and out of gutters – I can tell you, I was scared stiff from start to finish! But that old Dodge was a magnificent car and took the hammering. In fact, it was a car within a car – we took spares of just about everything.

Predictably, they got bogged a number of times, the wheels of the Dodge being too narrow for sand.

> To drive over a sandy creek the vehicle had to be put into bottom gear and the accelerator pushed to the floor. The engine roared like an aeroplane before take-off. It would shoot forwards into the sands and rock crazily from side to side. If you were lucky, you would get through it in one attempt. If not, out would come the coir mats and shovels. Sometimes the vehicle would get stuck again and again under a blazing sun with sand hot enough to raise blisters. Never once did I see John Flynn angry, or even frustrated. He simply set about solving the problem with good humour, hard work and infinite patience. I suspected even then that he was a great man.

When they reached Alice Springs, Flynn felt a tinge of pride as his nursing home in Todd Street came into view – it was magnificent! Sisters Pope and Small were there and soon the four of them were relaxing over a cup of tea.

In answer to Flynn's questions, the sisters assured him that all was fine and that the controversial ventilation system "worked a treat". In fact, their visitors multiplied on especially hot days.

They also had a cheery story for Flynn. It involved two prominent local men who had opposed the building of the Alice Springs hospital, claiming it to be too extravagant for such a poor region. They had expressed these opinions in the Northern Territory press, irking Flynn who at the time was working night and day to complete their hospital. He had not responded; he seldom rebutted criticism, preferring his life and deeds to do this instead.

Sister Pope laughed as she told him what had transpired since. "I wonder whether God has a sense of humour? Those same two men just 'happened' to be our very first patients, and both were so ill that they had to spend several days in hospital. We smothered them with care and attention, of course, spoiling them rotten. Since leaving us, both have given large donations to the hospital and each has become an active helper in our fundraising activities. Isn't that marvellous?"

"Certainly it is. I believe that the only way to get rid of enemies is to turn them into friends. Well done."

Later on, Flynn and Traeger lugged the equipment from the Dodge into the tiny engine room at the rear of the hospital. This included more than wireless gear because Flynn wanted Traeger to install the hospital's lighting plant, which would operate from the same generator as the radio sets.

"No more kero lamps," Sister Pope observed happily when the electric lights came on with a flick of a switch.

Next, Traeger set about constructing the "mother" wireless station, 8AB, on the opposite side of the room to the lighting plant. It was to be very powerful, 50 watts in fact. They spread out their equipment over two cramped tables, one for the transmitter and the other for the receiver. Then they waited impatiently for evening.

Dusk came at last. Flynn leant over Traeger's shoulder, watching him as he tried to raise Kauper in Adelaide. He began by trying voice telephony rather than Morse code.

"8AB calling 5CL. 8AB calling 5CL. Do you read me? Over."

There was no response. Traeger tried again. Kauper's voice then boomed out of their receiving set, startling them with its unexpected strength and clarity. "8AB, am reading you loud and clear. Very clear."

Flynn pressed Traeger's shoulder in a friendly gesture. "Congratulations," he said. 8AB was a reality, it was on the air!

Although "mother" was operational, Traeger spent many hours adjusting it to his high standards. He also spent time showing Maurie Fuss, the local telegraph operator, how to use it. He had agreed to man 8AB while Traeger and Flynn set up their "daughter" stations.

One bright Sunday morning, they loaded half a ton of Edison copper oxide batteries and mounds of other equipment into the back of the Dodge and set off for Hermannsburg Mission, 80 miles to the west. It was now 11 November 1926, and Traeger needed to be back in Adelaide by Christmas. The Dodge creaked and groaned under the load.

"The Edison batteries are good because they need so little upkeep," Flynn observed, "but they are too bulky for the bush. Also, they're filled with caustic soda, nasty stuff, and are too expensive. We will need to find another source of power before we can set up a radio network for the flying doctor. Some simple form of electrical generator would be best."

"I know," replied Traeger. "I think about it all the time. When I get back to Adelaide, I'll experiment."

They tossed ideas back and forth. The previous year Flynn had seen a Pathé Frères picture show in which the current for the projector had been produced by a man pedalling on a bicycle frame, a generator being mounted on the rear axle instead of a wheel. Traeger had heard of similar pedal generators being used by German soldiers during the First World War, but these had produced a very variable output, far too irregular for wireless work. The young man did have an alternative idea, though: "I have noticed how smoothly an emery grinding wheel spins. It's a heavy stone wheel which is spun by hand. Perhaps if I mount a generator on such a wheel, it will turn smoothly enough to give a consistent output. I'll try it out in my workshop back home."

Hermannsburg was an isolated Lutheran mission station, ministering to the Aborigines. Traeger felt very much at home with Pastor

155

Albrecht and his helper, Mr Heinrich. They were German Lutherans, like himself, and all had suffered the stigma of their German ancestry during the war. Traeger, for example, had not been allowed to fight for Australia, his nation of birth, in the conflict.

Flynn was far too excited that night to allow the conversation to dwell on matters German. He soon captured everyone's attention by painting word-pictures of all the benefits that wireless would bring to the Outback. Pastor Albrecht recorded later that his imagination was taken prisoner by Flynn that night. One of Flynn's more striking thoughts was: "I feel we have no moral right to our Inland if we leave it empty and undeveloped. The millions in Asia might find better use for it if we do not incorporate it fully into our nation. Wireless will do this more than anything else. Prospectors will be able to venture into desert areas with more confidence and mining settlements will spring up as a result. Commerce and transport will be co-ordinated with our great cities instead of operating independently. Radio will protect the safety of travellers, opening up the Inland to tourism. We will span the Inland with dots and dashes and sew it into our nation."

Mission-station Aborigines watched in silence as Flynn and Traeger raised their 30-foot aerial next morning. Flynn scratched around for timber and made a table for the set to sit on in the mission store.

Traeger went over to the table and put on the earphones. He made a quick check of everything, then began to tap out his staccato message using the Morse key.

"8AD [Hermannsburg] calling 8AB ['mother' station at Alice Springs]. 8AD calling 8AB. Come in 8AB. Over."

No reply. Traeger frowned. He was clearly surprised. He tapped out the message again, but apart from a buzz on the receiver there was no reply.

"Could that buzz have been a voice trying to come through?" Flynn asked hopefully.

Traeger shook his head dubiously, but nevertheless tapped out: "Say again. Speak louder."

No response, not even a buzz. Silence. Traeger pursed his lips, tinkered a bit with the regulators, then tried again, but to no avail.

"Do you think Maurie Fuss may have forgotten to stand by?" Traeger asked.

"I doubt it. He is the local telegraph operator so he's used to working to time schedules."

Traeger did exhaustive checks, including each one of the Edison cells. Everything seemed to be OK. He tried again. Still no response.

"I don't understand it. 8AB at Alice Springs is working. This one also appears to be working. Perhaps I should give it one further test."

Traeger then tapped out messages to distant amateurs, hoping that a "ham" in one of the cities might hear and reply. Again there was no answer.

"Perhaps no one heard," Traeger said. "On the other hand, it might be faulty equipment. I can't tell."

This session left the men dispirited and mystified. "There's nothing else for it, we must return to Alice Springs and find out what's happening there," Flynn decided.

Before they left, Traeger spent five days teaching the missionaries how to send in Morse code. Times were arranged for messages to be sent, the first to be at 5 p.m. on the Wednesday of their return.

The Dodge drew up to the hospital at Alice Springs a few minutes before the appointed hour. Traeger jumped out of the car before it had quite stopped, stumbled slightly, then ran into the lighting shed.

His eyes darted over the sets. The equipment seemed fine. Then he saw that Maurie Fuss had put the wrong coil into the receiver – 8AB had been tuned to the wrong wavelength! Snatching up the correct one, Traeger switched coils in a flash and heard the wonderful sound of Morse code coming through the speaker.

Flynn entered the room at the lope and Traeger glanced up. The two men locked eyes. Flynn's face was beaming – he had heard. Traeger turned to the transmitter and sent a reply by voice: "8AB calling 8AD. Receiving you clearly. Over."

A jumble of Morse came back from Hermannsburg. The letters were too close to decipher. "Send more clearly," Traeger said, but to no avail. A hodgepodge of Morse was the reply.

"They're too excited, I think," Flynn said. "Tell them to slow down."

Traeger did. It was no use. He sent a final "Goodbye, see you at morning schedule", and closed down.

"Today is historic — I believe this is the start of our radio network!" exulted Flynn. "It means the flying doctor is a real possibility." That night, he found it hard to sleep. Too much adrenalin was pumping around his thin body.

Next morning, at 5 a.m., the dots and dashes from 8AD came through loud and clear and at a slow and steady speed. Albrecht and Heinrich had recovered their composure, which they had lost the previous evening when Traeger's voice had boomed through their loudspeaker.

Flynn asked, "Do you realise that we are now the world leaders in personal wireless? No-one else has achieved what we have done. We have set up a bush station costing under £100, one compact enough to fit on a small table providing the batteries are kept on the floor underneath. Yet, I'm afraid this is still not good enough for our pioneers and we must press on very fast."

Within two weeks, 8AD at Hermannsburg was tested by a problem that developed at the mission station. Mrs Albrecht had had a complication of pregnancy and had travelled down to Tanunda to have her baby. The doctor became concerned for the baby's health soon after delivery and did not want the baby to leave the hospital. What should Mrs Albrecht do — leave the hospital and return at the time prearranged with her husband, or change the travel arrangements and stay? As it would take too long to try to send messages back and forth by traditional means, she decided to try using the new radio instead. She sent her message to 8AB at Alice Springs by telegram, whence Traeger relayed it by radio to 8AD at Hermannsburg. Pastor Albrecht replied immediately to Traeger, by radio, that his wife should remain at Tanunda until the doctor was happy for her and the baby to travel together. Traeger relayed this at once, via telegraph. What would normally have taken days, if not weeks, was achieved in hours. (The baby, Helen Albrecht, grew up to become Hermannsburg's well-known wireless operator in later life.)

The time had come to set up another "daughter" station, which Flynn and Traeger did at Arltunga, 70 miles east of Alice Springs.

8AD (Hermannsburg) and 8AE (Arltunga) then sent messages to each other, without using the "mother" station at Alice Springs at all. This direct communication gave promise of banishing isolation and loneliness forever.

Flynn and Traeger tested 8AC, the Dodge Buckboard, in a number of isolated areas to investigate the possibilities of incorporating vehicles into a radio network. Flynn was delighted with the results, concluding that all vehicle users would one day have the option of using wireless for safety purposes. Among these, of course, would be his own patrol padres.

Both bespectacled, lean and conservatively dressed, Flynn and Traeger looked like a "father" and "son" at work, Flynn the taller, older "father" and Traeger his tousle-headed "son". Traeger invariably wore dark, long trousers and striped braces, and no one ever saw him or Flynn in shorts, even on the hottest of days. By this time, the two men had developed a close personal relationship and would chat and joke with a relaxed camaraderie that the shy Traeger had never shared with anyone else.

They returned to Adelaide in December. Flynn immediately put Traeger on staff as the "AIM Field Radio Engineer", at a salary equivalent to his own. He believed that his protégé could do the impossible and put a wireless network in place for the flying-doctor experiment. "One of my greatest discoveries" was how Flynn described him.

Before returning to Sydney, Flynn held a short meeting with Traeger and Kauper to set goals for the development of the wireless network. A power source suitable for use in the bush remained their most vexing problem. It was decided Traeger should build two prototype generators; one would use a hand-operated spinning wheel and the other, using foot power, would be similar to a bicycle.

Flynn set four difficult criteria for a suitable radio set. "It must be simple enough for a child to operate, light enough for a woman to lift, powerful enough to receive and transmit messages from 500 miles as this will be the range of our flying doctor, and cheap enough for impoverished pioneers to buy. I would like it to come in at under £50 a set."

"You are asking for a midget miracle set, so small its cost disappears completely," Traeger mocked him.

"Just so," the older man replied equably.

Flynn made his epic announcement to the Board on his return to Sydney: "Gentlemen, we can give the bush a voice in the near future. This removes the last major obstacle to launching a flying-doctor experiment. I propose that we proceed with the experiment forthwith."

15

READY, SET, GO!

The year 1927 was a time of frantic activity for John Flynn. He threw himself into setting up the flying-doctor experiment. Officially, it was termed the "Aerial Medical Services (AMS) Experiment" because the medical profession objected to the title "flying doctor", feeling that it lacked dignity. The press, meanwhile, had no such finer feelings and popularised the original term.

Hundreds of details needed to be considered and Flynn was meticulous, wanting to avoid any hitches. To give just one example, in order to obtain permission for his plans for a radio network he needed to make approaches to the Postmaster General's Office, to the state governments, and the Federal Government, the Army and Air Force, the civilian aviation authorities and the police – not to mention seeking AWA permission to use certain equipment. Not only were some of these discussions difficult and protracted, but each of the other interested groups needed to be fully briefed on all progress made and decisions taken.

Flynn set Easter of 1928 as the date for the experiment to commence. He chose this period deliberately; its symbolism was not lost on Australians.

Five thousand pounds was needed before the experiment could proceed. Flynn was unhappy about canvassing for funds in such a hurry, his principle being:

> I have a great horror of professional canvassers, and feel that our revenue should be increased by natural growth, through the enthusiasm of those who become inspired to act sponta-neously. In this way we avoid that dangerous condition where our people complain that the church is always seeking for money, and attain the ideal where, as of old, the wise ones

come bringing gifts! [an allusion to the "wise men" who brought gifts to the infant Christ].

Mercifully, Andrew Barber agreed to take on the burden of raising the money in time. He had none of Flynn's scruples, being very direct. His view was that the pastoralists and industrialists would benefit from a flying-doctor service and so should be prepared to pay. He concluded public meetings by saying, "My friend, John Flynn, says that the money will come in time, but I prefer to see something more definite. As time is short and the need immediate, I shall accept cheques tonight."

Despite these efforts, Barber was forced to tell Flynn, a worried expression on his face, "We are not going to have the £5 000 in time. I've done my very best, but I'm afraid that I have failed. What should we do?"

"Oh? How much are we short?"

"Five hundred pounds. Look, I have shares in the family property. I'll guarantee £250 of that."

"That's very good of you. Thank you so much. I'll guarantee the rest."

This would be eight months of John Flynn's salary, an impossibly large sum for him to find.

"You never have any money," Barber protested, "and Traeger tells me that you keep buying expensive radio equipment out of your own pocket with what little cash you do have. You don't have the resources to guarantee anything!"

Flynn gave a whimsical little smile. For a few seconds he looked guilty, like a lad chided for having his hand in the cookie jar. He tapped his pipe, to gain time, then replied, "I established this mission on two qualities, faith and love. God has always provided the rations when we've needed them. By faith, I believe he will again. You get the necessary papers drawn up and I'll sign them."

"It was all too easy for Flynn to sign," Barber joked later on, "because he had no money. I stood to lose all of mine!"

All the while, Flynn was making landmark decisions about the first flying doctor: What type of doctor would be best? What sort of training should he have? What equipment and working conditions would he need? What should Flynn offer? How should the advertisement be worded to attract the right man? How should Flynn proceed through the minefield of medical etiquette to avoid offending the sensibilities of doctors and the Australian Medical Association? With the help of Dr Geordie Simpson whenever he could find the time, he rushed about seeing doctors and specialists for advice: in Sydney, Melbourne, Adelaide and Perth. Dr Holland, who ten years previously had dashed out to Halls Creek to try to save young Darcy, was one who spent many hours with Flynn, discussing the issues.

Who would supply the aeroplane and pilot for the flying doctor? Here the decisions were easier to arrive at because of the time already spent by Flynn investigating the options. He approached his old friend Hudson Fysh, with whom he had been meeting periodically since 1921. Could QANTAS come to the party, and under what conditions? The two friends hammered out a contract that was mutually satisfactory: the commonwealth government agreed to subsidise half the flying costs up to 25 000 miles, leaving the AIM to pay only the other half: should less than that distance be flown, the AIM would have to pay a rebate to QANTAS for the balance.

What would Flynn receive in return? Why not buy an aeroplane and hire their own pilot instead? Flynn explained his reasoning in a letter to a Mrs Munro.

> They [QANTAS] undertake to keep one of their most experienced pilots (already familiar with the country) in charge of this aeroplane, which will not be available for any other work other than medical ... This AMS plane will be painted to our own taste ... it will be our own in every desirable sense of the term as regards advantages – but, if it should be destroyed, the loss will be borne by QANTAS ... we will have behind us, in our service, no less than six aeroplanes of the same model in QANTAS' fleet! ... you will thus see that, so far as human resources can provide, the AMS is GUARANTEED TO FUNCTION WITHOUT INTERRUPTION. Once a month, or thereabouts, our AMS aeroplane will be put in dock for a thorough tuning up. Before it goes into dock, however, a facsimile machine will have taken its place in the hangar. The AMS pilot will sometimes be out of sorts, and sometimes on holiday, but always, in such an event, a colleague will step into his post.

He continued in a more flippant vein:

> It is likely enough that our original machine will be destroyed in some dangerous emergency, but, no matter: "The king is dead, long live the king." Another mail plane will at once take up the running, and our only worry will be, in the event of the doctor having perished with the plane, to get another doctor.

Hudson Fysh personally arranged for a DH50A to be specially fitted out for the flying doctor experiment. The biplane could carry four passengers with the pilot and could cruise at 80 miles per hour. It had a stretcher and another innovation, an undercarriage which was designed to lessen bumps on landing. Red crosses were painted below its wings and the name VICTORY on the fuselage. (Actually, a mistake was made with the name. Flynn had wanted VICTOR in honour of Hugh Victor McKay. VICTORY, though, seemed appropriate enough and so was left unchanged. H.V. McKay's family said they preferred it, in fact.)

A major decision remained to be made and that was where to base the flying doctor. In the absence of a radio network, the base would have to be somewhere with telegraph and telephone facilities, to enable those few pioneers with access to these to call him. Cloncurry, in Western Queensland, was a possibility because it had a government hospital to which the flying doctor might ferry seriously ill patients. From Cloncurry, where QANTAS already had an aerodrome, the flying doctor could service an area as big as New South Wales, not only for emergencies but with "clinic runs" to townships that had a reasonable population but no resident doctor.

Before a final decision could be made in favour of Cloncurry, its suitability would need to be determined by a visit, a task Flynn asked Andrew Barber and Geordie Simpson to undertake.

"I want you two to do much more than simply assess Cloncurry," Flynn told them. "I would like you to take steps to set up the infrastructure for our experiment. For example, encourage people to start preparing landing grounds. We also need an evaluation of the health of Inlanders, in order to give the flying doctor a picture of what he will be up against.

"However, your most important task is to sell the concept to the Inlanders themselves, and to any other medical personnel in the region. It is critically important that we harness support for the flying doctor. He could end up as a 'flying flop' if no one knows how to use him, or perhaps wants to. As soon as you return, Alf Traeger and I will do a similar trip to 'sell' radio to the pioneers. Hopefully, we will have some new equipment to test out by then. Getting a wireless network in place and operational in time is still our biggest challenge."

"What sort of progress is Traeger making?" Barber asked.

"I'm not certain. He is difficult to communicate with, being in Adelaide. Time is his greatest enemy. He has to make everything himself and it is all new and never been done before. He works at least 15 hours a day, sometimes 20 hours."

Flynn turned to Geordie Simpson. "Please don't forget your tools as well as your medical kit. I'm relying on you to keep the Dodge on the road for the next three months, because it is going to be a rough ride."

The travellers found that Flynn had not exaggerated: springs broke; valves burnt out; an axle cracked; not to mention at least a dozen punctures and numerous boggings. All the same, they visited hundreds of pioneers and passed on the message: "Prepare for a flying-doctor visit soon. Make your own landing strip, it's easy to do. Choose a narrow, flat stretch of land and clear it of trees and other obstructions."

In his survey, Dr Simpson found the Inlanders to be generally robust. Nevertheless, his services were needed at every stop.

When they finally reached Cloncurry, Andrew Barber wasted no time in calling a public meeting in the shire hall. Most who attended showed great enthusiasm for the scheme, though some questioned whether it was really necessary. The issue of safety was also raised. George Simpson addressed it eloquently: "Mr Barber and I have had a series of minor accidents to get here by car, and the struggle has taken us weeks. QANTAS has flown over this same ground for the past five years, taking only hours and not weeks, and has not had even one accident! Flying is much safer than horse, camel or motor car, as has been proven in your very own skies by the same QANTAS that will be transporting your flying doctor. Added to that, the extra speed and comfort of flying could well save your life or the life of a loved one."

Amazingly, the very next morning brought a crisis that encompassed the very questions brought up at that meeting. A miner at Mount Isa had a serious accident, injuring his spine and breaking his pelvis. To transport him 140 miles by car along rough roads to the Cloncurry Hospital would have been torture, perhaps even fatal. QANTAS was asked to fly a rescue mission to Mount Isa. When Geordie Simpson heard of this from Norman Evans, the QANTAS pilot, he offered to go with him to help. Evans accepted gratefully.

The news flashed through the community. Here was a real-life test of whether a flying doctor could be any good. The locals waited to evaluate the outcome.

On arrival at Mount Isa, Simpson examined the injured man. Evacuation to Cloncurry was imperative, but the mail plane standing by was not fitted out for this. Simpson made adjustments so that a stretcher could be accommodated, and ensured it would be safely anchored by arranging extra supports. Then he carefully directed the loading of the suffering man onto the aircraft and attended him during the flight. He was delighted at how comfortably the patient travelled. ("Fortunately, no one saw that I was horribly airsick," the doctor reported later to Flynn.)

On landing at Cloncurry, Simpson accompanied the miner in an ambulance to the government hospital, where he recovered.

Happily for Flynn he was very vocal about his experiences. "I suffered sheer hell, agony," he told everyone, "but that was while I was in the ambulance. Red dust had blown in drifts across the road and we had to crash through these like a boat through waves, spraying dust in all directions. Every jolt sent me through the roof with pain. In the air, though, it was like heaven: it was smooth and painless in comparison."

Flynn's busy pen sent news of this triumph to many newspapers, producing a positive response throughout the country. One unexpected spin-off was a flurry of donations for the experiment. These covered the outstanding amount and Flynn was not required to meet his guarantee of £250. The "rations" had come in time yet again.

Cloncurry was confirmed as the site of the first flying-doctor base. The next step was for Flynn to go there with Alf Traeger, who was keen to test out new equipment he had been building for the bush, including a lighter aerial which would be more efficient and simpler to erect. He also had plans to adapt the Dodge so that its generator could be run directly from the engine, without needing to be stopped and jacked up. This excited Flynn: if wireless worked successfully from a moving vehicle, he foresaw it would also be possible from a flying-doctor aeroplane.

Traeger's most promising step forward, though, was a simple hand generator which he turned with his left hand while sending messages in Morse with his right. Not only did it supply sufficient voltage, but the voltage was steady enough to send and receive wireless signals. This "smoothed-out" voltage resulted largely from "crystal control": Kauper had suggested that a quartz crystal be added to the circuit to allow a steady wave to be generated even though the voltage fed in was uneven. This "crystal control" was a revolutionary and major breakthrough.

Flynn had several surprises in store for Traeger during their two-month odyssey, one being the extent of his plans. They went to inspect sites Flynn had already determined would be radio outposts and introduced Traeger to the people there, including the Rothery family at Augustus Downs. "Have a good look around the home-stead," Flynn told him, "because this will be our very first outpost."

Most startling of all was an unexpected journey to Mornington Island, in the far-north Gulf of Carpentaria. Here was an isolated Presbyterian mission station, run by a friend of Flynn's, Reverend Wilson.

On the way, Flynn explained the reason for their trip: "In 1917 our head missionary there, Reverend Robert Hall, was murdered by Aborigines. His assistant was badly wounded. The wives and children barricaded themselves in. With the help of two Aboriginal lads, Gully and Mami, they repulsed attacks until the lugger returned to the island and rescued them, ten days later. In all those days of terror they could not communicate with the outside world. Dangers like those have probably passed, but the people still suffer shortages and epidemics on the island with no means of calling for help. I want you to put a wireless there as soon as possible."

Spending time with the gentle missionary families on Morn-ington Island, seeing their great sacrifices of love on behalf of the islanders, stirred something in Traeger. It awakened in him the true importance of what his radio could do for the bush; it added steel to his resolve. This was exactly what Flynn had planned it to do.

"Somehow, we must sell the concept of radio to Cloncurry," Flynn told him as, back on the mainland, they drove south. "Even if you produce the perfect network, it will be no good if the pioneers aren't interested in wireless and what it might do."

Usually a sleepy backwater, Cloncurry was abuzz with excitement when they arrived on the first Tuesday in November. They had unwittingly turned up on Melbourne Cup Day, the day of Australia's premier horse race.

"I'll have to wait a day or two before calling a meeting," Flynn grumbled to Traeger, "to allow this 'Cup fever' to die down. At the moment, that's all the locals can think about." Then he had a flash of inspiration. "Do you think you could string up an aerial and get the Melbourne Cup on the radio receiver?"

For a moment, Traeger looked startled by the unexpected question, then he grinned broadly as Flynn's strategy hit him. The sly old fox was going to popularise radio, all right!

Traeger rigged his aerial at the rear of the Post Office, where there was an open area in which a crowd could gather. He twiddled his receiving set, then turned to Flynn with a mock frown. "All I can pick up is classical music. Do you think that will do instead?" Flynn's face fell until he realised that Traeger was teasing. The younger man turned up the volume and commentary from the Flemington race-track boomed through.

"Turn it up even higher! Blast it out. I think that God has delivered Cloncurry into my hands!"

Within minutes, people materialised from all quarters, including the two nearby hotels. Many rushed away to call friends. Before the main race started, almost the whole town had gathered to listen.

It was an exciting Melbourne Cup. The roaring of the crowd of 100 000 at Flemington came clearly through the loudspeakers and added to the tension. The Cloncurry favourite was Trivalve, ridden by the famous Bobby Lewis. It seemed to be in with a good chance. How better to popularise wireless than if the local favourite was to win?

The race was a tantalisingly close one and the horses were straining towards the finish when tragedy struck. The receiver suddenly went dead! The crowd were silent, stunned. Traeger rushed to the set to see whether he could restore reception. "Horror of horrors," Traeger recalled later, "the earth wire had been broken, perhaps in a dog fight. I called out to Flynn: 'The earth wire! The earth wire!' and Flynn reconnected it just in time for the placings to come through, loud and clear." Trivalve, the local favourite, had won. A cheer went up from the crowd.

Flynn called a meeting the next night; the shire hall was full to capacity. He began by explaining the flying-doctor concept and the need for radio, and asked his listeners to form a local AMS committee, to support the work at Cloncurry.

Flynn ended the evening by inviting the deputy chairman of the shire to speak to Adelaide from the Dodge outside. A large number of the crowd were curious and tagged along – just what Flynn had hoped for. Unfortunately, the deputy chairman was overexcited by the novel occasion and launched into a 40-minute speech, mainly of thanks but nevertheless boring. At its close, Kauper reported excellent reception in Adelaide, as did an assortment of "hams" in other cities. The potential of radio for long-distance communication had been demonstrated effectively in Cloncurry.

A few more days were spent in the town. Flynn organised many aspects of the forthcoming experiment, including the setting up of a local committee.

"Soon all your hopes will be up in the air," Barber reminded Flynn on his return, "so we had better find the right doctor to do the job. What will you be looking for?"

"Ideally, he'll be a man of the knife, which is why our own Geordie Simpson won't fit the bill – he is not fond of surgery. The person we choose must be highly trained and command respect within his profession, to give the service standing. In his character, he should be tough but tactful. He will also need a sense of mission to put up with the difficulties that must come. I have described our ideal. Of course, we may have to settle for less."

Flynn placed an advertisement in the *Medical Journal of Australia* for 24 December 1927. Interestingly, he required the successful applicant to "give radio medical advice", revealing how optimistic he was that a wireless network would be operating within that first experimental year.

The salary offered to the successful applicant was £1 000 for the year, plus travel expenses and insurance cover. This compared well with other job vacancies for doctors.

Flynn was pleased to receive 23 replies, most from doctors saying they wished to do something "worthwhile". He confided to Hudson Fysh, "We have various doctors wanting to accept, all apparently very fair. Also one big fish nibbling. I may give the line a hard tug shortly and see if he will come out of the water."

This "big fish" stood above the rest because of an excellent reputation as a skilled surgeon. A strong and vigorous man, he possessed a forceful but likeable personality and that sense of mission that Flynn considered to be essential. The doctor wanted to dedicate a year of his life to Flynn's concept because he had been unable to serve in the last war. It would mean leaving his wife and three children behind, and a large medical practice, but he was keen to accept the challenge. This outstanding applicant was Kenyon St Vincent Welch. He was duly appointed as the first flying doctor.

"How successfully can a doctor make the transition from the soft life of a city practice to the harsh life of the Outback?" Barber wondered.

"We're about to find out," Flynn replied.

16

FLYNN'S FIRST FLYING DOCTOR

D̲r Welch was taken aback by the media attention he received on
his appointment: Flynn had done his job well and newspapers
glamorised this "history-making" first flying doctor. Elaborate send-
offs were arranged in Sydney, Melbourne and Brisbane. Typically,
Flynn stayed out of the limelight, nor did he go to Cloncurry to
introduce the new doctor to the people there. He had decided Welch
could look after himself and would be better left to do so.

Hudson Fysh, meanwhile, had the task of selecting the first Flying
Doctor Service pilot. Arthur Affleck was chosen because he was
brave and skilful, and also sensible and cautious. Furthermore, he had
flown the mail run for QANTAS and was familiar with the localities,
a vital attribute. For example, the "landing strip" at Urandangie was
the main street of the township, reasonably safe providing the only
telephone lines were still those between the hotel and Charlie
Thomas' store and that no new ones had been put up. Then, unless
a dog was sleeping in the street, a plane could set down comfortably
and, having lost speed, could turn around near the stockyards and
taxi back into town. A new pilot would not have this "local
knowledge".

Affleck would have to navigate the *Victory* mainly by sight. He
would use rough road maps, if available, balanced on his knee;
otherwise he needed to be able to recognise local creeks, hills and
bush tracks. For this reason, night flying was impossible. When
visibility deteriorated, he would try to find his way by flying close to
the ground.

Hudson Fysh met Welch in Longreach and introduced him to
Arthur Affleck. Soon the doctor and pilot were winging their way to
Cloncurry. Welch strained to see the nature of the land he had come
to serve as it floated past below him, unwinding its way as if to

infinity in all directions. The region was in the grip of a devastating drought. There was no sign of green and the trees were barren and gnarled after being ravaged by starving stock. That hot, dry, red land was where he was to practise, among those decrepit houses and tired-looking settlements.

A reception committee greeted the doctor as he clambered out of the aeroplane at Cloncurry. He was just shaking hands and introducing himself when a car drew up with a screech, covering everyone with fine dust. The driver was the doctor from the local government hospital, who rushed over, apologising profusely, and spoke to Dr Welch.

"It's rather rough to ask you to come straight away to the hospital, but I have a man waiting for an emergency operation. I would very much like you to assist." Dr Welch excused himself, the civic welcome was deferred, and he drove away in the car with the local doctor.

"The fellow cut his throat 50 miles away and was brought in by truck, having bled profusely. He's on the operating table right now," he was told.

"Mmmm. Loss of blood, a good case for air transport had we only been here a day earlier, don't you think?" Welch commented.

The local doctor shot Welch a sharp look, he thought, but he put it from his mind.

The operation was a success. Following it, Welch was whisked off to a reception at the courthouse. He had barely had time to recover from his welcome and settle himself in properly, when the first call came to which he needed to respond by air. It was from Julia Creek, 85 miles away.

Captain Arthur Affleck cranked the propeller of the *Victory* until the engine fired. He secured his flying goggles, gave Dr Welch a "thumbs up", and clambered aboard. Flynn's dream was about to become reality.

Welch and Affleck found over a hundred people waiting to meet them at the rough new airstrip at Julia Creek. Many were armed with their cameras and were keener to see and touch the aeroplane than to meet the new doctor! Welch attended to the two patients needing surgery at the Bush Nursing Home, then saw a number of other patients. With plenty of daylight hours remaining, he stayed to give the ambulance men an impromptu lecture on first aid and to share a cup of tea with local citizens. His professional manner and assurance won their confidence.

Not everyone accepted Welch as readily. The eight government doctors who practised in tiny hospitals within his flying range received visits from him and offers of his services for consultation. He assured them that he would not rob them of patients; he would limit his work to areas they did not service. Most of the eight greeted Welch cordially, but some were discourteous. Could it be that his superior training and reputation made them feel threatened? Whatever their rationale, these responses upset him.

By the end of his first month, Welch had flown 3 000 miles, given four anaesthetics, held two consultations and attended to 37 other patients. This was unspectacular, but a promising start. He was champing at the bit, wanting more work, but realised that the AMS needed time to become known and trusted.

Welch had been appointed Honorary Medical Officer at Cloncurry Hospital. He looked forward to helping because, as he told Flynn, "Cloncurry is no place to spend idle time." To his chagrin, though, he was only asked to help on rare occasions, and even these invitations stopped.

Then came a typhoid epidemic. The Cloncurry Hospital was stretched far beyond its limits and men were dying for want of medical attention. Aware of the crisis, Welch offered his services personally to the Medical Superintendent, who curtly refused them.

Eleven men died during the epidemic. Welch resigned his position at the hospital in protest, then wrote to Flynn to explain. He ended his letter philosophically: "I feel sure that a little bad blood has been generated, but it will absorb like most inflammatory lesions."

Flynn was angered at the rejection of his flying doctor because it threatened another of his dreams. He hoped that the interest in the Flying Doctor Service (as it began to be titled) would attract medical men of far higher calibre than were generally prepared to serve in the Outback. He looked forward to these flying doctors becoming free consultants to local medical services, thereby raising the whole standard of help on offer to his beloved Inlanders. "If something could be done along the lines now simmering in my mind, the flying doctor would be the supreme medical authority throughout the whole area," he wrote. What he had not anticipated was that professional jealousies could threaten this plan.

Concerned that Welch's morale might have been damaged, Flynn wrote a supportive reply. In it can be seen a leader who has been stung into making personal criticisms, something unusual for him, as he was among the most accepting of men. He never directly fired an employee, for example – though he had been known to make suggestions of alternative ministries when a man proved to be unsuitable. In his reply he said:

> I think I can understand the situation – a case of absurdities arising from fear inherent in the man's weakness. Heaven only knows what thoughts chase one another in the back of his mind; he has evidently been determined to grasp all the kudos which may be had out of the typhoid crisis. As things stand, no one can dispute with him whatever credit there may be for eleven deaths ... It seems to me that you did the only thing possible in resigning your appointment as Honorary Medical Officer. I hope you will not worry about this matter.

Flynn then shifted his emphasis, suggesting their gaze should sweep

> the horizon rather than the outhouse-infected foreground. As far as the AMS is concerned, I am not at all pessimistic, and I hope you, yourself, will be incapable of that ... but as a friend of Cloncurry, my heart is very sad indeed ... If you can pardon me for saying it, I do try to be swayed only by considerations of a permanent nature, and to ignore the yelps and snores of the moment ...

To further encourage the doctor to take the long view, Flynn added a postscript, asking Welch to join him for tea in a hundred years – then they would have a better perspective on the crisis!

It would not need a hundred years to find how things would turn out for the Flying Doctor Service. Nor, sadly, would it take that long to evaluate the life of the doctor at Cloncurry who had been so obstructive. Flynn had wondered what thoughts chased one another in the back of that doctor's mind while watching men dying of typhoid. Similarly, we may wonder what he might have been thinking when he placed the pistol to his skull a few years later, and pulled the trigger.

Would the flying doctor be able to demonstrate his value, despite the slow start? The tempo of work increased as Welch's surgical skills became better known, in line with Flynn's prediction. There was the boy who had a shotgun blast to his stomach: Welch operated on an improvised operating table by the light of oil lamps. An old lady's finger was wrenched apart and left dangling by two tendons: Welch snipped the tendons and took her to hospital to clean up the stump. Operations were needed on a stockman who was gored by a maddened bull, a man wounded by an axe blow into his skull, an elderly bushman who had walked off the top storey of a hotel late one night ... and so on.

Flynn wanted publicity to "ginger up" support. Most of the work, while sometimes dangerous, was only what might have been expected. A few unusual cases were newsworthy, though. One was that of old McNamara.

Despite his 80 years, McNamara went out on a 50-mile cross-country ride with Tom Lucas, his son-in-law. The horses were picking their way carefully through an uneven gorge when McNamara's shied, perhaps at a snake. The horse slowly went right over onto its back, crushing McNamara.

Tom leapt off his horse and rushed over. The old man was unconscious and obviously seriously injured: Tom could see at least a broken leg, a broken shoulder and perhaps some broken ribs. That dribble of blood coming out of the mouth and nose might mean nothing much, or it could mean internal injuries, Tom did not know. What should he do?

Under a blazing sun, with great difficulty, he managed to manoeuvre the heavy, comatose man into the shade of a rock overhang. He then rode out for help.

Nine miles of struggle brought him to Squirrel Hills Station. Barely pausing to change horses, he galloped ten miles, then changed to a squeaking and clattering spring cart. The target of his frantic ride was Glenholme Station, because the Champneys who lived there owned a motor car. Tom believed that the flying doctor was

McNamara's only hope, but the nearest telephone was 50 miles away, at McKinlay, and it would take a car to cover that distance in a reasonable time.

Miss Champneys agreed at once to drive her car to the telephone, her father accompanying her.

Tom wheeled the fresh horse he had borrowed and set off towards Interavon Station. He left a message and directions there for McNamara's son, and returned to the old man.

His main problem was how to carry McNamara out: a bush stretcher would not support his 17 stone for long. What could he use instead? An unusual idea came to him: why couldn't he take out a bed and use that? After all, a bed supported McNamara's weight every night, so it must be strong enough. Tom knew he could not carry the bed legs and mattress, but he certainly could take the iron frame with its base of wire and springs.

Thus it was that a man and a horse, with a cumbersome bed frame attached to the horse, undertook a nightmare journey of nine miles through difficult bush in the dark, stumbling over many obstacles.

Welch and Affleck, meanwhile, had problems of their own. The directions given by Miss Champneys were too imprecise to find her, so they decided to go first to McKinlay and speak to the locals. This they did, receiving mud maps and descriptions. They knew no landing strip had been prepared, but deduced a flat area by a stock route must be where Miss Champneys awaited them.

They followed the stock route, flying low. "There'll be no smoke to show us wind direction this time," Affleck said. "We'd better circle a few times until I can work out the best approach." Usually, he organised for there to be a bonfire of gidyea and coolabah branches onto which an old tyre could be thrown to provide a twisting column of black smoke to guide him. On this occasion, though, he had not been able to speak to Miss Champneys to make such a request. (In a later incident, a desperate father threw each tyre from his own vehicle onto the fire in turn. The final tyre was burning when the flying doctor appeared overhead!)

Affleck identified the landing spot and was relieved to see a motor car waiting nearby. After a dummy run, he put the plane down. It bumped about, but came to a stop safely.

The car took them ten miles into the hills to a "soak", a hole containing muddy water set in the otherwise dry McKinlay river bed. There they were to await the patient.

It was midday and felt like a furnace. Welch took out his clinical thermometer which showed the mercury right at the top at 110 degrees Fahrenheit. This was the limit of the thermometer; what the true temperature was, he could only guess. He had recently treated an Aboriginal man who had walked across this type of hot territory in order to consult him. The man had burns and blisters on his feet in addition to the original complaint.

Meanwhile, the previous night Tom had reached McNamara. The old man was conscious, but in terrible pain. At first light, Tom cut saplings to act as splints and set the leg as best he could. He also bandaged the broken shoulder. Next, he cut down sturdy branches and lashed these along the length and sides of the bed frame to serve as carrying handles. He was helped in this by McNamara's son and two other helpers, who by then had joined him. It was close to midday before they were ready to set off.

Each carrier knew that he must not drop his corner regardless of how much his hands and shoulders ached. Each constantly readjusted his level so that the bed remained more or less horizontal, whether going up ridges or sliding down slopes. It was exhausting work and the party soon needed to rest. How would they ever manage nine miles of this torture? The answer had to be one step at a time – and don't think of the task ahead!

Around 6 p.m. Welch decided to wait alone for the rendezvous. The others drove off to the Champneys' home, about 17 miles distant.

Sunset splashed the sky with a pastel pink. Then darkness came abruptly. Welch heard a horse approaching from the direction of the hills. It was stumbling a little because the night was so dark. When the animal drew close, Welch saw that the rider was leading a second horse by a length of rope.

"Are you Dr Welch?"

"Yes, I am."

"Would you like to come to where we have carried the old man? We think he needs your attention right now."

Their horses picked their way carefully up the gorge, sometimes slipping but never falling. The yellow glow of oil lamps greeted their riders at around 8.30 p.m. The exhausted men of the carrying party were resting up and had a billy on the boil. Welch examined the patient, but there was little he could do under the conditions apart from rearranging bandages.

Welch provided a graphic description of what occurred next.

> I suggested waiting for daylight, but, after a short discussion, they decided to push on, and asked me to lead the horses and light a track. The river bed and hillsides were covered with large masses of spinifex, and, as this was as dry as tinder, it blazed up twenty feet almost immediately a match was thrown into it. I walked on ahead, and for four miles we had a blazing trail to show the way. The night was hot and muggy and, at intervals of about a hundred yards, the bearers were forced to set down their burden and rest a few minutes. No complaint was made by the patient, though he must have suffered acutely when now one and now another of the men tripped over a rock or stumbled from weariness. The blazing spinifex lit up the craggy hillsides and glowed red on the rock faces.

> At last we reached the hut at Squirrel Hills, and the men, quite worn out, lay on the ground to rest until daylight. We had nothing to eat.

> At daylight, we lifted our patient, on his stretcher, across the back of a Ford and drove him ten miles to the aeroplane, it being impossible to find a nearer landing place ...

> Owing to the patient's great weight, we had a tussle to get him into the cabin, but in spite of his severe injuries he showed the greatest hardihood in trying to help us – seven men pushing and pulling.

McNamara was flown to Winton Hospital. Two months later, Affleck had reason to call at the hospital. He noticed a "tall, bearded figure walking with a stick". It was McNamara, well on the road to recovery. A further two months and the octogenarian was mustering cattle again. A slight limp was the only remaining sign of his traumatic experience.

Before Flynn publicised McNamara's rescue, he secured the old man's permission. Flynn was always careful to be strictly ethical in this regard. Permission obtained, the account captured popular imagination. It was followed by others of a similar heroic nature.

These successes were a source of encouragement to isolated AIM nurses, who hoped the service might expand to incorporate their areas. The flying doctor might have grabbed attention, but the nurses still shouldered the bulk of the Outback's medical burden. In that year of 1928, there were 11 of Flynn's nursing homes in service. They treated 581 inpatients and 1 797 outpatients, and drew 164 teeth. Sixteen babies were born in one hospital alone. As with the flying doctor, all these ministrations were given free of charge, in Christian love, regardless of colour or creed.

Australia's perception of flying changed forever in 1928. Bert Hinkler flew solo from London to Australia in February. In May, the flying doctor made his first emergency flight. Also in May, Charles Kingsford Smith and Charles Ulm flew from America to Australia. These exploits captured public attention, and the image of the aeroplane as a dangerous toy, useful mainly in wartime and for stunts, changed to that of a reliable and very fast mechanical marvel.

In 1928, Flynn's beloved father died. "Already, I miss him terribly," Flynn confided to Andrew Barber, "but I also have complete confidence that we shall be reunited in the next life. That hope alone makes the sorrow easier to bear."

There followed an exciting change in Flynn's personal plans: he would take a year's sabbatical leave, starting in February 1929. His Board insisted and would not countenance his excuses any longer. They noticed how tired he always looked, not having slowed down long enough to recover his strength after building the Alice Springs Hospital. It was rumoured of John Flynn that he had not taken a day's leave in 20 years and certainly no one could remember him doing so. Now, just as Christ had once told his disciples to "come aside from the activities of life and have a rest", Flynn's colleagues instructed him to do the same. When friends discovered that he had no money because he had put it all into the wireless experiments, they quietly raised sufficient for an overseas holiday. He put up token resistance, then set February as his date for sailing to Europe. But much remained to be accomplished before then.

With Flynn leaving before Welch's year was due to end in April 1929, the decision whether to continue the experiment was urgent. Despite its visible value, there was a feeling among many in the Church that this was not really missionary work and it was thereby misusing valuable funds. Meetings to discuss the matter were set for early February, to culminate with a vote.

A series of unexpected events heartened Flynn. First was an anonymous cheque for £1 000! Then came enthusiastic letters of support from the Prime Minister and the Governor-General.

When Flynn stood to address the Board, he related some simple stories of how the flying doctor had saved lives. "Yet it is the elimination of dread that is our greatest gift to the bush," he told the members. "Mothers need the security each day, and especially at night, of knowing that the flying doctor can come to their aid." Then he read out a message sent from Cloncurry: "The AMS has been a great boon to the outlying areas and we wish to express appreciation of its benefits, and sincerely trust that arrangements can be made for its continuation."

Realising the strength of the opposing view, Flynn pointed out that the true value of the flying doctor could not be assessed until a radio network was in place: he felt certain one could be started soon. Why not continue the experiment for a further year and defer a final decision until then? This seemed a sensible compromise. It was put to the vote, and passed.

Flynn was delighted. He wrote at once to Traeger to inform him that the Flying Doctor Service would be closed down unless a radio network were in place very soon.

Traeger, meanwhile, had been making exciting progress. He had abandoned the hand-generator concept in August in favour of pedalling. A generator attached to the rear wheel of a bicycle had proved very successful, especially when crystal control was added to the circuit. He had then miniaturised the pedalling system, bolted it to the floor and encased the gears in oil to ensure smooth, dust-free movement. His exceptional skill in winding armatures enabled him to produce suitable generators. The final product would be more expensive than the hand generator, but the total cost of a "baby" set would still be under £50.

Flynn received a note from Traeger in November. "Come and see the real 'Victory' before you go on your holiday trip." Knowing how reticent Traeger always was, Flynn realised he must have made a major breakthrough. He bought a train ticket to Adelaide at once and arrived at Traeger's workshop in a state of high expectation.

The young man greeted him with his shy, cautious smile and took him inside. He pointed to a neat black box covered with dials and sitting on a table. Underneath, bolted to the floor, was a shiny pedal generator.

"There it is."

"How easy is it to use?"

"Women and even children should be able to generate sufficient power," Traeger assured him. "Its greatest advantage is that it frees both hands to operate the Morse key."

"Mobs of thanks," Flynn said slowly. It was all he could say for a few moments, being overcome with emotion, knowing what that wireless set would mean to the bush.

Once he had recovered his composure, Flynn tested the radio for himself. He was delighted with it. He made Traeger return home, put on his best suit of clothes and sit at the set for a historic photograph.

"How soon can we get the network started?" Flynn asked.

"I don't know. Each set will take a long time to make, then we must take them into the bush and teach the pioneers how to use them. There is a lot to it."

Back in Sydney, Flynn worked late every night to leave AIM business in good shape for Barber, Simpson, Traeger and the others in his AIM Family. He had complete confidence they would do a good job in his absence.

It was in a happy frame of mind that he made final arrangements for his holiday. Friends gave him a further monetary gift the night before he was due to sail, leaving it late so that he would have no opportunity to buy further wireless equipment with the funds.

Flynn nearly didn't make it to the ship in time, being engrossed in fixing some items he had not had the time to repair earlier. His friends virtually manhandled him into the waiting car and then onto the boat. Just before sailing, he yelled out his final thoughts about things that still needed to be done. As the ship slipped away, he tossed the group on the quay a vital set of keys he found in his pocket – it only just missed falling into the water! Then he waved cheerfully at those who had gathered to wish him farewell. "A happier smile was not seen amongst the other 800 passengers," Jean Baird observed with satisfaction.

At 47, John Flynn had lost none of the childlike enjoyment of life that had always been one of his most endearing characteristics. This was going to be the holiday of a lifetime, packed with happy memories – he would make sure of that.

17

Networks

Ever since childhood, John Flynn had wanted to visit the Middle East, the lands of the Bible where Abraham, Moses and Jesus Christ had walked and lived. Now this dream came true. He captured the variety and moods of what he saw in a series of sensitive photographs.

He then went on to London, where a great surprise awaited him: he had been appointed as an Australian delegate to the First International Congress on Aerial Medical Service, to be held shortly in France. Flynn was fascinated. He had not expected sufficient interest elsewhere in the world to have warranted such a conference.

More surprises were to follow: a large number of countries had sent delegates and the flying-doctor experiment was widely known among them. People clamoured for information. Flynn was bemused to find he had somehow gained an international reputation greater than that he enjoyed among Australians.

The conference gave Flynn news of the international scene: that the air forces of Sweden, Poland and Siam (Thailand) flew doctors to emergencies, using military planes as air ambulances. This reminded him of his own unsuccessful attempts to involve the military 11 years previously.

By popular request, Flynn gave out some statistics on the Australian Flying Doctor Service: "You can fit the whole of Europe inside the Australian Inland, and still have miles to spare," he told delegates, "so you can readily appreciate why we need doctors who use aeroplanes." His listeners were surprised to hear this; they had not realised that the Australian Outback was so huge. Flynn smiled a little ruefully. "Nor have most Australians," he said.

He also quoted the impressive statistics for Dr Welch's year of service: "Fifty emergency flights, saving at the very least four lives and treating 255 patients. He held 42 consultations with colleagues and visited 26 settlements which would otherwise have had no visit from a doctor that year. His aeroplane, the *Victory*, is made of linen cloth stretched over a wooden frame and looks flimsy, yet he flew 1 500 miles without mishap. On only one occasion did bad weather prevent him from flying to an emergency. All in all, gentlemen, an unqualified success."

After the conference, John Flynn made his way to Ireland and investigated his ancestry. His maternal grandparents had emigrated to Australia in the 1850s, while his father's side also had strong links with Ireland. Flynn spent happy hours with his mother's relatives, the Ewarts, in Belfast. He sought out old letters and other memorabilia that helped him to picture better that mother whom he had never known, but whose photograph he still carried everywhere with him.

Next he visited Germany and Switzerland, where Flynn savoured the magnificent mountain scenery, finding it restorative and inspirational. "Do not quarrel with the much abused 'dull days', they are the most restful invention I have ever come across," he wrote.

Then came his trip to America, whose scientific advances fascinated him. Typically, Flynn collected in that country hundreds of cuttings and booklets on a plethora of subjects that might have application to the Inland: dam-building, animal husbandry, reclamation of desert areas, aeroplane design, and much else.

Throughout his holiday, Flynn was kept up to date with the progress of the AIM by mail. The great challenge facing it was the need to get a wireless network operating. He followed developments with prayers of hope.

Alf Traeger, meanwhile, had told the AIM Board early in 1929 that he was ready to establish the "mother" station at Cloncurry, together with a sprinkling of "daughter" stations spread through outlying areas. These "daughter" stations would comprise pedal-powered units costing under £50 each. As each had both a "transmitter" and a "receiver", they were referred to among AIM staff as "transceivers". The term became widely used in the press after Traeger placed both transmitters and receivers inside the same rectangular box.

A control switch separated the transmitter on the one side and the receiver on the other. Later Traeger added a wireless receiver with which coastal radio stations could be listened to as a third position on the dial, a masterstroke in his campaign to popularise the technology. The final result was far in advance of anything similar in the world. (The Royal Air Force had been labouring in this field for years and had at last produced a portable set. But it was far more expensive, bulky and complex than Traeger's, required trained operators, and had a range of only 30 miles. Traeger's radio had a range of at least 300 miles – anything less would have been useless in the Australian bush.)

The Board was impressed with Traeger's progress and approved his plans. He would need someone to help, to take Flynn's place as an assistant. The job went to Harry Kinzbrunner, a young acquaintance of Traeger's. Kinzbrunner would remain in Cloncurry to operate the base station while Traeger travelled and established the outlying "daughter" stations. If the pair managed to establish a working network, Kinzbrunner would become the base operator in Cloncurry and Traeger would return home.

The Cloncurry station, call sign VJ1, was constructed in the vestry of the local church. At the official opening on 6 June 1929, a crowd of some 300 curious locals gathered. Traeger was too nervous to make a speech. Instead, he demonstrated the capability of the station by contacting Harry Kauper in Adelaide with voice transmission. Kauper's reply came loud and clear and the crowd clapped. Then Traeger relayed music from the new commercial radio stations situated in the coastal cities, a wise strategy. The bushmen's interest rose markedly.

Leaving Kinzbrunner to stand by in Cloncurry, Traeger travelled with patrol padre George Scott to Augustus Downs, 180 miles to the north, to install the first of the "daughter" stations. Flynn's dream of a radio network was about to undergo its acid test.

The initial challenge was to install a 60-foot-high aerial. This great height should, Traeger hoped, make reception and transmission more reliable in the bush. Next, he set up the transceiver indoors and bolted the pedal generator to the floor.

Traeger then asked Mrs Gertrude Rothery, the manager's wife, to test the generator by pedalling while he measured power output with his instruments. This was a clever ploy as Mrs Rothery was surprised and pleased at how easily she managed to generate sufficient power.

Traeger knew that the manager's wife was the person most likely to use the wireless consistently, so he taught her the rudiments of Morse code. The big moment for testing arrived on 19 June 1929. Traeger asked Mrs Rothery to send the first message to Cloncurry: "Hello, Harry" (Harry Kinzbrunner was receiving).

The operator looked nervously at the Morse key. "Go on, try it out," Traeger encouraged her. So she did. Kinzbrunner's voice boomed out of their speakers in reply, startling them and making them jump. They looked at each other, then grinned. The flying doctor network had begun. (Later, Harry Kinzbrunner told them he had received "Hell. O. Hell. O. Harry," but then he always was a bit of a wag!)

Two days later, Augustus Downs sent its first telegram. It was hammered out in Morse by Mrs Rothery to Kinzbrunner, who then fed it into the official telegraph system en route to the AIM office in Sydney. The first message read:

> Greetings by wireless service from Augustus Downs, first station installed. Manager, family and station deeply appreciate services rendered ...

It was immediately sent overseas to Flynn by Jean Baird. Flynn was deeply moved by it and he wrote a letter of congratulations to Traeger within minutes. No one else appreciated as fully as he did what Traeger had achieved.

Mrs Rothery reported later that the pedal wireless was the "biggest thing" that ever happened to her and her family in the bush. It allowed them to communicate with the outside world and to call up the flying doctor.

One "daughter" set was a long way from providing an efficient radio network, though Traeger at once set about installing others. Each installation required travel time, plus from ten days to a fortnight to familiarise the Outbackers with the equipment. They would appear keen until he began to teach them Morse code, at which point most men would remember an urgent need at some distant part of the run and would disappear. A number always stayed, however. They found Traeger a patient and gentle teacher who would only move on once they were confident and competent.

Birdsville's extreme isolation can be assessed from its having neither telephone nor telegraph, nor was there any for 250 miles around. It had once applied for a telephone system, but had been told it would cost £70 000, an impossibly large sum – and now the AIM was intending to give them wireless for nothing. The sisters at Birdsville practised Morse every day for a month before Traeger came, longing for the day they could seek help from Dr James Spalding, the flying doctor at Cloncurry who had replaced Dr Welch.

Within a month of the wireless being installed at Birdsville, 40 telegrams had been sent by residents, through Kinzbrunner at Cloncurry, to the outside world. This shows the joy with which the region welcomed their release from silence. Some messages were personal, but many were commercial, as in ordering equipment or arranging business deals. Flynn's prediction that wireless would help to open up the Inland was already coming true.

Not long after, the new equipment was needed to save a life. Sister Gilbert became seriously ill in Birdsville. Sister Pearson immediately resorted to the radio, to raise the flying doctor. The radio would not work! She desperately approached townsfolk to help her repair it, but no one knew how to. There was nothing else for it – they would have to drive Sister Gilbert through the desert for 250 miles to reach Boulia, where there was a telegraph.

Traeger rushed to repair the set at Birdsville. Then the sad news arrived from Cloncurry – Sister Gilbert had died. He was shocked. Flynn's dictum returned to him with great force: In the Outback, it is either an aeroplane or a coffin.

A young friend named Jesse Shackleton had travelled down to Birdsville with Traeger to help him. The heat was oppressive, so the two went for a swim in the Diamantina River to cool off. Shackleton got into difficulties and drowned.

This double tragedy proved too much for young Sister Gwen Pearson. She broke down in Traeger's arms and wept. Just as overwhelming, she would have to carry on alone in this forbidding land until another nurse could be found to help her. Traeger was moved to tears also, both for her situation and for Jesse Shackleton.

These two deaths underlined to Traeger the danger of life in the Outback, and how important it was for his radio to operate efficiently. He was discovering all sorts of unexpected difficulties in the situation: termites ate his wooden radio cases, dust somehow got into radios and stopped them operating, aerial guys became loosened when flown into by large bats called flying foxes and inquisitive probing by children and adults caused malfunctions.

Traeger left Birdsville determined that no set of his would ever fail again when a life was at stake. Once back in Adelaide, he would put the sets inside metal cases, not wooden ones, and ensure they were dustproof and, as far as possible, secure from human mishandling. He would drop the sets several times from shoulder height in case they fell off horses or cars, to check they still functioned. Everything that could be done would be done.

—

George Scott and Alf Traeger bobbed and rolled on the *Morning Star*. They were going to Mornington Island, to fulfil Flynn's promise to the missionaries there. On arrival, they received a rapturous welcome from the mission families and excited Aborigines alike. That night, Traeger's attention was caught by strange markings on the wooden walls of the mission station. "Those are spear marks," he was told. "Eleven years ago women and children huddled together in this very room, terrified for their lives." The next day, Traeger had the satisfaction of releasing Mornington Island from its bondage to silence.

While returning on the lugger, Scott typed out a summary for *The Inlander* of the results of their wireless work. He included a vivid description of Traeger testing whether he could communicate satisfactorily with Cloncurry from the ship:

> By September, 1929, eight sets had been distributed at various strategic points ... The simplicity and adaptability of these sets will be appreciated when it is realised that one of the sets can be set up and operated in a few minutes, and that in the most unlikely of situations. For example, at the moment of writing, the set is standing upon a small table in the cabin, a short aerial is stretched from the masthead through a porthole to the set, the counterpoise is strung around the cabin bulkhead, and yet, with this primitive preparation, Mr Traeger is in constant touch with the central station at Cloncurry.

George Scott preached to his awestruck congregation back in Cloncurry while travelling with Traeger. Later, other patrol padres followed suit.

By the time of Traeger's return to Adelaide, Dr Spalding was regularly "on air" giving consultations. A "digger" with lots of war experience, he was outstanding at getting people to talk about their troubles. The skills he developed in radio diagnosis and treatment often saved the need for expensive flights. Radio also reduced his periods of inactivity and boredom.

Besides the telegrams, the "daughter" stations had already transmitted 60 000 words of general conversation by 30 November that year. It was still only five months since the first "baby" set had been installed at Augustus Downs.

No longer was Flynn's bush dumb, nor were pioneers isolated from help. No longer did homesteads suffer from lack of companionship. Flynn's great battle against loneliness, which started with the Mail-bag League in 1908, was close to being won.

The years of "chat radio", leading ultimately to "talk-back radio", were about to begin. A kind of "togetherness" grew in the backblocks.

—

Search and rescue procedures in the Outback were about to be revolutionised. In a well-known example around that time urgent messages from the "baby" set at Hermannsburg helped save the lives of three members of Harry Lasseter's final expedition searching for a fabled gold reef. Lasseter himself, unfortunately, perished.

There was an amusing side-benefit to the radio revolution: it reduced rustling and cross-branding of cattle, practices so common as to be almost respectable. Men on stations reporting in at the 6 a.m. "rooster session" would describe on air their intended work and movements. If they did not report in, or were seen at the wrong place, this caused good-humoured exchanges and sometimes real suspicions. Stealing one another's cattle wasn't so easy any more!

The new pedal set led to no small interest among the Aborigines, although some did not immediately grasp its purpose. One man observed, "That fella bike no good. Missus ride him all day, come up nowhere."

In February 1930 Flynn returned to Australia, much invigorated by his holiday and bursting with enthusiasm. His immediate desire was to see Traeger's network in action. However, there was an accumulation of business awaiting his return that had to be given priority. This included delicate negotiations with the Postmaster General's Department to regularise their radio network. George Simpson, who had begun the negotiations, reported his frustrations: "The PGD seems to regard the pedal set in the nature of a toy. To them, 'official efficiency' can only exist in a set costing much money and making a great deal of noise. The fact that ours is miles better than theirs seems to make no difference."

Flynn's negotiations proved very worthwhile, though tedious. The final agreement was more than the AIM might have reasonably expected – money received from telegrams sent through the wireless network would be shared equally between the Post Office and the AIM. This unexpected revenue enabled Flynn to continue selling the sets for the cost of their components: installation costs, servicing by AIM staff, Traeger's own salary, travel and other expenses were not included in the pricing of the transceivers, since otherwise the pioneers could not have afforded them.

Traeger reported to Flynn by letter:

> As a rule, the folk are puzzled as they always seem to think of a wireless transmitting station as costing hundreds of pounds. In several instances they have remarked that it seems too good to be true.

The radio man, who looked like a simple country boy, spoke of the joy he felt when giving the pioneers their "big surprise".

Flynn, champing at the bit now, hoped to travel to the Inland in May, but a financial crisis arose that prevented him: the government were cutting expenses and Flynn was required for "shuttle diplomacy" to and from different government ministers and departments. Australia, and the AIM, were threatened by a worldwide economic failure, the Great Depression.

Though he was chained to organisational duties, John Flynn's restless vision drove him on. A new enterprise was a comprehensive map showing every pioneer's dwelling, a map so detailed both the flying doctor and his patrol padres could work from it. A helper wrote a charming pen picture of Flynn at work on that map in the jungle that was his office, trying to assemble a mountain of data into a single document.

> It has been a tremendous job, keeping him going practically every night and every holiday without exception, as well as the weekends. He now says the idea is worthwhile, and that, if it is all gone over again carefully, and all the information checked once more, the chart should be quite a good one! Of course, he will be using it as it stands, unless the fairies provide us with sufficient time to make it all over again ...

It was November, nine months after his return, before Flynn escaped from Sydney and visited the Inland. In Cloncurry, he spent some hours with the AIM's new radio operator, Maurie Anderson. Anderson had been a ship's radio officer and was a radio buff whose expertise enabled him to maintain the local "daughter" stations, a great help to Traeger. He had the ideal personality for the job: infinite patience, a cheerful manner, enthusiasm for radio and a compassionate heart. He quickly won the affection of the Out-backers and became a local identity.

"The bush may be backward in some ways," Maurie Anderson told Flynn, "but not as regards world news. In that department, we are often a day ahead of the cities."

"How is that?"

"I'm a radio 'ham' and I make notes of world news each night, plus things other 'hams' tell me from around the world, then I relay this over our early morning program."

Flynn's thoughts flashed back to the excitement of his Birdsville nurses when he presented them with a pile of old newspapers. These were their first papers for six months and they were starved for news. Now, thanks to Maurie Anderson, they would be among the first in Australia to hear the latest.

"We are ahead in another way, too."

"Oh? How?"

"A person in Sydney or Melbourne who wants to send a tele-gram has to make their way into town, fill in a form and pay for it there and then. Here, they can sit at home and pedal through a telegram whenever they want. They can pay later, too."

Flynn smiled. Maurie Anderson had just the kind of enthusiasm he liked. His respect for the man deepened as he watched him in action. Often the messages received were indistinct and badly spelt, so much so that a dozen repeats were sometimes needed before the sender was satisfied.

A further thrill for John Flynn was flying in the *Victory*, with Arthur Affleck and Dr Bill Cornford, who was filling in as flying doctor until a more permanent appointment was made.

Dr Cornford was a strange man. Very short and slight, he appeared to have a chip on his shoulder and was altogether a prickly customer. He always carried an automatic pistol in his hip pocket, where it was easily visible. As a doctor and a person committed to saving lives, he never explained why he carried such a lethal weapon.

Affleck noted with concern that the tiny doctor seemed to take an intense dislike to the tall, gangling Flynn. This response was peculiar as Flynn was universally liked, even by most of his critics.

On a day that was so hot you could smell the rubber of the aeroplane tyres before take-off, Affleck flew Dr Cornford and Flynn to visit nearby Kynuna. Twenty minutes up, Affleck felt drowsy from the heat. Once, some months previously, under similar conditions, he had dozed off for a few seconds until a deep voice had boomed through the intercom asking why the plane was "dancing about". This time, though, there was no chance of his snoozing because a loud explosion rang out. It sounded like a pistol shot!

Affleck was instantly fully awake, alert, heart pounding. "Oh no!" he thought. "Cornford has shot John Flynn!" He felt the skin crawl at the back of his neck. If the man had gone mad, he could even now be planning to use his pistol again.

Affleck strained his ears, but could hear nothing unusual. He eased open the small round door between him and the passenger section just a fraction and put his nose to the crack – no smell of cordite. Now what? He eased the door open a bit further and very slowly peered through it, careful to make no sudden movement in case he "spooked" the mad doctor.

There was a movement in the cabin. Both occupants turned to peer at him and raised their eyebrows. He shook his head, then closed the tiny door once more. Settling back in his seat, Affleck chewed his lower lip and thought deeply. Both men were very much alive, thankfully. It could not have been a pistol shot he had heard.

The situation was very confusing. The motor was purring away, so nothing had happened to the engine. What, then, had caused the loud report? The only thing he could think of was a tyre exploding. This did not seem likely because tyres exploded with the heat of friction when landing or taking off; he'd never heard of one going "bang" in the air. "First time for everything," he decided, when no alternative explanation presented itself. Perhaps the exceptionally hot day was to blame?

The pilot looked down at the rough, sunbaked land below them with its few stunted trees. They would have to crash-land. With only one wheel, their chances of survival were small: the "dead" wheel would "catch" and throw them violently sideways, causing the aeroplane to tip over or cartwheel. Their one slight chance was to land at a proper airport with an exceptionally smooth runway. Perhaps he could balance the plane at touchdown on one wheel long enough for it to slow down before "catching".

Affleck spent long minutes pondering which of his two ears had heard the noise the louder, to ascertain which of the two wheels had exploded. He could not decide. Finally, he tossed a coin. His favourite candidate was the starboard wheel, but the coin showed the port side. The pilot sat and pondered this result for a few moments. It did not feel right, so he decided to toss twice more. Both tosses came down in favour of the starboard. He stopped tossing when he had the answer he favoured.

Affleck decided to put down at McKinlay rather than Kynuna: the strip was bigger, perhaps smoother and would more likely have a wind blowing across his line of approach. Such a cross-wind would help to buoy the plane up on the one remaining wheel.

A communicating tube ran from the outside cockpit to the cabin. One old bushman had thought it was a urinal and had caused some havoc. The pilot had to shout down this not very efficient device to warn Flynn and Cornford to prepare for a crashlanding. "If Flynn dies in a crashlanding, will the flying-doctor experiment die too?" Affleck wondered.

He circled McKinlay, cutting speed as much as he could before starting his approach to land. Even then, the ground seemed to accelerate up at them. He tilted the aeroplane slightly so that the portside wheel would touch the ground first – providing, of course, that it was there at all!

There was a slight jerk as the wheel made contact with the ground. His guess had been correct. He coasted in on the one wheel as far as possible, every yard helping to slow their speed.

Finally, gravity had its way and the aircraft dropped onto where the second wheel should have been, but wasn't. It gripped at that point and swung sharply to the right on the good wheel, then jerked to a bone-shattering halt. They had survived, a bit shaken but none the worse for wear.

Flynn commended Affleck for his remarkable skill in landing them safely, then spoke as a propagandist: "I would prefer it, gentlemen, if this story did not get into the newspapers."

On return to Sydney, Flynn pondered an emerging threat to the flying doctor. Everyone could see the benefits of the scheme, but the world was already in a bad recession and donations were dwindling. Philanthropic enterprises suffered first in tough times.

Of one thing Flynn was certain, an exceptional successor to Dr Cornford was vitally important, a man who would do such an outstanding job that no one would want to close the service down, a man who himself might help in fundraising. Flynn had a number of applications on file, but none appeared to fit the bill.

"The Flying Doctor Service might 'crash' unless we get the right man," he told friends. "Our next appointment is going to be crucial."

18

ALLAN VICKERS

John Flynn was pondering the need for an outstanding successor to Dr Cornford when a visitor called to see him. He rose to greet a sandy-haired young man of medium build, with an alert face and a sparkle in his blue eyes.

"Dr Allan Vickers! It's been several years since I last saw you. How have you been keeping?" Flynn's memory for names and faces was remarkable.

Vickers' mind went back to their meeting four years previously when he had been one of the applicants for the inaugural flying-doctor position – at that time he had recorded:

> Flynn bade me welcome in a matter-of-fact voice with a slight drawl, backed up by a cheerful smile. But most of all, I was conscious of a close scrutiny by a pair of clear grey eyes, which I felt were busy taking stock of me and I hoped that his first impressions were as favourable as mine. He talked of the future. He certainly did not seem to be one to rest on his laurels and past accomplishments were of comparatively small interest ... But he was full of the great need of those who live in the Inland ... I felt that I had met a most inspiring personality; a man whose dreams might well come true in spite of the obvious difficulties; a man with whom it would be a pleasure and an honour to be associated.

The inaugural position had, however, been given to Dr Welch. Allan Vickers had gone into private practice in Queanbeyan instead.

It was now January 1931, and Dr Vickers had recently accepted a scholarship to specialise in surgery in England. With a few days to kill before sailing to Japan on holiday then on to England, he decided to see how the flying-doctor experiment was progressing. He had heard little about it in the interim.

Flynn was only too happy to tell him, in the course of which he spread out a map on his desk. "Come and look more closely at what we are doing at Cloncurry," he invited. Within a short time, Vickers found himself offered the flying-doctor position there.

"No, sorry, Mr Flynn. My plans are all made. To study surgery in London has been a goal of mine for years now."

"Yes. That's good. Quite good. Let me show you now how we plan to extend the Cloncurry service until the mantle of safety covers the whole of the Inland." Flynn took up a pair of dividers. "I have set these to scale for a radius of 300 miles, the distance each flying doctor base can service comfortably, though Welch went much further afield on occasion. How many bases do you suppose we would need to cover the Outback?"

Vickers did not respond, but watched, fascinated, as Flynn measured his circles out over the map.

"There you are. Under ideal conditions, only six to eight bases will be needed. That is not too great a dream, is it? Imagine – just six bases would bring freedom from fear to every brave pioneering family!" Flynn looking up, fixing his gaze on Vickers' blue eyes. "However, we have only one base at the moment, not six, and that is in danger of sinking. It has been subsidised by £1 000 out of AIM general funds already. Unless something can be done, we may be forced to suspend operations. If that were to happen, I believe it might never start up again. We need the right flying doctor to guide it through this crisis.

"I know the flying-doctor concept is a good one and I've got a strong faith in these matters. There's a special Providence that looks after good causes. Providing your cause is thoroughly good and you are working like the devil, not simply waiting for something to turn up, you'll get your breaks when things look at their blackest. Don't ask me why God works like that at the last minute, but He does. It has happened a number of times before and it will happen again."

This was Vickers' first exposure to a naked faith prepared to fly in the face of logic, and it made a deep impression on him. He wrote later:

> There was no doubting the simple faith of the man and the conviction with which he spoke. "Dreamer" and "visionary"

he had been called, possibly with some justification, but I now had my first glimpse of the faith and tenacity of purpose with which he backed his visions and which in the past had enabled him to transform them into reality.

Would Flynn's faith formula work now that the whole world was in the grip of the Great Depression? Vickers was unsure. What did strike him was the fortunate timing for the flying-doctor experiment in the first place: had it been attempted even a year later, the concept would have been rejected because of the tightening financial situation. Perhaps there really was a "Providence" looking after the scheme? Though not particularly religious, Vickers found himself wondering.

Flynn held out another carrot to the young man. "You mentioned at our last meeting that you had a personal interest in wireless. Well, I have just had an exciting thought. How would you like to experiment sending radio messages from the *Victory* to Maurie Anderson on the ground? It's never been done before as traditional wireless sets are too large to take up in aeroplanes. Ours could be right, though. Think of the possibilities that could open up – minute-by-minute reports on the patient you were flying to attend, perhaps even mid-air consultations about other patients."

By the time he and Flynn parted company that evening, Allan Vickers had decided to cancel his holiday in Japan

> and go up to Cloncurry, at any rate, for a few months – but I kept my booking on the ship to England just in case! In addition to medical duties, I was asked to look into the matter of how much money we could raise in the Cloncurry area while Mr Flynn would strain every financial nerve in the south. We would keep our fingers crossed for the future of the service.

Flynn was delighted, sensing Vickers was the man for the hour. He rushed the young doctor around to see Dr Spalding "who, having served for a year as a flying doctor, proved to be a mine of practical information".

A few days later, when Flynn was saying farewell, he commented, "You will have good company in Cloncurry. Mr Whitman, the chemist, has two very nice daughters." Vickers grinned, and thought he would see for himself.

Vickers was collected at his hotel in Brisbane

> by a well-dressed young man and rather wondered at the superior calibre of the car drivers employed by QANTAS. He remarked that my suitcase was somewhat big and heavy for an air traveller, but I dismissed his comments rather airily. When we arrived at Archerfield [which was then the main Brisbane aerodrome] someone said "Good morning, Mr Fysh", and I realised that my driver was none other than the already famous Hudson Fysh, Managing Director of QANTAS! My face was a bit red!

Vickers' mettle was immediately put to the test as he and Arthur Affleck tried to fly out from Archerfield. Their first flight was aborted when thick cloud prevented their landing at Toowoomba, so they returned to Archerfield and sat around on petrol cases until trying again that afternoon. This time storms forced them back.

The team tried again next morning, and their tail skid struck a tree-root which had not been properly grubbed out, Archerfield being a new aerodrome. Despite this minor accident, they made it into the air safely, only to find that the elevator controls were jammed. The machine went on climbing, up and up. Eventually it would stall. Frantically, the men moved everything in the cabin as far forward as they could, including themselves. To their intense relief this ploy got the nose down sufficiently for them to return to Archerfield. It is a mark of Vickers' commitment that he was not fazed by these trials. At the fourth attempt the aircraft got away successfully.

It was a surprise to the newcomer that Affleck flew seated behind his passengers, in an open cockpit exposed to the elements. "It must be tough on you when it rains, or in the bright sun, while we all sit in comfort in the cabin," he commiserated.

"Suits me, Doc," came the cheerful reply. "If we ever hit anything, that old engine has got to come back through you before it gets to me. I'll probably walk away from it, but you?" He left this open-ended question for Vickers to ponder.

Immediately on arrival in Cloncurry, Vickers visited the government hospital.

The hospital stood by itself, more than a mile from the town. As I was later to find, this was common practice in Western Queensland towns, and was intended to isolate cases of infectious disease, especially typhoid fever, epidemics of which occurred every few years. Only two years before there had been a severe epidemic in Cloncurry and there were many deaths, both white and Aboriginal. On entering the hospital, I came face to face with three Memorial Tablets, all in memory of doctors who had died there in the not very distant past. I sincerely hoped that I would not be the inspiration for a fourth tablet.

The following afternoon, Vickers received his first emergency call. He was soon extraordinarily busy. Could lack of funds really close down the Flying Doctor Service? That would be a tragedy! He encouraged the local committee to intensify fundraising and also secured a few local donations himself.

Vickers had a novel idea while attending patients at Kynuna Hospital, 120 miles from Cloncurry. The hospital was in the care of the efficient Matron Pass, but was too small to attract a full-time doctor. Might not the government employ him as the Resident Medical Officer of Kynuna? He could fly in to service its needs on a regular basis.

He wrote to Flynn that same night with his idea. There was something else on his mind, too: the time had come for him to decide whether to go to England, as planned, or to continue in Cloncurry. Flynn's most recent letter told him there had been no significant increase in donations to the service, and that the Board would be unlikely to send another doctor to Cloncurry after he left. This information put the young doctor in a dilemma: he was convinced that a flying doctor was vital and had become attached to his bush patients, "who were putting up such a good show in the face of all their difficulties". On the other hand, he did not want to miss the opportunity to specialise in surgery.

Vickers paused in his writing. He paced about the hotel room for a while, then settled back to his letter. He said he hoped his idea of supervising hospitals like the one at Kynuna might improve the AIM's financial position. In any case, he would stay on for a full year, if the Flying Doctor Service should survive that long.

Before he could change his mind, he wrote a second letter, this one to the shipping agent, cancelling his trip to England. The die for his future was cast.

Flynn contacted George Simpson on receiving Vickers' letter, to tell him the good news. "Now we must do our utmost to keep him aloft."

"It is the flying costs that are crippling us," Simpson pointed out.

"I know. I have been talking to Fergus McMaster and Hudson Fysh about that. We might arrange for the *Victory* to fly mail for QANTAS twice a week from Cloncurry to Normanton. It's a wretched decision to make in case an emergency arises while the aeroplane is out, but QANTAS are in trouble like most other companies and can't simply cut costs without getting something in return. You and I will then need to pray that no serious emergency arises while the *Victory* is otherwise engaged."

The lack of an aeroplane for a day-and-a-half each week was a worry for Vickers, too:

> It was constantly on my mind that an urgent call would find me without a plane, but it was remarkable how we got away with it. Several times we delayed His Majesty's Mail to fit in a medical call. At other times, people had to hold the fort with medical advice by radio until the plane got back to Cloncurry and we could go out to see them. Fortunately, the tragedy that I feared didn't eventuate.

On 8 July 1931, George Simpson came to see Allan Vickers. The two doctors had met before and had a liking for each other. After initial greetings, Simpson got straight to the point. "I bring bad news from the AIM Board. We have to scale the AMS down and perhaps suspend operations. In these depressed times, it's proving too expensive."

Vickers replied in a rush, in an agitated, staccato voice. "They can't do that. They need to come out here and see for themselves what this service is achieving. To stop now would be to return to ... to ... to the silence and fear and tragedy that was here before we came. What does Mr Flynn think about this?"

Simpson hesitated slightly before replying. He decided to brief Vickers fully. "Officially, Mr Flynn will support what the AIM Board decides; it's a question of loyalty. I don't mind you knowing that he spoke strongly against the motion during the debate about it. Surprisingly, though, he is not panicking. He believes that if we continue to play our part, the service will survive somehow. Nevertheless, he felt he owed it to you for you to be told the official position as soon as possible, in case you might want to reverse your decision and still go to England."

"That's thoughtful." There was a brief silence while the young doctor pondered the situation. Then he shook his head and said emphatically, "We cannot walk out now, it would be abandoning those we are committed to serve."

"That is exactly what Mr Flynn said during the debate," Dr Simpson remarked.

"Well, he's right. The next tragedy that happened, the locals would wonder why the AMS had deserted them. The AIM would lose credibility throughout the Inland, and would deserve to. We must hang on, as long as possible."

There was another brief silence while Simpson thought deeply. Vickers' vehement determination to carry on had caught him by surprise. It sparked fresh hope in him. He said, "The Board will take some convincing. What might you suggest?"

"Take them letters from local people. Many have told me what a boon the AMS is — get them to put it down on paper. That should convince the Board."

"I'll do that. It won't solve our main problem, though. How can we continue to operate at a loss?"

"I have some ideas about that and so has Maurie Anderson. We need to pool them and come up with some survival strategies."

Simpson, Vickers and Anderson settled down for a series of lengthy discussions. Slowly, a plan evolved. Vickers and Anderson felt that many people outside Cloncurry might not have donated to the flying doctor because they had never been asked to. Vickers would send out a circular letter explaining the emergency and inviting them to contribute. He could also try to set up local committees in small centres like McKinlay, Normanton, Urandangie and Burketown with the purpose of organising functions to raise donations.

Finally, as a gesture to the Board of their faith in the service, Vickers and Maurie Anderson offered to take a reduction of ten per cent in their salaries.

Simpson gathered a number of letters of support for the Flying Doctor Service, spending a month away from his practice to do so. Flynn discussed these with him before Simpson prepared his report for the Board. "This letter from Police Trooper Hall will impress the Board most of all," Flynn said. "The police are generally respected and considered reliable witnesses. Trooper Hall is three hundred miles from the nearest hospital, lacking medical expertise, but doing his best to help the sick and injured that are brought to him. He ends by saying he has a vivid recollection of 'several instances being very hard pressed for assistance – assistance forthcoming in every case only from the flying doctor, and in each case, only just in time to avoid loss of life'. We can't want a better recommendation that, can we?"

"No, and it will prove to the Board that lives will be lost if we stop operating. I shall compose a very strong case for continuation," Simpson replied.

He was as good as his word. His report said, in part:

> The Aerial Medical Service has fulfilled from its inception all that the promoters originally expected of it ... A "Mantle of Safety" has been spread by the wings of the "Victory" and home life is being made possible where never before. It would be a tragedy if the AMS had to be withdrawn now.

Tragedy or not, the Great Depression was merciless. Even the buoyant Flynn became worried, writing to Traeger on 19 June 1931, "It will hardly be necessary to tell you that these times are causing us much anxiety ..."

In July 1931, while awaiting the Board's decision as to the future of the AMS, Vickers received a call for help from the mission station on Mornington Island in the Gulf of Carpentaria. This was the place where Traeger had noticed spear marks on the wall while setting up the pedal set 20 months earlier. The missionaries were battling an epidemic which had already taken the lives of several Aborigines on the island.

Vickers did not want to fly to Mornington Island unless it was absolutely necessary, so he conducted a series of radio consultations instead. However, certain symptoms and complications were unusual and he feared further loss of life, especially as the missionaries had run short of drugs. He decided he would have to go.

This raised a series of problems. Firstly, no aeroplane had been there before – the coastal strip north of Burketown was uninviting mangrove country, while the trip across the water was an unknown hazard. A forced landing anywhere would be disastrous.

Vickers telegraphed QANTAS for approval. They refused, quoting Hudson Fysh's policy that:

> The first essential for the AMS during the experimental period is to prove the service is safe and reliable. Without that, it will collapse. It is by far our most risky operation, using a single-engined aircraft which has already had to make periodic forced landings owing to engine trouble.

Vickers remonstrated, saying the risk needed to be taken because so many lives were at stake.

After a short delay, QANTAS requested £1 000 guarantee as they feared for the safety of their aeroplane. Vickers knew the AIM did not have £1 000 for such a mission – the fuel alone would strain their resources!

All this time, lives hung in the balance. Vickers was receiving further disturbing reports from Mornington Island. He had to do something, fast. He paced around, thinking. Only Hudson Fysh could change his own policy, so he decided to telephone him.

Fysh was very sympathetic, saying he would seek permission for the flight and that he would speak with George Simpson. That same evening, he telephoned back and said QANTAS had dropped the requirement for a guarantee and that the Civil Aviation Authorities had given clearance for the flight.

Next, Vickers telephoned Flynn. The journey was going to be very long and expensive. "You must go," Flynn told him. "Go, even if you use all the money we have left. Go, they need you. I'll make sure the money is available." This was another occasion when Flynn quietly added a significant part of his salary to the fund.

Vickers records:

> Arthur Affleck and I took off next morning. We had a tail wind and made good time to Burketown, where we refuelled. Then we flew west along the coast, looking for Bayley Point, from whence we would head out to sea. The wind was very gusty

and increasing in strength and the dust clouds were beginning to swirl and rise from the dry claypans some four thousand feet below us. As a consequence, the flying was bumpy and the visibility poor.

Dust was always a danger as it could choke the single engine. It was intensified by the south-east monsoon until it formed blinding clouds. The tiny aircraft was tossed about like an insect in a storm.

We hadn't much idea what Bayley Point looked like and it was not easy to be sure of it. We had expected to see Mornington Island from the Point, but all we could see was dust.

Turning north, we struck out over the sea. The air was now thick with dust and the chain of small islands which was to be the guide to our destination loomed but faintly through the haze as we passed them. They are all low-lying and flat, little more than mud banks. All that we saw from time to time was the encircling ring of white-crested rollers, driven by the wind.

When a dark shape appeared, Affleck called out in relief, "I think that's it!" He buzzed around the island until they located the mission station below, then set out for the adjacent Denham Island, on which the missionary had told them there was a large claypan. They found it easily, as it had been marked out by a giant cross laid out in white seashells. After a successful landing, they drove their pegs in deep to secure the plane against the high winds and roped it securely.

The channel between the two islands was sheltered from the full force of the winds. Nevertheless, the sea was very choppy with the high wind whipping up whitecaps. The crossing in a dinghy was rough and the two men were drenched with spray by the time they arrived at Mornington Island. Reverend Wilson quickly steered them through a welcoming crowd and took them to the mission house, where Mrs Wilson had a hot meal waiting.

"I am so glad you have come," Mrs Wilson greeted them. "Besides the sick adults, we have 18 critically ill children. Perhaps you could see them immediately after lunch?"

During the meal, a group of about 50 Aboriginal children assembled at the back steps and asked to see the visitors. When Vickers and Affleck appeared at the door, the children burst into songs of welcome, harmonising perfectly. Vickers was charmed by the happy enthusiasm of the youngsters.

From then until late that night, the doctor was extremely busy: examining, diagnosing, prescribing and advising the missionaries on the care of the sick. He began again at daybreak next morning, working until satisfied that the epidemic would be brought under control.

The return flight was into the teeth of the wind. Occasionally the plane dropped around a hundred feet in the turbulence before coming to a bone-jarring halt. The men were buffeted about, jerked this way and that, and thoroughly exhausted by the time they reached base.

Wireless contact with Mr Wilson allowed Vickers to monitor progress. Very sick Aborigines kept coming in droves for help and the drugs ran low again. A number of these bush Aborigines had new symptoms and the missionaries requested a second mercy flight. Flynn and Vickers were willing, of course, but QANTAS was again hesitant.

Vickers remembered something he and John Flynn had discussed at his interview for the job: the possibility of carrying a radio on board the aeroplane. This would allow their position to be known during flight over uncharted mangrove swamps, something that would reassure QANTAS. Alf Traeger happened to be at Cloncurry on a servicing visit, so he set about building a small transceiver from components he had with him. It used dry cells and was very compact, though its signal would be weak.

Traeger doped an aerial into the leading edge of the upper wing and he and Maurie Anderson ran a series of successful tests on the ground.

QANTAS cleared the second flight. It was decided that Maurie Anderson would fly while Traeger operated the base radio set. Unfortunately Anderson became airsick, but struggled on gamely, sending and receiving in Morse. It worked!

This was the first occasion, 8 August 1931, that radio was used successfully on a medical flight anywhere in the world. From that time, QANTAS allowed Vickers to fly in any direction he chose.

Vickers was delighted to find that every one of the patients he had seen on the previous visit was recovering. He turned his attention to new cases.

The bush natives had obviously been more seriously affected than the mission people by the epidemic illness. This was probably partly on account of their poor living conditions and consequent malnutrition; and partly because of the difficulty of treating them adequately. Apparently many of them, when they began to feel feverish, made for the nearest water hole to cool down. The result can be imagined – it would not be surprising if they developed pneumonia and consequently died ... But they were a cheerful lot, once they got used to me.

He continued treating the bush Aborigines the next day, building bridges towards them so that they would accept further help in the future. The following day he flew out.

How successful had he been in the long run? Would the foundations he laid bear fruit in the future? An old Aborigine later recalled:

From the time Mr Traeger set up the wireless on Mornington Island and the flying doctor came down to us, from that time we on the Island stopped dying and began to live.

When they stopped in at Burketown on their return flight, Vickers learned the good news that he had been appointed Medical Officer of Burketown and Kynuna Hospitals. The question still remained, though – would the AMS be forced to scale down or suspend its operations? When would the Board decide?

The minutes of an AIM Board Meeting in August 1931 give the answer – the AMS would be continued at all costs! It was noted that more than the work of the flying doctor was at stake: a withdrawal would mean the end of the wireless network as well, thereby returning the Outback to silence.

This bold decision was one of the Board's finest. It flew defiantly in the face of the Great Depression. To most critics, it was illogical and had little chance of success "bar a miracle of finance".

19

Flying into the storm

John Flynn and Andrew Barber tried everything they could think of
to steer the AIM through the financial storms of the Great
Depression.

Then came a body-blow. The Federal Government removed its
subsidy on mileage flown. Flynn was profoundly shocked and
disappointed at this decision. Didn't the government realise the
importance of the flying doctor and the radio network to the
development of the Inland?

Flynn lobbied as hard as he could, seeing every politician he
thought might help to reverse the dropping of the subsidy, but to no
avail. He was told that "the extraordinary circumstances of a worldwide recession prevent the government from supporting the Flying
Doctor Service further." How he would love to stand up in Parliament to challenge that decision, to tell them what was being
achieved economically for Australia by the AMS!

A disturbing thought then came to him: what if the Queensland
Government followed the example of the Commonwealth?
Queensland had first granted the AMS £1 000 in 1930 and Flynn was
relying on receiving a similar amount each year. He sent Andrew
Barber to pre-empt such a decision by lobbying Queensland poli-
ticians. Barber was successful, and £800 was granted.

The Queensland grant was a relief, but other measures would
have to be taken. Flynn, ever the propagandist, prepared a series of
pamphlets, including one entitled "Don't Let The Flying Doctor
Crash!" Another tactic was to see if perhaps they could trim their
own costs further. Flynn telephoned Vickers to discuss possibilities.

"I was wondering whether you might not be able to cut flying
costs, while still doing a first-class job. Perhaps more can be done
through wireless consultation before you actually fly out?"

"I'm doing that already, building on the techniques pioneered by Dr Spalding,"Vickers reported. "To date I've treated gastritis, measles, whooping cough, scalds, sciatica, certain accident cases and even broken limbs without flying out – all of them successfully, I might add. I have even admitted and discharged patients without ever seeing them."

"I have picked that up from your reports," Flynn told him. "It's because you are so successful that I wonder whether your wireless techniques might not be developed even further?"

"The problem is diagnosis," Vickers said, "and panic jobs. If you can't diagnose on the information sent through, you have to fly out just in case. I have even flown out to treat what turned out to be chronic indigestion. Drunken brawls are a real curse: they leave blood all over the place, everyone panics and I am called in when all that's needed is a good clean-up and patch job."

Flynn persisted. "Perhaps you could develop new techniques of radio diagnosis, using the bushmen as extensions of yourself? Bushmen are extraordinarily observant. Why not work out an orderly sequence of observations for the bushman to follow, then use his eyes and fingers instead of your own. It could save you time, and also save us money."

Vickers did much work to develop this concept, becoming a master of "radio diagnosis", acquiring skills and techniques that he was later to share with other doctors from around the world.

With survival in the balance, might Flynn be able to renegotiate his terms with QANTAS? He hated doing it, but decided to try and put pressure on his old friend Hudson Fysh, now managing director. He arranged a meeting.

For once, Flynn was short and to the point. "We both know that the subsidy paid out to QANTAS by the government and by ourselves in the experimental years for miles not flown did much to keep QANTAS afloat."

"Yes, that's quite right, Father Flynn. The profits were good when we were struggling for survival. Mind you, that was only because there were no serious crashes. We could not afford insurance at the time and so we built a safety component into our charges to you. I would rather you didn't shout from the rooftops that we were in financial trouble."

"I shall remain very circumspect," Flynn replied, with a smile. "However, we're the ones now in the hole. That contract we have with you is a trap. You see, we are flying less mileage in an effort to lower costs, but are still paying you out for those miles not flown. Admittedly, this is less than it would cost if we actually flew them, but it is still more than we can afford."

"We must retain a minimum figure, Father Flynn. If we drop below a certain mileage, it becomes uneconomic for us to leave a pilot and aeroplane standing idle."

"These are extraordinary times, requiring extraordinary measures," Flynn countered. "If you dropped your minimum requirements to what we are more likely to fly in a year, say thirteen and a half thousand miles, you might not make a great deal of money out of it but you would keep us afloat. Look on it as an investment in the future, when good profitability will return to our relationship."

Hudson Fysh sat back thoughtfully and said nothing for a few moments. He was proud of QANTAS' association with the Flying Doctor Service. He would do his best to save the scheme from folding.

"I'll try for you. I'll put it to my Board," Fysh said at last. "I'm certain that Fergus McMaster, who has discussed your problems with me, will want to keep the flying doctor aloft. With his support, I just might swing it."

"Thank you. Would you ask your Board one further thing at the same time?" Flynn continued. "Please ask them to lower the cost to us per mile flown by 25 per cent. Put it to them that these are only contingency measures until sanity returns to world economics."

Fysh shifted in his chair. "I'll do my best for you," he promised, "but these are tight times for us too. I don't know which way the Board will decide." In the event, the QANTAS Board turned up trumps for Flynn, granting both of his requests.

Flynn met frequently with Andrew Barber to discuss ways of raising support. "Please approach the graziers again. They use our radio network for commercial reasons all the time. Let them know that they may lose the network. Try Sidney Kidman, not to give money himself, but to organise fundraising events."

This Barber did most successfully. The rodeo organised in Adelaide by Kidman, a large landowner, attracted 40 000 spectators and raised £1 000 for Flynn's work.

"All the same, I am still concerned for the long term," he told Flynn at their next meeting.

"Don't be concerned. People are big-hearted when they see a need, even if it means going short themselves."

"That's just it, they don't see our need. The problem is our image. The public thinks we are funded by the government and don't know how essential their contributions are. We need publicity in the cities, to widen the base for our funding, but that's not happening."

"Our work takes place in the bush, which is why it is largely ignored by the city press," Flynn pointed out. "We can't blame them for that."

An incident soon to occur would change all that. It took place at Croydon, an old mining town in far North Queensland, at the base of the Gulf of Carpentaria. In February 1932, Jock Williamson, a Croydon hotel manager, struggled to service his old kerosene refrigerator. He bent low over it in concentration. Suddenly a ball of flame enveloped him, followed by a large explosion. Williamson was blown right out into the street, together with the side wall of the building. Startled residents found him still alive but his face dreadfully blackened and distorted. Both eyes had been badly burned and his skull was damaged.

Vickers flew to Jock Williamson early next morning. He reported:

> I found that he was blinded in both eyes. One eye was hopelessly injured, but the other seemed to hold out some hope of recovery if only he could be transferred quickly for treatment by a specialist. Moreover, it seemed imperative to get him out of the intensely hot and steamy climate which would have been a big handicap to his recovery. To take him to Cloncurry would be very little better as far as climate was concerned. The ideal place for him would be Brisbane – but Brisbane was over twelve hundred miles away! Could we afford such a flight in the present state of our finances? I knew that it would mean scraping the bottom of the barrel, but to Brisbane we decided to take him.

The doctor made this decision after discussion with Eric Donaldson, his new pilot since Arthur Affleck had gone tobacco farming. Donaldson advised him that they would have to stop to refuel at least three times and would be in the air a difficult 20 hours. There was an added complication:

> His [Williamson's] mother wished to come with us. That would mean she would occupy the only seat on the aircraft, the one on which I usually sat. An empty petrol case would have to serve me for a seat. It wasn't exactly comfortable as the bulk-head against which my back rested sloped the wrong way and vibrated rather badly.

They set off, refuelling at Cloncurry. Bert Reeves, the QANTAS ground engineer there, took Eric Donaldson to one side. "You're very heavily laden and the air is extremely thin in this heat. I doubt you will make it off the ground."

Discussion followed as to how they could lighten the aeroplane, but there was not much they could jettison.

"Bert was right. We aren't going to make it!" Donaldson thought as the *Victory* chugged down the airstrip, struggling to build up speed. Reeves, watching in trepidation, fully believed that the *Victory* was going to crash. He leapt into his truck, started it up, and wheeled it around in order to chase down the runway to the projected crash site. To his immense relief, though, the *Victory* reappeared from behind the trees along the river – flying low and slow like a bumblebee, but aloft.

> We encountered strong head winds and were forced to stay the night at Winton.
>
> During the night, it became apparent that in addition to his eye injuries, Williamson was also developing lung symptoms, probably due to the inhalation of gas from the explosion. I had little rest that night as he had several bad turns and his condition was obviously becoming worse. After much thought, it was decided to continue the flight to Brisbane as holding out the best chance for his recovery.

By this time, Vickers knew that this was no longer a dash to save a man's sight alone, it was a race against death! He telephoned Brisbane with details of Williamson's deteriorating condition.

Somehow, the press got hold of the story. Brisbane, Queensland's only major city, had never been touched by a flying-doctor emergency before. The media eagerly awaited the outcome.

The race for survival was knife-edge. Vickers administered morphine and drugs and tried to keep his patient as comfortable as possible. By now Williamson was burning with fever and his life had begun to slip away. His mother watched her son's face wordlessly, her own a picture of despair. Could they possibly reach Brisbane in time?

> We had to land every few hundred miles for fuel and the heat on the ground was terrific [around 40 degrees centigrade]. As the day wore on, Williamson's condition became worse and worse. Finally, in the late afternoon when we were only two hours' flying out of Brisbane, he died. The wings of death had proved too fast for those of the *Victory*.
>
> I was dog tired and utterly dejected. My petrol case seat had been far from comfortable and it had been a distressing experience watching the patient die cooped up in the small cabin with his mother looking on helplessly. I had spent a lot of our precious money and the trip had ended in failure.

A flare path had been lit for them at Archerfield. Eric Donaldson put the aeroplane down with his customary expertise. It was 9 p.m.

Vickers was bemused by the bevy of reporters and photographers who rushed over to the aeroplane and began to question him. "I am sorry to report that my patient is dead," he told them wearily. "Time and distance won. Please be considerate of his mother. She has sat in the midst of a cyclone and watched her son die." Wasn't it bad enough to have been defeated? Were they now going to publicise the flying doctor's failure and make the service look incompetent?

By the time Vickers flew out next day, the "race with death" theme had been taken up by all the major newspapers in Australia, some with streamer headlines on the front page.

John Flynn phoned Vickers, partly to cheer him up but also to give him some surprising news. Donations were flooding in to the Flying Doctor Service in all the major cities!

"Why? I expected quite the reverse!"

"It's empathy. Everyone is battling and the pathos and tragedy in your flight has struck a chord with their own situation. Perhaps it has shown city dwellers the true plight of their country cousins, I don't know. In any case, there have been a number of offers from individuals to start support groups where we have not had them before. This is just what we need. Oh, and a number of newspapers have been asking me if we could supply them with further stories from your work in the future, which will give us publicity in the cities."

"I'm no writer, Mr Flynn."

"I know, but they will employ correspondents in Cloncurry itself. All you will need to do is talk to them, giving details of cases and flights. Of course, do not give details that would be unethical. Try to keep an eye on what they write, too. We don't want to glorify the service, we want readers to receive an accurate picture."

"All right, I'll try. Do you really think it's that important?"

"Yes, I do."

The young doctor took to recording details of his flights on brown paper "airsickness" bags in order to have ready copy for eager newshounds on return. Most of his flights were routine and of no great news value, but every now and again a rescue mission had the elements that made for a good story and kept Flynn's work in the public eye.

Thus it was that Australia read of a doctor who divested himself of his clothing to wade across the flooded Mitchell River, in order to reach a desperately ill child. The rescue team had been forced to land on a narrow ridge because of difficult conditions over Dunbar station. Even then, water had sprayed out behind them so that they had looked more like a boat than a plane landing! They set out immediately on the 12-mile hike to Dunbar. En route, they were met by a group of guides and carriers sent out from Dunbar station to help them.

Stripping down before entering the waters of the Mitchell, Vickers noticed a young Aborigine looking up and down the river for crocodiles. It was dusk, the favourite time for a crocodile attack. The Aborigine assured Vickers, "No one bin taken by a crocodile for long time now."

"You go first then," Vickers rejoined.

"All right. Crocodile, he no eat blackfella!"

With that, the carriers and guides entered the water. Vickers followed behind more gingerly.

When halfway across, the aborigine who was carrying Vickers' bag noticed how the doctor was looking suspiciously at every floating object. He tried to reassure Vickers by saying, "Crocodile not too bad. Him bin taket horses lately, but no white man."

Vickers was not reassured one jot:

> In my imagination I stood on at least a dozen crocodiles before
> I reached the far bank!

With just a few metres to go, the guides broke into a run, shouting out, "Crocodile catchem last one over!" Vickers laughed and retorted, "No bin catchem this one!" and splashed along at his more sedate pace.

The child had been unconscious for two days when Vickers reached him:

> His mother's reaction to our arrival was pitiful to see. Three days before she had sent off a telegram asking me to come. The telegram had to be carried eighty miles by foot over flooded countryside by a young Aborigine. The mother had no way of knowing whether the telegram had arrived, or whether we were on our way, until we had flown over the station about two hours previously. For those three days, she had watched her child becoming more and more comatose and she was nearly frantic about his prospects. For over three days, he had not recognised anyone, nor had he taken any food.
>
> On treatment overnight, the child improved considerably. Next morning I decided to take him with me to hospital.

This would require the seven-year-old patient to be carried the twelve miles back to where the plane had landed. Vickers improvised a stretcher out of two poles and a couple of corn sacks for the trip. The lad was carried across the flooded Mitchell on the shoulders of his father and a stockman. The stretcher was returned and the mother and her babe-in-arms were hoisted high in it by the strong Aborigines, arms above their heads.

The boy from Dunbar Station recovered completely, but had to wait seven weeks before the station car could get through the flooded roads to take him home. It was this kind of detail in Vickers' accounts that helped city dwellers to conceptualise life in the Outback.

In the public mind Vickers became the symbol of the Flying Doctor Service. His success in tricky situations gave a lift to readers during the gloom of the Great Depression. "It would be a great blow to our popularity if something should happen to Dr Vickers," Flynn said publicly.

A flying accident had to happen sometime, though. The conditions in which they operated were too dangerous to escape forever.

Their first serious accident happened when the plane failed to lift on take-off. Vickers was thumped against the wall of the cabin, injuring his arm. The smell of fuel told him they could be enveloped in a fireball at any moment. The sick eight-year-old boy he had just collected was crying softly; Vickers comforted him with his good arm and spoke reassuringly to him for a few valuable seconds, then tried to force his way out of the hatch. He found that the crumpled top wing of the biplane was pressing against the hatch and he could not budge it. Then he heard movement.

"Is that you, Eric?"

"Yes. I was thrown clear. Look, I can't budge this top wing. You're trapped, I'm afraid, unless you can force the hatch yourself."

The distress of his young patient, Les Webster, made Vickers struggle the harder. Using his back against the hatch, and bucking like a wounded bull, he managed to create a tiny gap. Further gigantic heaving made a space wide enough to pass Les through to Eric.

"Take him well away from the aeroplane right now and stay with him. Do not return to the plane," Vickers ordered. He and Eric had become fast friends and he was concerned that Eric might return to the aircraft to help, leaving the patient by himself. What would happen to him if they were both killed in an exploding plane?

Vickers had to ignore shooting pains of protest from his arm as he kicked and heaved. The top wing lifted further, little by little. He finally scrambled out and stumbled away to a safe distance. Fortunately, the plane did not explode and QANTAS sent a replacement immediately.

Despite his arm injury, Vickers decided he must operate on Les that afternoon. His diagnosis was acute appendicitis and he dared not wait. The operation was a success. (Les Webster later became a Convair Captain with Trans-Australia Airlines (TAA) and a good friend of Vickers. Not surprisingly, he was an ardent supporter of the Flying Doctor Service.)

While Vickers was winning national media coverage, Flynn's fame was also rising. The year 1932 found him the subject of a best-seller, *Flynn of the Inland*, by Ion Idriess. Flynn was not interviewed for the book, which was a well-written reconstruction rather than a history. Its subject was tolerant of the mistakes because it popularised the work of the AIM. Personal fame meant nothing to Flynn. He would laugh at the "hero" status accorded him by the book and refer to it as "my mythical self". He wrote in a letter:

> That book has overwhelmed me. People rise out of the paving stones, as it were, to talk about our problems. Most of them expect, in response to their greeting, a little lecture which might be called "All Over Australia's Frontiers in Five Minutes".

Flynn of the Inland, Vickers' exploits, the efforts of Barber and the speeches of Flynn and Simpson all helped to popularise the AIM. Consequently, donations to the organisation rose in 1932 despite worldwide recession.

Ion Idriess, like many others, had wondered why the man who had championed family life so vigorously had never married. He hinted in his book that it was because of a tragic romance. In fact, it was nothing of the sort; it was simply because of Flynn's "weird life", as he described it himself. His correspondence is packed with phrases like "My life is not my own, it is booked out for the next three months". It was not that Flynn was unappreciative of the opposite sex, but he was too frantically busy and "on the wallaby" to be able to develop relationships. He felt the lack keenly and wrote plaintively to George Simpson, when congratulating the latter on his engagement: "My lot seems to have been cast outside the glow of a fireside: but I have the sense of appreciation none the less, and hope that you will reap all I have missed in that quarter."

There was only one woman with whom Flynn spent any quality time, whose sensitivity and sense of humour was similar to his own, who understood his visions and methods so well that he could leave even the most delicate of negotiations to her, who knew his innermost feelings because she helped him to compose hundreds of personal letters every year, whose fierce loyalty had been so valuable when he had been "in exile" from his Board in 1926 – his personal secretary, Jean Baird. As the years passed, he found that rather than dreading a return to his cluttered office, he looked forward to the time he would be spending there with her.

Flynn's impish humour is seen in a *Memo From the Superintendent – Private and Confidential* that he sent throughout the AIM in 1932. It read, in part:

> For a very long time I had been expecting Miss Baird to break down under the strain of her responsibilities as secretary – a strain not always reflected in her countenance. Considerably more than a year ago, I had tested her attitude towards a transfer from the secretarial chair to more varied, interstate activities ... Thereafter Miss Baird agreed that the most satisfactory way in which she might render the wider service was under my name.

This mysterious memo caused a frenzy of conjecture in AIM circles. What did he mean by Jean Baird coming "under my name"? Was the old fox having a laugh at their expense or was he indeed planning on getting married?

In fact, both! Congratulations poured in when the news broke officially. Flynn was now fifty-one years old, Jean Baird in her late thirties. Most friends had decided Flynn was the perennial bachelor and were caught completely off guard by his announcement, one writing about the "intense joy" he had felt watching the surprise on certain faces at the news.

The Flynns did not have time for a proper honeymoon: there was too much to do. Jean went to live with him at the Metropole Hotel in Sydney until somewhere more suitable could be organised, although that was low on Flynn's priority list. He put somewhere to live in the same category as food and material things – necessary, but unimportant. So much of his life was spent travelling that a home base had seemed irrelevant. It took months before Jean could wean him into a place of their own, a third-floor flat near Hyde Park.

Travelling was still Flynn's life and Jean often went with him. Nevertheless, much of their life, of necessity, was spent apart. Despite this independence, friends reported that their mutual affection was touching and their companionship close.

Jean was so self-effacing that people frequently did not know who she was: one lady was delighted to hear that Jean had worked with the AIM in Sydney. "Oh, really?" she had exclaimed. "Then can you tell me something about this sweet young thing Flynn has married?" Jean's correspondence is sprinkled with similar humorous observations.

Flynn could be very pleased to have found a wife whose heart beat so close to his own concerning the AIM and whose faith and outlook on life was similar to his. They made a happy pair.

He did not to know, then, how important her love and support would be to him in the year that lay ahead – the most difficult year of his life.

20

FIGHTING TO SURVIVE

For the AIM 1933 began well, with its first seaside camp for deprived Inland children held near Adelaide. The camp was a great success, and from that year it became an annual event.

The dark clouds of financial storms still threatened Flynn's work. Contributions to the AIM had improved, but did not keep pace with increasing costs.

Flynn worked quietly on an unusual fundraising scheme for some months. Only when he was sure it would work did he discuss it with Andrew Barber. "Allan Vickers has been getting a lot of exposure in the press and is becoming quite well known. He cuts an adventurous and romantic figure. In these tragic days, he has become a symbol of hope – a cavalier sparring against doom and gloom."

"And our donations have improved because of his popularity."

"Do you think," Flynn asked Barber, "that people would come in droves to hear him, even in the big cities? Doctors have a certain mystique that interests the general public, so they should find him doubly interesting."

"Do you mean as a speaker? Has he ever done anything like that before? Would he even consider it? I doubt he wants to leave his work to become a glorified fund-raiser."

"He has been a successful fund-raiser on a minor scale around Cloncurry, so he is not against the practice. My concept is for him to do deputation work in the cities. I first broached the possibility in a letter."

"Oh? And how did he respond?"

"Much as you expected. He protested that he had never done anything similar before, but I explained he wouldn't need to develop much material because he has a wealth of anecdotes to tell, and they were what people most wanted to hear. After much persuasion, he's agreed to do it. I believe this is so important that I am changing my personal program for next February and March to accompany him."

"It's a good idea," admitted Barber, "but we need more than the few hundred we could hope to raise through a series of talks."

Flynn's grey eyes became guarded. "As I had hoped, the itinerary has filled up. We'll do a tour of all the major cities, bar Perth − so I think we will raise more than just a few hundred pounds, more like a few thousand."

"Poor Vickers! Has he seen the proposed itinerary yet?"

"Yes. We spoke for several hours on his way through Sydney on leave. He protested, of course, saying he'd expected to be speaking to only a few church groups and schools, not in large halls in front of state governors and suchlike. But he's a fine man and he'll do it well. He'll have plenty of time to plan while he catches trout in the Geehi."

"What else might we try? A grand tour with Vickers will help, but the hole we're in is deeper than that."

He might have known Flynn would have something up his sleeve. "Archdale Parkhill, Minister for the Interior, visited Vickers last year in Cloncurry. He was impressed with what he saw and promised to try to restore the Commonwealth Government subsidy for us. Nothing's happened to date, but I've been in contact with him and others in the government. It's early days yet, but I'm praying that they may want to hear our flying doctor for themselves in Canberra."

"You mean this dream of yours to stand up in Parliament and tell them to support the Flying Doctor Service? Come now, Flynn, that really is far-fetched."

"It's one of my less likely dreams, but who knows?"

Allan Vickers, meanwhile, pondered his proposed series of lectures. Flynn had told him: "Don't try rhetoric, be yourself instead. Be natural. Tell them yarns from your own experience."

A few yarns, eh? What if he got tongue-tied and forgot what he had to say? He looked over the itinerary, two foolscap pages of typescript. He was due to begin at the prestigious Commonwealth Club in Adelaide. His eyes roamed over what would follow: talks to the British Medical Association, to Rotary, to rallies, press gatherings, on radio programs ...

"Had I known in advance what was in store I'd never have agreed, and John Flynn knew it!" he grumbled to himself. There was no escape now, though, so he learned four stories by heart. If he was required to give a long talk, he would use all four. If a shorter one, perhaps only one or two. Bad luck if anyone came to hear him a second time!

Fortunately, the Albury Apex Club heard of Vickers' plight.

They were courageous enough to invite me to address them, and I was able to inflict my first public address on a sympathetic audience. Albury Legacy and Rotary Clubs and the Albury Branch of the CWA [Country Women's Association] joined in the spirit of the thing. By the time I arrived in Adelaide on the 7th February 1933, I was gaining a little more confidence.

Nevertheless, he had a serious case of stage fright before his first talk in Adelaide. His hands were clammy, his throat dry. What if people couldn't actually hear him? Perhaps he would forget what to say and look like a complete fool.

He began badly, speaking far too fast because of nerves. "He's like a Vickers machine gun," commented one listener within earshot of John Flynn, who was in the audience.

Luckily, the young doctor quickly worked out what was going wrong. With a conscious effort he slowed himself down, but still continued at a "jog" as that was his natural style, even in private conversation. He spoke quickly, emphatically, but with verve and humour.

His listeners now began to understand him and warmed to what he was saying. Waves of applause washed over him as he finished up. His first large public meeting had been a success!

Over the next eight strenuous weeks, Vickers found that:

Flynn was a tower of strength, he put me up to several little tricks of the trade. He also pointed out that I had been born with a voice which, without effort, would carry into the far corners of large halls. He said, "That voice should not have been given to a doctor at all, but to a minister or a politician who has to earn his living by the sweat of his tongue."

Crowds swelled at meetings and donations began to flow in.

One person who heard Vickers speaking on that tour, in Brisbane, was Fred McKay, a man destined to play an important role in the AIM. Fred recalls of Vickers: "He was shy – and great. He had real incidents to relate, and the romance of it all became visible in a real flying doctor."

Carefully Flynn orchestrated the press releases concerning Vickers. He deliberately introduced him to men of influence and wealth, hoping that the word would get back to Canberra that here was a young man worth listening to.

Flynn spent much time on tour discussing his vision for the Flying Doctor Service with Vickers. Characteristically, this would be late at night when the doctor was dog-tired.

> Mr Flynn's enthusiasm was most infectious. Already he was visualising not only consolidation of the Cloncurry base, but the extension of our work to other areas! Long after public meetings had closed and everyone else had gone home, we talked far into the night – usually over coffee until the last café closed, then as we walked along the street.

The tour was drawing to a close when something very exciting happened.

> Mr Flynn came to me one morning waving a letter which he had just received. Colonel [later Sir] Thomas White, then Minister for Trade and Customs, had written on behalf of the government inviting us to visit Canberra to address the Members of Parliament!

Flynn chuckled when he saw the alarm on Vickers' face. "Don't worry, my friend. It will be like addressing any other crowd, which you have learned to do so well. This will be our opportunity to save the Flying Doctor Service, there won't be a second chance like it."

They spent the time on the train to Canberra discussing tactics. Vickers must still supply some anecdotal material to underline the great value of the Flying Doctor Service, but their emphasis would need to change.

"The Federal Government is not concerned, directly, with the provision of medical services to the Outback. That is the responsibility of the individual states. Their concern is for national issues.

Therefore, we must sell them on our contribution towards nation-building, towards the settlement and development of our vast open spaces," Flynn explained.

Flynn and Vickers stood at the door to Parliament with Colonel White, who introduced them to the members as they came in, when along came one whom Vickers recognised at a glance as the famous "Billy" Hughes, whose face had been the delight of cartoonists almost since he could remember.

Billy Hughes had been the Prime Minister who had first supported the flying-doctor concept in parliament in 1921 and had pushed for the original government subsidy. He was still a supporter of their work.

> He stopped for a moment and, poking his finger into my waistcoat, said, "This had better be good, young fellow. I have given up my golf to come here," then stumped on into the room.

This was hardly the confidence boost Vickers needed at that moment!

"I must warn you that the economic situation is very bleak," Colonel White told them. "Parliament is in no mood to distribute largesse. However, I am pleased to see that more than half the members have come to hear you, including seven cabinet ministers, which is a sign of interest in what you are doing." Flynn nodded and smiled thinly at hearing this, but did not comment.

After gracious introductions, the floor was handed to Vickers. "Now is the time to put our best words forward," he thought to himself.

Vickers' weeks of public speaking had been excellent training for this very moment. He controlled his nervousness by a supreme act of will, then spoke powerfully about the value of the work of the AIM.

> I concentrated on the need for Australia to settle its nearly empty north and west if it wished to support its moral right to hold those areas permanently. To be really effective, settlement must be made by men with their wives and families rather than by men alone. To enable this to be done efficiently, isolation must be broken down and medical security assured. In the

pack-horse settlement days, this had not been possible, neither had the motor car provided the answer, but our combination of radio and aircraft was pointing the way! We had proved at Cloncurry that the scheme would work. The time was now ripe for expansion on a nationwide scale, for which at least six additional bases would be necessary.

Flynn rose slowly to address the House. He was a stooped man nowadays and looked ineffectual when compared to the dashing figure cut by Vickers.

What John Flynn said that day was anything but ineffectual. With a few bold strokes, he painted his visionary pictures of what was possible. He then cheerfully proposed that government supply a subsidy of £35 000 pounds to the AMS to "seed" this future. Only he could have stood before Parliament during the Great Depression and proposed such a bold expansion.

While the members were chewing over Flynn's proposal, he gently pointed out that for the Cloncurry base to continue, the restoration of the Federal subsidy was vital. This did not involve £35 000, just a small fraction of that amount.

It would have seemed churlish, after the great vision that had been shared with them, for Parliament to refuse such a trifling request. During the vote of thanks, several congratulatory speeches were made. Their good friend Mr Parkhill said, "If the Acting Prime Minister finds that certain money for the proposal has to be put on the Estimates, I am bound to say it ought to go through the House without opposition." It had worked. Flynn's tactics had worked! On his way out, Billy Hughes growled at Vickers, "It was. Now for that golf." It took the bemused Vickers a few moments to work out that Hughes was following up his remark an hour earlier that the talk "had better be good, young fellow".

> I was very glad that the terrible Billy wasn't dissatisfied. Who knows what he would have said if the sacrifice of his golf had been entirely in vain?

Flynn was elated. Unfortunately, the Prime Minister and Treasurer were both away in Western Australia, so nothing definite could be decided right away regarding the subsidy. However, Flynn and Vickers left Canberra confident that it would be restored soon because they had won a great deal of support.

The speaking tour drew to a close. Several thousand pounds had already come in as donations, and the vital subsidy was likely to be restored soon. The tide had turned. Vickers recalled:

> As we parted in Sydney, Mr Flynn made a little speech which I shall be able to hear until the day I die. "Allan, I think you know about my belief that there is a special Providence which does not allow good causes to fail – that when things look blackest they get their breaks. How, otherwise, would there have come walking into my office two years ago, when the tide was ebbing very low, a doctor who had been given a voice which carries such that he who is in the most distant corner can hear! Thanks for everything."

It is interesting to note that while Flynn sometimes addressed Barber, Traeger, Vickers and Simpson by their first names, only Barber ever used Flynn's first name in return, and then only in private. The others always addressed him as "Mr Flynn".

Vickers was soon back in the thick of things, doing what he loved best: "Hardly was I back in Cloncurry when the fun started. On several days, in quick succession, I found myself trying to deal with two or more urgent calls at once …" He was not too busy to enjoy the thrill of victory a short time later when Flynn telephoned with the great news that the Federal subsidy had been restored.

In a different context Flynn was also frantically busy. Cloncurry was the first flying-doctor base, still experimental. Flynn's plan was to spread a network of bases right over Australia, which would require the permission of each state involved. Having just won over the Federal Government, his next challenge was to gain the support of the separate state governments. How could he best achieve this?

Flynn targeted the Premiers' Conference of June 1933, a month away, which each state premier would attend to discuss issues of mutual interest. As he would not be permitted to address the Conference himself, he needed one of the premiers to do so on his behalf. The most obvious candidate was the Queensland leader, William Forgan Smith, because Queensland was already benefiting from the service at Cloncurry.

How might Flynn secure the support of Forgan Smith in the short time available? He wrote a letter asking that he raise the issue, and requesting a personal interview. To ensure that Forgan Smith had access to the facts, he included a lengthy statement of the achievements of the Flying Doctor Service.

Flynn was not granted his request right away. Instead, he was invited to talks with lesser lights in the government. He had expected this. At each encounter, he stressed the importance of a face-to-face meeting with Forgan Smith. Finally, his persistence had its usual reward and a short interview was scheduled for 25 May.

The Premier was extremely busy. Fearing he would not have enough time with him for a thorough briefing, Flynn employed a typical Flynnian tactic. He perused details of the Premier's intended schedule for the rest of that week and noted that it included the opening of a church fete on 26 May, the day after his interview. Flynn arranged with the minister involved, Reverend James Gibson of Ithaca, to share the opening of the fete with the Premier. That would give him the extra time he needed!

As Flynn had predicted, the official interview was too short. Forgan Smith agreed to put forward the case for expansion of the Flying Doctor Service, but was not adequately briefed to do this properly.

The next day, after the official function at Ithaca, Flynn and Forgan Smith settled down to afternoon tea. Flynn soon had the Premier engrossed in flying-doctor business, and fed him dreams and visions of future possibilities. To his Board he wrote confidently after this informal discussion: "Our overture will be presented with care and emphasis."

It was. Forgan Smith's motion was debated at the Premiers' Conference and a resolution passed in which the Premiers approved of the expansion in principle, but wanted a detailed plan of how this could be done.

"We must supply them with a plan, who else could?" Flynn pointed out to Dr Simpson. "This is a crucial step – one small error in what we propose now may become a major stumbling block later. We must have it sewn up before next February when the premiers are due to meet again."

Flynn's vision centred around a unifying concept:

> The essential things for the success of the Flying Doctor
> Service are co-operation under one ideal and name round
> which great traditions will accumulate; one sentiment which
> will give power to its life; and one purpose which will
> guarantee support for the weaker branches by the stronger.

This ideal needed a very special plan. Flynn consulted many
people and began to stitch ideas together.

In June 1933, John Flynn was awarded the Order of the British
Empire (OBE). Letters and telegrams of congratulations flooded in
from all over Australia. The honour came at one of the busiest times
of Flynn's life. Not only was he working flat out on flying-doctor
business, but he was also planning nationwide twenty-first birthday
celebrations for the AIM and a report for the General Assembly of the
Presbyterian Church, both for September. He simply could not spare
the time to attend any of the three investitures by which the
governor-general was to present his OBE! He wrote painful letters of
apology.

Finally, a letter from Canberra resolved his dilemma:

> Governor General's Secretary informs me you will receive
> decoration from His Excellency at a later convenient date, but
> without ceremony.

Flynn finally received his OBE in December that year. It was
presented without ceremony at the Australia Club in Sydney.

Meanwhile, Flynn was making landmark decisions regarding the
future of the Flying Doctor Service. Its official name would be
expanded to become the Australian Aerial Medical Services (AAMS).
A federal body would oversee national policy, to which each state
would send its representatives. However, ninety per cent or more of
the planning and decisions would be left to the local organisations,
which would best be aware of their own needs and resources. To
ensure greater efficiency, it was decided to preclude government
involvement other than in a supporting role.

These decisions produced a great paradox – for the Flying
Doctor Service to become national, it could no longer remain an
arm of the AIM. Vickers explains this:

If the AIM were to undertake its development alone, progress would surely be slow because of the limited funds available. Moreover, with control vested in any one section of the community, the movement would not easily attain the national prestige and support for which we hoped.

That he would have to give the Flying Doctor Service away worried Flynn not a jot. It was something he had always suspected should happen. Certain members of the Presbyterian Church were unhappy with this decision, though. The Church had poured in funds, time and effort with little reward to date. Now the Flying Doctor Service was financially viable and growing in prestige, reflecting well on Presbyterianism. Flynn wanted to hand it over just when the Church's investment was beginning to pay dividends.

He quickly realised that this opposition from within the Church was extremely serious. The General Assembly in September would no doubt make a decision on the issue, and as it met only every three years, that decision would have to stand for that length of time.

What should he do? He decided to prepare a document to enable the transfer of the Flying Doctor Service to secular control – a very sensitive issue. He put it in a letter to a friend, "God guide us through this valley of fog and mystery!"

Vickers notes, "Mr Flynn now put on a tremendous burst of activity. By some magic, he produced a draft Memorandum and Articles of Association." This plan was passed as suitable by the AIM Board and was then ready for its big test at the General Assembly.

Flynn now turned to his trump card, Allan Vickers.

> Considering that I might help to turn the tide, Mr Flynn persuaded the Executive to invite me to Melbourne for the AIM Demonstration [birthday celebrations] which was to be held in September at the same time as the General Assembly.

> Furthermore, should the hoped-for authority be granted by the General Assembly, Flynn planned that he and I should forthwith visit Western Australia [where interest had been shown in forming a second flying doctor base].

> Flynn wrote to me: "This may look like 'stepping on it', but it seems to be impossible to succeed unless we dash around from

centre to centre to get preliminaries finalised before the gains won at the Premiers' Conference have suffered from the attrition of time. We MUST get our colleagues to realise that there is a tide in the affairs of the Flying Doctor Service, and that tide is now!"

Vickers did not let Flynn down. At the General Assembly, he gave an impressive slide presentation of his work, and then spoke with great conviction of the need to expand the Flying Doctor Service as soon as possible. He left the Assembly to ponder a haunting question – were they prepared to accept the responsibility of preventable deaths on their consciences if they were to slow down the expansion of the Flying Doctor Service by keeping it under Church control?

After very little debate, the General Assembly gave Flynn exactly what he wanted, the authority to create and become a member of "a new organisation of national character to establish and maintain Aerial Medical Services adequate for the isolated areas of Australia".

Victory! Vickers recorded his reaction.

> To the everlasting credit of the Church, it saw the light of Flynn's wisdom and, having spent much money and effort on these enterprises in their risky pioneering stages, it gave away these outstanding examples of practical Christianity on the eve of their fulfilment.

When Flynn arose to speak at one of the AIM's birthday parties, he paused first to look around the room at the members of his "family", men and women with whom he had shared so much of his life. "Well," he exclaimed, "it is too marvellous to see those boys and girls that I sent Inland now middle-aged and stout, and some of the boys with hair thinning on top!"

At that point some wag called out, "What about your own?"

"Oh no," he replied. "Mine is the result of matrimony!"

Flynn enjoyed the twenty-first celebrations, but his mind kept wandering to Western Australia and the challenge of starting new bases there. The tide was right, the time was now.

21

GOING WEST

On the long trip to Perth, John Flynn and Allan Vickers had time to talk in a more relaxed fashion.

"Have you thought about my offer for you to head up the work in Western Australia?" Flynn asked.

"Yes, I have, but there's a problem. As you know, Lilias and I intend to marry next February."

"Ah, yes. She's the young lady I told you to look out for, the pharmacist's daughter. My taste is impeccable, don't you think?"

"I am very grateful, though I must say that in the absence of thousands of pretty girls thronging the streets of Cloncurry, and being a doctor and having only one pharmacist to do business with, we might still have noticed each other."

The two men laughed.

"What is the problem concerning Lilias, Allan?"

"She doesn't like the bush, so I might take up a city practice again." This would be a serious blow to Flynn's plans. The multi-skilled Vickers, capable of meeting any challenge, was ideal for Western Australia.

In Perth the two men were excited by the enthusiasm they encountered for the plan. Vickers then went north to seek out possible sites for bases. The state would need at least two.

Flynn stayed on in Perth, to set up an Advisory Committee. He found many good people willing to serve, including the same Dr John Holland who had tried so hard to save Jimmy Darcy's life at Halls Creek.

At the committee's inaugural meeting, Flynn introduced his "Eight Points of Agreement", a hastily compiled set of guidelines for the extension of the Cloncurry experiment to other states. It was a delicately worded document that enshrined the concept of a national body with uniform standards, but still accommodated local freedom to solve local problems. Although the debate was lively, the committee finally endorsed and adopted it. So far so good!

"Both Port Hedland and Wyndham would make good flying doctor bases," Vickers reported on his return. "It is hard to say which should be first; both are needed badly."

"I want to start both right away, but the Perth committee will be hard-pressed enough getting just one going. I have a plan, though," Flynn said. "Victorians are exceptionally warm-hearted, why should we be robbed of having a flying doctor base simply because our state is so small? I believe we should sponsor a base in Western Australia. It's not an entirely novel idea; I asked Andrew Barber to look into it a while back. Despite returning to a Church ministry, he still does a lot for us."

"Mmmm, it's an interesting concept. What would be the logistics of running a base interstate?"

"We've been running Cloncurry in Queensland from Sydney in New South Wales, so it is quite possible."

The next tricky step was to secure state government approval. To their surprise, the West Australian government accorded the two a parliamentary luncheon. This was followed by a letter to Flynn from the premier:

> The government of this state is prepared to co-operate in the formation of a NATIONAL Aerial Service for Australia, and anything we can do to assist in that direction will be willingly undertaken.

This stunningly successful visit under their belts, Flynn and Vickers went on to Melbourne. Here Flynn pursued his concept of Victorians sponsoring a base out west. At a round table conference organised by Andrew Barber, the Lord Mayor Mr Gengoult Smith electrified the crowd by describing how his own life had been saved at Flynn's nursing home at Halls Creek. After an endorsement like that, Flynn found it easy to form an enthusiastic committee, which went on to decide to adopt Wyndham, in the Kimberleys, as its flying-doctor project.

There were now two flying-doctor committees wanting to get started, so Flynn had to produce a national constitution that would tie all bases into one fine service.

———

Allan Vickers and Lilias Whitman were married in early February 1934, in Cloncurry. They set off by train to Sydney on the start of their honeymoon, which was to Hong Kong and further east.

When the train chugged into Rockhampton, the newlyweds were surprised to find the Kerr family there to greet them. Young "Pixie" Kerr, whose life Vickers had saved twice, curtsied and presented them with a beautiful basket of fruit for their journey.

"You will continue as flying doctor on your return, won't you?" Mrs Kerr asked Vickers.

"I'm not certain yet of my plans," he replied.

There was a good-sized crowd to meet the couple in Sydney where they were feted that night at a party thrown by the AIM Family.

During the evening, Flynn pulled Allan briefly to one side. "I am hoping still that you will accept the challenge of transplanting the flying doctor into Western Australia."

"I can't commit myself, but I'll come and see you immediately I return."

The *Taiping* sailed out of Sydney Harbour and put into Brisbane on the first leg of its voyage. Vickers was surprised to find reporters waiting for him at the quayside. They wanted photos of the newlyweds. Most of all, they wanted to know what the young doctor's future plans were.

Next morning, the *Courier-Mail* ran a long article on Vickers' work, describing some of the more dramatic incidents. However, many readers found the "P.S. From Mrs Vickers", tacked on at the end, to be even more interesting:

> I think Allan will still be the "flying doctor" after we return
> from our honeymoon. To me – and to hundreds of families
> "Outback" – he will never be anything else.

On being shown the article, Flynn commented, "I think Lilias is listening to Allan's heart, in which case we won't lose him!"

He had been forced to miss Allan Vickers' wedding because it clashed with the 1934 Premiers' Conference. The previous conference had asked for a plan for the orderly development of the Flying

Doctor Service interstate, and this is what Flynn had to have ready for them. It involved projecting the Flying Doctor Service into the distant future, then producing a constitution to secure that development – a tricky challenge, as any mistake could produce enormous problems later on. The conception had to be broad enough to allow each state virtual autonomy as to how it ran its own Flying Doctor Service, yet compact enough to weld all the states into one national service.

As always, Flynn turned to an array of experts to feed him information, but the final synthesis was uniquely his own. No one else in the world could have produced the brilliant 40-page document that resulted. Besides providing a tight legal and organisational framework, it took careful account of human foibles. As he put it:

> It must be secure from petty jealousies, personal kingdom building and party spirit. So many walks of life will be involved in each new base over the years, it will need to be able to serve a multiplicity of personalities. These constraints make the task long and difficult.

When George Simpson commented that Flynn had done little else for three months other than the constitution, Flynn replied, "Things that crawl first often fly later! That is, provided nothing has harmed them in the embryonic stages. My patience will be rewarded by the speed of events once we are ready to 'go over the top'. At that point, I can stop being a constitution builder and become a public advocate for it instead. I can't tell you how much I am longing for that day!"

Flynn appeared to Simpson to be tired, lined and care-worn. Nevertheless, the national constitution he produced was a visionary document. It stands, almost unchanged, to this day.

Would the national constitution be acceptable to flying-doctor committees in the individual states? Flynn decided he would have to prove this before the premiers met. He pushed his Victorian supporters to adopt it and declare themselves the Australian Aerial Medical Services – Victorian Section. This was done formally on 9 February 1934, just days before the premiers discussed the AAMS.

Flynn had wisely kept each leader thoroughly briefed about developments in the eight months since the previous conference. Once again, he selected William Forgan Smith to put his case to the others, asking him to seek a "benediction of a general character", so that future progress would not be too circumscribed. In this, Forgan Smith was successful; the resolution passed down by the Premiers read:

> This Conference approves of a general co-operation of the governments of the Commonwealth and the states with a view to furthering the Australian Aerial Medical Services scheme.

Although this sounded very vague to Simpson, he found Flynn was delighted with the wording. "It may prove even greater than my expectations," was his judgement. "We face a minefield up ahead, and need to be free to pick our own routes through it."

"Like the jealousies Welch faced from doctors when he went to Cloncurry, is that what you mean?"

"Yes, and many other problems besides," replied Flynn. "That's why we must secure Vickers for Western Australia: his experience, intelligence and diplomatic skills will give us our best chance of success there."

Until Vickers returned from his honeymoon in April, there was little more Flynn could do about starting in Western Australia, so he turned to other AIM matters.

He was cheered by Alf Traeger's latest breakthrough – two-way voice transmission for up to 500 miles! Despite Traeger's ingenious automatic Morse keyboard of 1931, many pioneers had steered clear of wireless because of difficulties with code. The final impediment was now removed.

Flynn set about planning to network many more Inlanders into his mantle of safety. There would be a delay until the following year while the new sets were being developed, so he made fresh maps to show, in his words:

> every habitation and the number of children, men and women in it, even the lonely hut of the single man hundreds of miles from his nearest neighbour. The AAMS plans to effect a communicating "point" with ALL of these habitations.

He dreamed of a new caring community coming about as a result.

I cannot see every Saltbush Bill, in his bough shed, bothering to purchase a set, but I can envisage a comprehensive network where every man in the Inland is within twenty miles of a pedal set. Wouldn't it be marvellous if those with sets took care and concern over every person within a twenty mile radius?

He sent AIM personnel on a giant survey to update his information and started on the new maps. Flynn loved his maps and an old leather map-case became his constant companion in his travels. He would whip a map out at the drop of a hat to illustrate a point, spreading it over any available surface, commonly using railway seats and the floors of hotel lobbies.

On returning from his honeymoon, Vickers went to see Flynn. "I'll take on the challenge of Western Australia," he told him. He was keen to go immediately to Port Hedland to start the base there, but Flynn pointed out there were foundations to be laid first – money to be raised, state and local permissions to be sought, promotion of the service to be done, suitable aircraft to be organised. In short, all the things he had done so carefully before sending Dr Welch to Cloncurry had to be repeated for Port Hedland.

In order to keep Vickers occupied, Flynn arranged for the new Victorian Section of the AAMS to employ him as their Chief Medical Officer, to advise and plan and also to raise funds, at which he had proved adept. Leaving the two parties to get on with the job, Flynn set out to join Skipper Partridge, to renew his acquaintance with the Inland and the sunburnt apostles he had stationed there. He had neglected the far-flung AIM patrols and nursing homes because of the demands of the Flying Doctor Service, but relished the chance to return and see for himself what progress had been made.

He and Partridge travelled many hundreds of miles over the next five months, going "everywhere in nowhere, for the love of the Inlanders". Once more Flynn slept in his swag under the stars, or on a dirt floor in a home, or next to the chooks. The two men wrote letters and reports by hurricane lamps, baptised children in water-holes, and collected water in billy-cans to wash their clothes.

Being a patrol padre seemed a romantic lifestyle until a man started to live it – then the flies, heat, multiple difficulties and dangers robbed it of much of its glamour. Transcending all the discomforts, though, Flynn's men knew they were doing what God wanted. In modern parlance, they experienced a high level of job satisfaction.

Flynn was delighted to observe how his wireless network was helping women to overcome loneliness. Daily sessions between neighbours had started, soon to expand into extensive "galah" sessions as voice telephony became more readily available. (Galahs were screeching grey-and-pink cockatoos with an unfair reputation for garrulous stupidity. Traeger inadvertently named the "galah" session in 1935 when sending wire to Birdsville to strengthen the aerial from collapsing under the weight of galahs. At the same time, he advised the nurses there to start a chat session "just like the galahs on your aerial".) Pedal and chat, pedal and enquire about your neighbour's children, pedal and ask for advice ... pedal the world into your home. The homestead was a silent prison no longer. Distance and isolation collapsed like the walls of Jericho.

Flynn also renewed old acquaintances, collected data and expanded his vision for the Outback. "A patrol like this is an ideal antidote to an overdose of the AAMS," he wrote to Jean.

By the time he returned to Melbourne he was rejuvenated. This was just as well. In his absence, a series of mini-crises had blown up and required immediate action. The first involved Vickers, who was on the verge of returning to private practice.

"A series of problems has prevented any real progress and we seem to have bogged down," he told Flynn. What I want is to get out to Western Australia and make a start, but that could take years at the present rate of progress and I'm not prepared to wait."

"What are these problems?"

"The Director General of Postal Services is hedging on granting permission to create a wireless network in Western Australia with unlicensed operators. Various other permissions are also slow in coming. Alf Traeger has work planned for the next eight months on the Cloncurry network, let alone starting another. He calls himself an "agitated ant" and his health is suffering from overwork. The biggest problem, though, is that QANTAS are not operating in Western Australia. The government has accepted the tender from MacRobertson Miller Aviation Company to do the mail run, but they don't have an aeroplane suitable for a flying doctor. It sounds like they want a prohibitive amount of money to sign a contract with us."

Flynn lit his pipe and took a couple of thoughtful draws on it before replying. "I'll solve all those problems in time, Allan, every one of them. My concern right now is for you. How would it be if I twist a few arms and secure you a government posting as a doctor somewhere in the north of Western Australia? Then you could go almost immediately and practise your profession, but in your spare time you could be laying foundations for the Flying Doctor Service to come."

Vickers was persuaded to stay. By October, he found himself employed as Medical Officer at Broome, which lay between the proposed flying-doctor bases at Port Hedland and Wyndham.

He enjoyed the medical challenges of his new position. He also promoted the Flying Doctor Service (FDS). Further, he planned suitable landing sites and the wireless network. Then he arranged for Traeger to come and establish "mother" stations early the following year. At last, events were on the move.

Traeger encountered many difficulties in trying to set up stations in Western Australia, not least of which were the problems of distance and having to cart everything with him. Then, when he finally began work, it was so hot that spanners raised blisters on his hands, and he was forced to limit outside labours to before 9 a.m. and after sunset. Even in these excessive temperatures, he still wore his long dark trousers and striped braces!

Port Hedland went to air in October 1935, and Wyndham in May 1936. This base was officially opened by the Prime Minister, Joseph Lyons.

These delays in communications did not prevent Vickers from getting involved. Though employed simply as a medical officer, he thrice chartered an aeroplane to effect a mercy mission: shades of George Simpson's flight to Mount Isa to rescue the injured miner before the flying-doctor experiment started. In the same way as Simpson's mission, Vickers' flights led to widespread comment among pioneers and an awakening to the potential of the Flying Doctor Service.

Allan Vickers' restless brilliance sought other ways of serving the community. Appalled at the dangers to which the pearling vessels were exposed, he considered ways they could be incorporated into a wireless network. He also made provisional plans for a search-and-rescue operation by air for missing seamen. This paid dividends in April 1935 when there was a cyclone and various pearling luggers went missing. Vickers reacted with typical speed and decisiveness, using chartered aircraft to carry out a successful search for the missing boats. Once again, residents were awakened to the enormous potential of wireless and aeroplanes in rescue work.

The Port Hedland base appealed to Vickers and he decided to be the flying doctor there. What, then, of the "Victorian" base up at Wyndham? Aware how important it was to select the right man, he began a personal search which uncovered a quiet, unassuming doctor from Perth who loved flying. Ralph Coto had his pilot's licence and owned a tiny de Havilland Hummingbird for personal use. Within an hour of talking to Dr Coto, Vickers was convinced he had found their flying doctor. Coto, though, wanted to fly the aircraft himself and was disappointed to hear of Flynn's dictum, "One man, one job".

"You see," Vickers explained, "the needs of the patient have to come first in our work. There have been a number of emergency cases where I have had to administer first aid in flight, to save a life. Imagine if I had been flying the aeroplane at those times."

Eventually, Coto was persuaded to serve as the flying doctor at Wyndham, leaving the piloting to someone else.

"You know," John Flynn observed to George Simpson, "there is one aspect of the Wyndham base that I find especially satisfying. It will service Halls Creek, where Dr Holland went to try to save young Darcy. Holland pointed this out to me in a recent letter."

Fittingly, Halls Creek was the destination of Coto's very first mercy flight, on 19 August 1935. A telegram from Sister Anderson at the AIM hospital there requested he attend a stockman, who had just arrived with a very serious hand injury.

Dr Coto flew from Wyndham at 11.30 a.m., arriving over Halls Creek three hours later, a journey that normally took three days by car. This startling comparison was spoken about throughout the Kimberleys, which had not forgotten what had happened to Jimmy Darcy 18 years earlier.

The stockman was flown back to Wyndham and his mangled hand was saved. Dr Coto later received a letter of congratulations about this incident from Dr Holland. (Strangely, Dr Holland had said in 1917 that were he to go to Halls Creek again, he would fly. As life turned out, he never went to Halls Creek again, but his support of the AAMS enabled another doctor to fly there instead.)

A few days after the Halls Creek mercy flight, Coto had the satisfaction of saving a life, that of an Aboriginal child at Forest River Mission. Australia's second flying-doctor base was well and truly operational.

Within a short time of Dr Coto commencing with the service, Flynn read a flying-doctor report concerning Halls Creek that gladdened his heart.

> The amount of midwifery occurring in the Kimberleys is at present remarkable, considering the population. However, the influx of young and newly married couples that is occurring must end in results like these.

"You know," he pointed out to his wife, "it was at Halls Creek that Miss Madigan reported an old prospector who was moved to tears when he saw a white baby. It was the first white baby he had seen in sixteen years. Times have certainly changed."

An extraordinary incident took place when the Port Hedland base was opened on 30 October, three months after the Wyndham base.

During the official ceremony, in the midst of the speechmaking and handshaking, Dr Vickers was called away to the radio. This was the first emergency call in Western Australia. The "mother" station had only just come on the air and the first "daughter" station had been installed in isolated Warrawagine, 200 miles inland. A badly injured Aborigine had arrived there only minutes before, having been carried a long distance through rugged desert by his tribesmen.

It took Vickers several minutes to calm Mary Miller, the manager's wife. Once composed, she supplied him with the information that the man had fallen out of a tree while seeking honey and had a badly injured spine. This was not a case Vickers could leave to radio diagnosis – he would have to fly out immediately. What about the official opening ceremony? Well, he would simply have to excuse himself.

The official guests watched, goggle-eyed, as the pilot ran out to the aeroplane and warmed the engine, closely followed by Vickers carrying his black doctor's bag. The aeroplane had been named the

John Flynn, and Vickers could not suppress a smile when he thought how much the real John Flynn, the arch-propagandist, would have enjoyed the drama of that moment. "Flynn could not have staged this better himself!" he decided, as he turned to give a final wave to the watching guests before boarding the aircraft.

When they landed at Warrawagine and disgorged from the belly of the plane, the naked tribesmen who watched expressed their wonderment in a chorus of grunts. Vickers, in turn, was equally surprised to find them completely naked.

"It was like magic hearing you on the wireless, and now to have you drop out of the sky two hours later!" Mrs Miller greeted the doctor. "Recently, it took several days to get help when my own child was sick. I can't tell you what a relief it is to know that I can call on you. Until today, I have had to act as doctor to a dozen station hands and any number of wandering Aborigines. I have no knowledge of doctoring and we keep little in the way of medicines."

Vickers treated the injured man and then had him carried on a stretcher to the waiting aeroplane. The tribesmen watched impassively, then set up another chorus of grunts as their brother disappeared into the plane. As Vickers recorded:

> I treated the patient and had him strapped in the aircraft while his blood-brothers, in all their naked wildness, looked on …
> What they reported when they arrived back at their camp can only be left to the imagination.

The Aborigine recovered and was sent back "good as new", but this time in some clothing. What his fellow tribesmen thought about that is not on record either.

Mrs Miller was soon on the air again with another emergency, this time concerning a very sick Aboriginal girl. Vickers asked her to accompany the child to Port Hedland; though scared at the idea of flying, she agreed. It so happened that weather conditions were stormy that day and the tiny aeroplane bucked and bounced like an insect buffeted by the wind.

Mrs Miller was very relieved when they landed safely at Wyndham. She was to become an ardent supporter of the FDS and travelled widely as a speaker and fund-raiser, eventually receiving an MBE in recognition of her selfless input into the service.

From Port Hedland Vickers kept an expert eye on events at the Wyndham base. He instructed Dr Coto how to conduct diagnosis and treatment by radio, and soon Dr Coto was treating five times as many patients by radio than the number to whom he had to fly.

Vickers did much to promote the concept of a "mantle of safety" over the whole Inland, and shuttled between east and west as its main spokesperson. During one of his trips "east", in September 1935, he spoke to the fledgling Goldfields Flying Doctor Service at Kalgoorlie, advising it concerning the work of the AAMS. Later, he returned and helped with planning and addressed public meetings. As a result, a vigorous and efficient arm of the AAMS was established in Kalgoorlie.

Vickers often met with Flynn and Simpson to hammer out policy.

> We would meet at George Simpson's house in Melbourne and talk at large about the Flying Doctor Service, past, present and future – but mainly of the future. As we talked Mrs Flynn, an expert stenographer, took down any points of importance while Mrs Simpson provided the creature comforts in the way of drinks and supper. These meetings would go very late. By the following morning, Mrs Flynn had typed for each of us an excellent précis of the night's discussions. At these meetings, much of the future course of the Flying Doctor Service was plotted. If there is any one place which can be regarded as the spiritual home of the Service, it must surely be the home of George and Nesta Simpson.

The flying-doctor bases in Western Australia were soon respected and recognised as outstanding successes, thanks largely to Allan Vickers. It is fair to say that Vickers had become to the Flying Doctor Service what Plowman was to the patrol padre system, and Nurse Bett to the nursing homes: they were all archetypes, serving as the image, personality and standards for all who followed. Not all flying doctors were gallant swashbucklers like Vickers, but each aspired to the same compassion and dedicated professionalism.

The time was now ripe for Flynn to promote new flying-doctor bases across the Australian Inland. Other problems, though, were calling for his attention.

22

FRED McKay, heir apparent

"Our nurses in Birdsville are still struggling along in that dilapidated old Royal Hotel, George," Flynn said to Dr Simpson. They are doing a grand job, but would do an even better one with proper facilities. It's not fair to put off building them a new nursing home simply because I'm so involved in flying-doctor work."

"How do you intend going about building a new hospital so far out?" Simpson asked.

"I've drawn up the plans already, but need someone to supervise the project from start to finish."

"I hope you aren't considering going there yourself, as you did to Alice Springs?"

John Flynn laughed. "No. My Board would never allow that nowadays. My challenge is to plan a new patrol which would incorporate Birdsville, then our new patrol padre would supervise the building of the nursing home. He'd have to solve problems at Cloncurry too. The base there badly needs organising and oversight."

"What about our need to federalise the AAMS? That's vital too. We must give strong leadership and direction to the new committees springing up, otherwise we could find ourselves with lots of little schemes, badly planned and organised, which could shortly fizzle out."

"I know. That has started already, unfortunately. Perhaps our only solution is to get a federal council up and running to oversee the flying doctor work. My dilemma is that I don't have the time it would demand."

"I'm also pushed for time, but I'll work with you on it."

George Simpson was as good as his word. Despite his thriving medical practice, he spent countless hours travelling, talking and writing articles about the need for federalisation. He was held in high regard throughout Australia and all interested parties paid close attention to his suggestions. Dr Vickers wrote later:

> George Simpson's quiet deliberation and consciousness of the needs of the present were a perfect complement to John Flynn's somewhat intoxicating enthusiasm and habit of thinking several years into the future; so that they made a splendid team.

The Federal Council of the AAMS was formed officially in July 1936. By that time, six flying-doctor bases were operating successfully. When eight representatives met at this inaugural gathering, it was a moment of great triumph for both John Flynn and George Simpson.

Guided by Flynn, the Federal Council at once addressed problems with the wireless network. Traeger's brilliance meant that he frequently brought out improved models of his radio sets. This was an expensive process, the radio arm of the AIM showing a huge loss of £15 000 by 1935. It also made servicing and maintenance by AIM staff extremely difficult, meaning that obsolete radio equipment mounted up throughout the Outback. Flynn's "advisory committee" of specialists dealt with the situation by standardising all equipment and wireless procedures. (Different areas could still tailor programs to local needs, though. Broken Hill, for example, operated a very successful bushfire control system over the wireless.)

Flynn's genius for inspirational communication led the Federal Council to develop its own broadsheets, leaflets and, ultimately, an excellent magazine. This bound the developing sections together into the one great tradition that the founder had always envisaged.

In Western Queensland Flynn set up the infrastructure for a vast new patrol, but could not find a patrol padre. Everywhere he travelled, he asked ministers if they knew anyone who might be suitable and one name kept coming up as a possibility – Fred McKay. Young Fred had been raised on a property near Mackay in Northern Queensland, made friends easily, could ride a horse, was good at practical things and had performed well academically at Brisbane's Emmanuel Theological College, winning a scholarship to Edinburgh to further his studies.

Flynn arranged to be invited to speak at the Southport Church, where Fred McKay was the Home Missionary. Fred was pleased when told there would be an unexpected visit from John Flynn. It meant he would not have to prepare sermons that Sunday!

His thoughts flashed back to the only previous time he had heard Flynn. It had been at the 1928 Federal Assembly of the Presbyterian Church in Brisbane; Fred, a young student, had attended out of interest. He had not been particularly impressed: Flynn's voice was too monotonous for his liking, although he had enjoyed the stories.

To Fred's surprise, Flynn's speech that day had been followed by virulent attacks on the AIM from the floor: it had not built any churches, its work was not "spiritual" enough, aspects were racist, its activities cost too much money, wireless and medical care should be left to the government to provide, its superintendent was too often absent from his office, and so on. As a trainee minister, McKay immediately sat up and took notice. How would the famous Flynn answer such stinging criticisms? What could he possibly say?

Flynn had not lost his composure, appearing to remain relaxed. In response he simply told another round of real-life stories about the AIM and its ministry. Puzzled, Fred was on tenterhooks, waiting for Flynn to address his critics. He never did, at least not directly. It was as if their criticisms had never been voiced. Yet, somehow, they began to assume petty proportions in the light of the stirring events being described. Once comment from the floor ceased and Flynn had finished, there was a warm round of applause.

The younger man had thought much in the interim about how Flynn had dealt with his opponents that night. He concluded that Flynn had been very astute. By not tackling the criticisms directly, he had avoided open conflict and polarisation of opinions. The case histories he had outlined in his "defence" were impossible to argue against either: they had happened and that was that. All that was left to the listeners was to decide whether they liked what had happened, or not. Yes, Flynn had been very clever. Fred looked forward to his sermon.

Once again, however, he was disappointed with Flynn's preaching. The man spoke with conviction but without fire, and had a tendency to ramble. Nevertheless, the congregation appeared to enjoy him.

That night, Flynn asked whether he and McKay might not have a yarn before he had to leave for Brisbane the following morning.

McKay's heart sank. Monday was his day off and he had planned to swim and surf. When he mentioned this to Flynn, the visitor immediately offered to come down to the beach and talk there!

The sea was perfect for surfing and Fred really enjoyed himself. Flynn watched, contentedly smoking his pipe.

Eventually, Fred dragged himself out of the water and walked across to Flynn, a towel around his waist. He could not help thinking how incongruous Flynn looked on the hot sand in his smart suit and waistcoat, stetson hat and boots.

Fred settled down beside his visitor and listened as Flynn started to tell him about the AIM. He began by describing episodes of AIM ministry, interspersed with insights into the vision behind the work. Fred became interested.

After a couple of hours, during which Fred said little, Flynn mentioned that he was looking for the right man for a new patrol in Western Queensland: "Someone to mooch around Coopers' Basin country up as far as Cape York, to penetrate some new and pretty wild areas for us, to build a new hospital for our brave nurses at Birdsville and to oversee the Cloncurry flying-doctor experiment." He did not offer the position to Fred, yet the unspoken challenge was there.

Fred let the fine sand run through his fingers as he listened. Flynn took up a handful too, let it fall through his bony fingers, then looked directly at Fred said, "You know, the sand out at Birdsville is a lot lovelier than this." Something leapt inside Fred when he heard these words. They had a mysterious effect on Fred McKay that he cannot explain to this day.

Finally, Flynn left to catch his train. As he strode along the sand Fred followed behind, stretching out his legs and trying to follow in Flynn's footsteps.

Fred McKay found that Flynn's challenge would not leave him. Was this a sign that God wanted him to be a patrol padre? As the days passed he became increasingly certain of this, but struggled with the decision which would involve such a radical change of direction. He decided to confer with his fiancée, Margaret Robertson, a trainee nurse at the Brisbane General Hospital.

During a stroll in the park he told her of his meeting with Flynn and the strange effect it had had on him. "You know, Meg, my mother dedicated my life to the Lord's service when I was dying as a child. The doctor had given up hope, so she called out to God to save my life and in return pledged me to His service. I think the AIM may be that service. I never intended to work in the bush, so this may be a shock for you. It is for me too."

It was no shock for Meg. She told him a surprising story. Her father, Hubert Robertson, fresh out from Scotland in 1913, had become fascinated by the AIM and found out all he could about it. Before Margaret was born, in 1915, her parents had agreed to dedicate the baby to the work of the AIM. This they duly did, and told Flynn so when he came to stay with them six months later. Mr Robertson then made his baby daughter a member of the AIM's Inland Legion of financial supporters by placing a pound note in her hand to pass over to John Flynn. "Now you are a member of the AIM, called to serve and support our mission," Flynn told the baby solemnly when he had managed to extricate the pound from her grasp. "So you see," Margaret concluded, "I, too, am called to the AIM."

"Do you realise that would mean your coming with me to Birdsville once you have finished your training?" Fred asked her.

"Yes! Birdsville, or Edinburgh, or Timbuktu!"

Fred McKay had reservations as to his own suitability, being only 28 years old. Was that too young to be dealing with rough, tough Inlanders? He expressed these doubts to Flynn, who wrote him a masterly reply, dismissing his concern.

> While it may look odd to appoint one so young to a position of such possibilities, it was not nearly so odd as my appointment to the position of AIM Superintendent – an atrocity which was perpetrated before I had reached the age of thirty-two. The late Dr Meiklejohn ... once pointed out that, however handicapped a young man might be in his experience, he was frequently endowed with a charm of youth which carried him into places that an older man could not penetrate.

He then proceeded to deal with McKay's feelings of inadequacy.

> My own belief is that no man is sufficient for any task handed out to him, but that if he faces the task, the Great Father, day

by day, supplies all rations as they become necessary. A man does not start out ready-made. He is the product of countless emergencies, bravely met and overcome – each of which leaves in his personality its own deposit of wisdom and power.

After contemplating this letter with its insights, Fred McKay decided to accept the position. When preparing himself for his first patrol, he applied to Flynn for detailed instructions.

"I'm not going to tell you what to do. You're an ordained minister of the Church. Go out there and listen to people, just listen. That way you will begin to see what you should do, then do it."

A great deal of valuable advice, McKay was to discover, was encapsulated in these few words.

At his first big mustering camp, he helped brand cattle until he was exhausted. On the third night, the cook, a bit of a wag and a lapsed Catholic, said to him, "If you're a padre, why don't you conduct a church service for us?" and called out to the men to gather around.

The camp-fire yarning stopped and the men came over. They would give the young padre a hearing because he had proved himself. McKay panicked – what should he say? No sermon he had preached before would be suitable. He could not even read from the Bible for lack of light.

"Listen to people," Flynn had said. Well, they had been speaking much about the branding, so he would continue on the same theme. He spoke about how Jesus Christ put his own brand onto those who followed him, and the importance of that brand. He used Flynn's name in the sermon to ensure their attention, a ploy that appeared to work well. It would have been inappropriate to sing anything, so he ended by saying: "Let's say the Lord's Prayer together." Then he got a shock – only he and the cook knew it!

The cook told the men he was going to take up a collection for "the padre", then passed around a tin plate. It arrived at McKay with a big slab of raw beef on it, as a joke. Everyone laughed, Fred included. He felt deeply satisfied with the way things had turned out. For many of those men, this was the first time they had heard the message of God's love and forgiveness.

"Never miss a race meeting," Flynn had advised McKay. "You will meet everyone there." He made sure to attend the meeting at

Innamincka, his first. The policeman who had punted him and his car over the Cooper River recognised the padre. He stood up on a box and shouted out over the crowd, "Hey, you lot! Everyone, be quiet for a moment. This here is Fred McKay, the new AIM padre, one of 'Flynn's mob'. Come and hear what he's got to say."

Here? At a race meeting? What did one say at a race meeting? McKay was helped onto a large petrol drum from where he could see the dozens of faces looking up at him, expectantly. Remembering how Flynn's name had been well received at the mustering camp, he used it again.

"If our good friend John Flynn were here today," he started, "he would say what a privilege it is to be with you all, sharing the fun and excitement of this meeting. Flynn sends his greetings. He also sends out patrol padres like me to be where he cannot be, an extension of his own hands. Yet, you know, Flynn himself is only an extension of the hands of the greatest friend a man could have, the rough hands of a carpenter from a little village called Nazareth. This friend healed people. He forgave the sins of people. He died on a cross to become saviour of the world." McKay kept it short and sharp, and they listened.

That day the padre discovered a key to his ministry, that the name of Flynn was an open door into the hearts and minds of the Outbackers.

Flynn had told him that "our radio valves tell a parable to the bush and our flying doctor shows them Christ". If McKay thought this was an exaggeration he was soon to change his mind. At a race meeting he attended at Gregory Downs a stockman was seriously injured. McKay dashed to his radio and summoned the flying doctor from Cloncurry; this stopped the meeting, and the bystanders witnessed every step of a dramatic rescue. As the plane departed, its shadow cast a cross which raced along the ground and over their feet. One old-timer pointed the stem of his ancient pipe towards the aircraft. "That bloke's the flying Christ," he declared.

John Flynn joined Fred McKay in 1937 on a trip to investigate the medical needs of the Cape York country. He had a second motive for being there – the Queensland Government was contemplating its own Flying Doctor Service, as a replacement for local doctors in outlying communities. Flynn was appalled: a Flying Doctor Service should supplement local medical services, not replace them. His pleas to this end were ignored by the government. What could he do? The Queensland plan would be very expensive. Perhaps he could prove that private endeavour and philanthropy would be cheaper and more effective? To support this contention, Flynn was looking at the possibility of starting a new flying-doctor base in the far north of the state.

Fred learned much about his leader during their trip north. For example, he found that Flynn's genteel habits included changing into long pyjamas each night and hanging his underclothes on a nearby tree. In the morning, he would shave and dress in suit and waistcoat, always looking immaculate in a land where no one else did. Only in extreme heat would he remove his jacket; his waistcoat, never.

One night, the pair made camp early and McKay had dozed off. He awoke later to hear Flynn talking, but not to him. He listened, astonished, to discover that Flynn was praying for his AIM colleagues, mentioning each by name. His prayers were humble but confident, using well-chosen words. Was private prayer the key to his phenomenal success?

At Dunbar, Flynn spent three days talking to the locals. He then went ahead and planned a hospital suited to Dunbar's conditions. It amazed Fred that Flynn could find out so much in so short a time, simply by chatting!

His investigations at Normanton convinced him that another flying doctor was needed who could also serve as Medical Superintendent of both the Normanton and Croydon hospitals. During these discussions, McKay noted a Flynnian technique for overcoming opposition to his plans. "He walked around the objections, almost as if he had not heard them, and kept returning to the main objectives. He never deviated from the big picture." It took time, but it seemed to work.

The next job was to raise money to fund a new flying-doctor base. Flynn decided to approach Artie Fadden in Brisbane, administrator of the large J.S. Love estate, in which £3 000 had been left for approved Flying Doctor work. (Fadden later became Federal Treasurer.) Flynn and McKay drove to Brisbane to arrange an interview with Fadden, not an easy task with so busy a man. At the meeting, Flynn yarned away for over an hour, lighting and relighting his pipe. Not once did he mention Normanton or why he had come to see Fadden. Finally, Fadden had to close the interview, arranging to see Flynn again the following day.

That night, McKay received an unexpected phone call from Artie Fadden. They had known each other since childhood because their families were friends. "What does Flynn want, Fred? When you bring him to the office tomorrow, he'll have to tell me what he's all about. Look, I'll give him what he wants, within reason, but I can't spend much more time with him. Please try to make him say what he wants."

In the car the next morning, on the way to the meeting, McKay told Flynn that Fadden had telephoned and that "he'd like you to put any proposition you have to him straight away". Flynn smiled enigmatically but said nothing.

After they had filed into Fadden's office and sat down, Flynn did not even light up his pipe. Looking directly at Fadden, he voiced his request for support for the Normanton and Dunbar projects. Fadden immediately gave him what he wanted. After a few further minutes of pleasantries, Flynn and McKay left.

In the car returning to the hotel, Fred's curiosity got the better of him. "Why didn't you ask Artie for the support yesterday?" he queried.

"Because he wouldn't have given it to me yesterday. He'd have said 'no' yesterday. If you sense that a person is going to say 'no', don't ask. People find it hard to reverse their decisions." Flynn smiled knowingly as he said this.

The next step was to appoint a flying doctor for the new base. Dr Jean White, who had the best qualifications and references, was selected. Her appointment as the "world's first woman flying doctor" made her the darling of the press. A vivacious but unassuming Christian girl, she was taken aback by all the attention.

She soon proved herself an efficient doctor and was liked and respected at the Croydon Hospital, but serious problems developed at Normanton. Venereal disease was widespread in that community and the men there did not want to be examined by a "sheila". They asked the AIM to remove her. McKay, as the missioner on the spot, was called on to deal with a deteriorating situation. Worse still, he had unwittingly wheeled an Aboriginal woman into a "whites only" ward of the local government hospital which had caused an uproar, despite her "having a close blood relationship to a prominent local cattleman". The locals claimed that the AIM was insensitive to their needs, with the upshot that the Hospital Board terminated Jean White's appointment.

What should he do? McKay's initial reaction was one of outrage – look at all the trouble they had gone to, only to be rejected! He telephoned John Flynn to discuss the crisis. "We will not withdraw from the area, Fred," was Flynn's reaction. "We will continue to serve the people of Normanton and build our bona fides there. Don't look on this as a failure, but as a 'successful failure'. We've miscalculated the sociology of the local situation, so we must learn from our mistake and build for the future. Always look beyond next Christmas. Dr White can continue her flying-doctor work and also run the hospital at Croydon. She will have plenty of work to do, all of it most valuable."

Despite this bad start, Jean White and the new flying-doctor base proved their value in a series of mercy missions. Dr White became known as "Santa Claus" because she often arrived laden with gifts for those she had come to serve. Her skill, compassion and love won her adoration, almost adulation.

In the light of Jean White's success, the Queensland Government abandoned its plans to replace doctors with a Flying Doctor Service of their own. Flynn had won another battle for the good of his pioneers.

The Normanton criticisms amused Flynn and Fred when they discussed them again later. "I find it ironic," said the latter, "that we are accused of being 'racially insensitive' in Normanton, while in the *Messenger* earlier this year we were accused of racialism!"

"The Church is often caught in the middle in such debates, Fred. I also find it ironic, especially when we treat more Aborigines than white people in most of our nursing homes, all free of charge and in Christian love. I won't reply to the criticisms in public, though. We'll let our actions speak louder than words."

Flynn had often expressed concern for Aborigines. In his first edition of *The Inlander* in 1915, he used graphic photographs to draw attention to their problems, calling the situation "a blot on Australia" and asking that compassion, understanding and a "fair go" be accorded them, especially the black women who were badly treated by their own people. Flynn wrote this despite a generally hostile approach to Aborigines by the pioneers, so he was hardly currying favour with his own parishioners. Had God called Flynn to minister to Aborigines, the AIM would no doubt have been of a totally different character. The fact that the organisation did so much good for the indigenous population was almost incidental to its official work among pioneers. A sister mission within the Church had responsibility for caring for Aborigines.

John Flynn was non-racist. Other AIM staff did not necessarily share all his views. The freedom Flynn gave to his workers allowed for a variety of personal opinions which meant that some of the things done and said in the name of the AIM were not in line with Flynn's own thinking.

McKay saw Flynn's compassion for Aborigines, however, reflected many times in AIM actions. Once he and a nurse noticed a swarm of flies over a bundle of rags left by the side of the road, and stopped to investigate. It was a baby girl, an abandoned twin, covered in muck and half-dead.

"Nothing could have stopped that nurse," McKay recalls. "She was overcome with compassion, the same type of compassion that always drove Flynn, something that welled up from deep inside. She gathered up the smelly bundle and we raced away to try to save her. We thought we had failed, but were finally successful. Later, the tribe accepted her back."

The young minister discovered many surprising things about Flynn as they talked in their swags under the stars or bounced along in the truck. For example, despite his happy marriage and many friends, John Flynn was a lonely man. There were parts of him, of his vision, that even his friends could not comprehend, leading to the isolation of feeling "different". Apart from that, Flynn was "unusually unencumbered, innovative, free, open, ready to fail and learn, to leave behind, to be peculiar, to face misunderstanding – and yet to display in every situation the gentleness and courage of a Man of God".

Unconsciously, Flynn modelled the qualities of a spiritual leader to the enthusiastic new padre. One important lesson involved faith. The projected Dunbar Hospital was to be in McKay's patrol; both he and Flynn wanted it started as soon as possible, but the Board required all the funds to be in hand first. Flynn decided to confront the Board on the principle of faith, saying, "God has never let us down; I don't believe He will now. He has always provided the rations when we have needed them."

The Board would not yield; nor would Flynn, and the Convener nearly walked out. Instead, Flynn found an excuse to get up. "The mail should have come in by now, I'll go and check it quickly," he said, and made his exit. They all needed a breather.

A few minutes later Flynn returned, triumphantly waving a cheque for £3 000 sent by Artie Fadden for a hospital at Dunbar!

"Please don't introduce me as 'Superintendent', it sounds too grand," Flynn instructed McKay. "I superintend nothing, I superintend no one. I would prefer, but can't have, the title of 'General Encourager'." This humility permeated every aspect of Flynn's leadership. After McKay had overseen the building of the new Birdsville Hospital in 1937, Flynn came up for the official opening, together with three carloads of other well-wishers. Naturally McKay expected Flynn, as Superintendent, to conduct the program. "No," Flynn told him. "You're the padre here, you take charge of the proceedings."

Another salutary lesson came from Flynn's generosity of spirit. When the Methodist Church criticised his Inland work for not being evangelical enough, Flynn said nothing in defence. The Methodists decided to make up for this supposed lack by forming their own mission, the Methodist Inland Mission. Flynn leapt into action. Here was another group that might be of valuable service to his beloved bush. He wrote them letters of encouragement and offered them any support he was able to give. In this way he slowly built bridges to the Methodist leaders who had been critical of him. Later, he met with them and helped them in their work.

This same generosity was apparent in the way Flynn dealt with the swashbuckling Dr Clive Fenton, whom some saw as a threat to the whole flying-doctor concept. Dr Fenton had applied to be a flying doctor, but wanted to pilot the aeroplane himself, which was against Flynn's "One man one job" principle. Undeterred, he had borrowed money and bought his own aeroplane in which he pulled off some amazing solo mercy flights in the Northern Territory, capturing popular imagination. Did Flynn see him as a threat to his flying-doctor structure? When McKay asked, Flynn replied, "Fenton is no threat.

He's a one-off, and best of luck to him. We don't need 'one-offs' though, we're here to stay. We're building something permanent."

When Fenton was in danger of having his licence suspended for reckless flying, Flynn, by now highly influential, wrote a personal plea for leniency. The reason? If Fenton could not fly, some Outbackers might suffer.

What inspired McKay most of all about Flynn's modus operandi was that "he entered people's lives and served them every way he could, demonstrating the love of Christ in practical ways".

In turn, Flynn must have discerned some special qualities in the younger man because he remarked to Simpson, "I believe Fred McKay has leadership in him." Did the older man see in him the son he never had, as one biographer has suggested? Or was he "Crown Prince"? Whatever Flynn was thinking, typically he kept it to himself.

Flynn inspired a peculiar dedication in his AIM Family. One of them wrote:

> If you had worked with him for half a lifetime or for few or many years, the result was the same: always a keen desire to do anything he suggested. Many men can keep interest at a high level among the workers by their presence. John Flynn did better. Even though we knew we might not see him again for months, or perhaps years, the flame burned on. To have worked in the AIM Family was to belong for all time. Enthusiasm and desire to fulfil his wishes never died.

Prayer and example were important factors in his ability to inspire others, but Flynn also had the ability to sell dreams. As Professor Ronald MacIntyre of Theological Hall, Sydney, expressed it: "You listen to him, thinking what an impractical visionary he is, and before you know where you are you are helping him do it."

All the while, John Flynn continued to establish new flying-doctor bases. With Allan Vickers fully occupied in Western Australia, he and George Simpson had to do all the negotiating and preparation themselves, without the help of a bureaucratic staff.

As each base was completed, Flynn would inscribe its range of operation on his map of the Inland. With each new circle, the mantle of safety came one step nearer to reality. Now only Alice Springs required cover. How could he raise funds for a base at the Alice?

Flynn heard that Adelaide Meithke, OBE, wanted to establish a "flying sister" at Port Augusta, to commemorate the great work of pioneer women in South Australia. Miss Meithke was the dynamic president of the Women's Council and the concept was part of South Australia's Centenary Year celebrations.

As soon as he heard of her plan, Flynn arranged to meet with Miss Meithke in Adelaide.

Flynn found the secretary of the Women's Council, Phoebe Watson, with Miss Meithke. Nothing daunted, he soon had all three of them kneeling over a large map of Australia. Using his thumb as a pivot, Flynn drew circles with his forefinger around each flying-doctor base. "Each of these circles represents the range of the flying doctor at that base," Flynn explained. "Now, look at the dead centre of Australia, around Alice Springs. There is no cover at all for this area. Which region do you think your brave pioneering women of South Australia would have preferred to cover? Central Australia, where their fellow pioneers suffer for lack of adequate medical cover, or Port Augusta, where medical facilities exist already?" He gave the women his shrewd, measured look, checking for chinks in their armour. .

"The money has been raised in our state with an understanding it would be used in South Australia, not Central Australia," Miss Meithke countered. "Our flying sister would perform a service which is lacking in South Australia. She would fly to outlying areas and bring nursing and companionship to lonely homesteads. Flying doctors are very good, but sometimes women need to speak to another woman about the things that are concerning them."

"That has some merit," Flynn agreed. "However, listen to what a flying doctor can achieve. He is a pioneer himself, to pioneering women and their families. Our wireless also overcomes the chill of isolation out there." Flynn proceeded to describe incident after incident where the FDS had helped pioneering women.

It took many hours of persuasion, until early in the morning, before the two women were won over. Five thousand pounds, and other support, was given from Adelaide for the establishment of a base in Alice Springs. This began operation in 1939.

A mantle of safety now covered the Inland. Ironically, the Second World War was about to begin, threatening to sweep aside all Flynn's dreams.

23

WARTIME

"I am just a 'stoker' in the ship of the AIM," was how John Flynn described his role, but in 1939 the Presbyterian Church chose to make him their 'captain' by electing him to the position of Moderator-General. This is the highest office in the Presbyterian Church, with a three-year tenure. In his letter of acceptance, Flynn wrote:

> At such a turn of life's wheel, one is forced to realise one's limitations; but with the help of my brethren, and under the kindliness of the Great Father, I will do my share in the building of that mysterious Kingdom of our Lord and Saviour.

The AIM throughout Australia burst with pride at this appointment. So did many a bushman. "Our Flynn", as he was commonly known around campfires, had become a legend: "Flynn will try anything", one of their sayings went. "He would even try to make water run uphill. Tell you what, he'd get it halfway up too!"

The office of Moderator-General was more than ceremonial. It allowed Flynn to promote certain Church policies he held dear. One was the pursuit of Christian unity.

Flynn had always believed in a unity that cut across denominational ties, basing it on Jesus Christ's prayer for his disciples shortly before he died: "May they be brought to complete unity to let the world know that you sent me" (John: chapter 17, verse 23). Realising that the unity Jesus had prayed for needed to be visible, he commented:

> If the world sees theological discussion, it is not impressed and seldom even interested, but if it sees Christians of different denominations rolling up their shirt sleeves and labouring together on the same task, it is impressed. We must work together before we concern ourselves with theology: that can come later if we desire it.

This emphasis on first working together made Flynn's approach to ecumenism different. As he wrote: "It is a strange thing that some of the men who are keenest on corporate church union are deadly enemies of anything in the way of co-operation."

Flynn's approach to ecumenism had found little expression in the AIM because this was usually the only Christian ministry in a given area. As Moderator-General, however, he now had the opportunity to model how to achieve unity, and he selected Darwin for his attempt.

He decided that a recreational centre in Darwin for the troops stationed there was important. He had opened similar clubs elsewhere to supply an alternative pastime for heavy-drinking youngsters, with great success. Flynn met with Reverend John Burton of the Methodist Church, who agreed to co-operate on building the centre. The two worked so well together that they planned further joint projects. The Congregational Church joined in with them.

When the Inter-Church Welfare Club was opened in June 1940, Flynn organised a large turnout by the AIM. The whole complex was to be managed on a co-operative basis by Presbyterians, Methodists and Congregationalists. This proved such a success that it was a basis for the three denominations joining together to form the United Church in 1946 in the Northern Territory, and eventually the Uniting Church throughout Australia. It is significant that at the time of union in 1977 there was discord in every state except the Northern Territory, where the three denominations had been working together for over 30 years. Flynn's principle of working together before seeking formal unity had been validated.

—

Many AIM workers volunteered for the defence forces during the war and staffing shortages became critical. Holes threatened to appear in the mantle of safety. Flynn improvised: for example, Dr Harold Dicks became the first flying doctor to pilot his own plane. On one such occasion, he had to circle in the air and watch Port Hedland being bombed before he could land safely with his patient. (Harold Dicks was another of Flynn's "turn-around men" – he had been on his way to England to study plastic surgery when he came under the charismatic leader's spell. Instead, he became a fine flying doctor.)

Flynn was now a national figure. What part could he play in helping his country at war? He immediately placed the AIM on a war footing and at the disposal of the government. He donned khaki garb himself and the Inland saw him for the first time without a suit. But in his speeches, even during the blackest moments of the conflict, he expressed a positive optimism. For all the hustle and bustle and turmoil, nothing seemed to disturb his leisureliness of manner. What was the basis of his buoyant outlook? He expressed it this way in a letter to his wife: "I hope you are able to regard this ramshackle old world as the dream – very pleasant on the whole, but badly damaged by nightmares – and the unseen things as the Realities."

In 1940 flying doctor Gordon Alberry and his pilot, Captain Berry, went missing. Many search flights failed to find any trace of them. Perhaps this was the tragedy that the pessimists had predicted for so long? Flynn called the AIM throughout Australia to prayer, and pushed for the aerial searches to be intensified.

What had happened was that Alberry and Berry, blown offcourse, had crash-landed in flooded country as a result of engine failure and filthy weather. They had emerged largely unhurt and waded from the damaged plane, in waist-deep water, to a patch of higher ground. Their quick scrutiny had shown that the radio had been badly damaged in the crash.

The days passed without any sign of rescue. Alberry noted his own and Berry's weakening condition without proper food, only three milk tablets per day, and decided he must make a bid to walk out, although he did not know their location. All he knew was that they were somewhere between the Gregory River and Burketown. Captain Berry would stay near the plane in case it was yet spotted, although the chances of that seemed increasingly remote because they had been blown many miles off course.

A remarkable incident then occurred. A burst of terrible weather followed, so violent that it also blew a QANTAS aeroplane miles off course. The pilot was Captain Eric Donaldson, the ex-FDS pilot. When the cloud cover broke for just a few minutes, he was amazed to see the missing aeroplane right below him! He flew in a circle and saw a man waving frantically. He dropped some much needed food.

Alberry, meanwhile, had succeeded in reaching Punjaub Station. Hastily organising a rescue party, though exhausted, he stumbled off with them in the hope of rescuing Berry. Soon both men were safely back in Cloncurry and recuperating from their ordeal.

Also in 1940, and to his immense surprise, Flynn had a doctorate conferred on him by McGill University in Montreal. He was usually addressed as Dr Flynn from that time.

The war hotted up, leaving Australia in great danger from the north. As long ago as 1918 Flynn had issued warning that an attack against Australia would likely come by air from this direction. His call for the installation of an air defence system had been scorned by the military. Sadly, Flynn was proved right when around a hundred Japanese bombers droned in from the sea in early 1942 and pounded Darwin, killing 233 people and wounding 250 others. Sixty-four air raids followed, some on targets other than Darwin. Broome and Wyndham were pounded in a manner that suggested an invasion was imminent.

Australia had never before been under direct attack. Flynn immediately pledged the AIM to an all-out war effort; nurses, patrol padres and wireless staff served with distinction in the battle zones. AIM buildings became troop hospitals or were used as homes for Army nurses. Six patrol padres served as chaplains to the forces. Flynn travelled everywhere, giving encouragement, lifting morale.

Lacking an adequate wireless network themselves, it was humiliating for the defence forces that they were now forced to use Flynn's extensive network. General MacArthur himself wrote that Traeger's transceiver was "one of the most useful pieces of equipment for communication purposes over the spaces of continental Australia".

The Inlanders became the eyes and ears of the defence forces, their "guardian angels", reporting anything suspicious. They were given charts of silhouettes of enemy aircraft to enable them to report these accurately. Their instructions were not to mention on radio any Australian troop, ship or cattle movements, the weather or road conditions – or anything else that could be of value to an enemy "listening in". The people of the northern frontiers proved to be suitably discreet. An investigation in 1946 confirmed that "no information of value was ever let slip" over the radio network.

Transceivers were also used by the Army and police. The sets were now lighter and operated with a vibrator unit, so it was no longer necessary to pedal, though Outbackers still said, "I heard you on the 'pedal' yesterday ..."

A special clandestine operation using Traeger's transceivers was set up in Arnhem Land, in the north, to spy on and monitor Japanese troop movements. Maurie Anderson enlisted and was used in the north because of his expertise with transceivers. Full details of their activities are yet to be told.

The *Flying Doctor* magazine of 1943 reported one interesting case of civilian vigilance, regarding the suspicious use of radio by other unidentified civilians.

> The party [of civilians] was armed with a short wave wireless plant of the most compact and sinister appearance and manned by a foreign-looking gang, complete with all the outward signs and symbols of spydom as known to the best Authors. Even the "Man-With-Dark-Glasses" who haunts all secret service fiction was there ...

> A posse then went out, armed to the teeth with Owen guns, Tommy guns, Bren guns. Its first glimpse of the party it was trailing caused it hurriedly to jamb home its magazines and take off the safety catches. A very neat transmitting set certainly was operating, a receiving set ditto! (The "Dark Glasses" were also clearly visible.)

> Strange syllables floated down wind, which seemed to be of foreign and trans-Atlantic vintage, and the fact that the conversation sounded trivial made it clear that it was couched in a secret code. (That it contained no profanity made it seem certain that the villains were not Australian mountaineers.)

> Firmly clutching its weapons, the intelligence unit moved to the attack. The unresisting wireless crew was captured intact with all its materials! (including the "Dark Glasses")

> It proved, upon being sorted out, to consist of John Flynn showing some American visitors the mysteries of the flying doctor communication system!

Lighter moments such as these were welcome in wartime.

In 1942 the AAMS was officially renamed the Flying Doctor Service, which was the term most widely used already. (It became the Royal Flying Doctor Service, or RFDS, in 1956). In the battle zone, the FDS attended to war injuries, advised the military on possible airfields, flying conditions and resources in isolated areas, and became involved in covert operations, such as organising certain guerrilla groups. Pioneers and Aborigines came together as enthusiastic members of these groups, which helped to break down racial barriers.

What of Flynn's co-workers in the Flying Doctor Service, Allan Vickers and George Simpson? Could they take Flynn's concept of "air ambulances evacuating the wounded", first published in 1918, and run with it now? Both were too tied up in the early stages of the war to do more than discuss the concept with Flynn, but they kept the vision.

Lieutenant Colonel Vickers was sent to Perth and developed a fine, modern hospital there. Irrepressible as ever, he contacted Squadron Leader Simpson of the RAAF, and together they worked to adapt a twin-engined D.H. Dragon into an air ambulance. It carried a crew of three with eight wounded men, seven on stretchers and one sitting. The design drew heavily on their experiences with the Flying Doctor Service.

These air ambulances became the "working end" of Number 1 Ambulance Unit, the first of its type in the world. The unit saw distinguished service in the Middle East and the Pacific Islands, in one month alone flying 28 000 miles and evacuating 799 seriously wounded men from the front. Overall, it served to evacuate more than 5 000 casualties from the front line. Flynn, whose early interest in first aid, the Red Cross and saving lives had never waned, drew great satisfaction from these results. Not only had his friends produced the first air ambulance unit, but it was ultra-efficient and became the model for those that followed.

The interest of the defence forces in his transceiver brought Traeger's work back into the limelight. He was awarded the OBE in 1944. This extremely shy man, now 48, was overwhelmed when told he would be presented with his award by the King. He dashed around to his friends, asking what he could do to avoid it – his nerves had been so bad at his last public appearance, where he was simply asked to say a few words, that he had vomited. He could not bear the thought of a public ceremony, yet he did not wish to be rude. After weeks of agony, Alf Traeger arranged to be given his award privately and without ceremony.

Had he possessed an entrepreneurial spirit, Traeger could have made much money from his inventions. As it was, his financial affairs were a disaster. The FDS came in twice a year to sort out the shambles that characterised his business life. His bookwork was virtually non-existent and bits of paper and accounts were squirrelled away in boxes and drawers. The FDS's motive for helping was partly to prevent their communications expert going bankrupt, which could have spelt disaster for the whole wireless network. At each visit, Traeger would blink self-consciously at their censure, then get back to fiddling with whatever circuit he was working on at the time.

One publicised fact gave Traeger great satisfaction. Since the tragic failure of his set at Birdsville in 1929, no transceiver of his had failed during an emergency.

The FDS was making strides of its own. It had developed a standard medical kit in 1942 that was given to all radio outposts. This greatly facilitated diagnosis and treatment over the radio. For example, the doctor could ask the patient over the air to check out various parts of the body by referring to the chart which had been provided. Some Outbackers used their own ingenuity regarding the contents of the medical packs. One reported that he had run out of pills in bottle number eight, so had used pills from bottles five and three instead, as these added up to the same thing!

Vickers was honourably discharged from the Army in 1943, his asthma having caused him serious health problems. He returned to Queensland so that Lilias could visit her family and he could consider his own future. He was uncertain what course to follow, but thought to take up private practice as he wanted his children to grow up with the educational advantages of city life. He popped in to see John Flynn in Brisbane, who within minutes was asking him what he intended to do next.

"I'm not certain."

"Have you a job?"

"No, not yet."

"Yes, you have, as of this minute. We need someone to start a new base at Charleville. You will be ideal for that challenge."

Vickers protested, but his good friend eventually prevailed, as usual. He went on to set up the Charleville base from scratch, making a great success of it. (Incidentally, both Vickers' sons grew up to be respected medical specialists in their own right, despite their lack of schooling in the city.)

Allan Vickers' return to the FDS showed how much influence John Flynn still exercised, that he could assure Vickers he had employment "as of this minute". Flynn had become the respected "elder statesman" of the FDS. He sat in on policy meetings and his advice was constantly sought. The AIM maintained a close working relationship with the FDS – AIM hospitals and patrol padres were vital to the mantle of safety. The patrol padres carried out much of the radio installation and repair work during their ministry trips.

One criticism of Flynn during the Second World War was that he spent too much time on flying-doctor business. "We have married our daughter off to the Australian public," he responded, "but we still have our family ties." In fact, he was busy welding together the different state bodies into one cohesive national operation. This was an important role that only he could fulfil at that time.

In Vicker's view:

> Had there been no John Flynn, there would have been no Royal Flying Doctor Service today. People have said to me that even if John Flynn had not thought of it, a Flying Doctor Service would eventually have started spontaneously as aircraft became a more practical means of transport. But a FDS has not yet started in the USA, although that country is the most advanced in the world in its development of light aircraft flying, and American friends assure me that there is a very great need for an airborne service in parts of their country.

As the bloodletting stopped and peace returned, Flynn told Allan Vickers, "I can hardly wait for conditions to return to normal in the bush. There are things that need to be done that I couldn't get started because of wartime constraints."

Even in his sixties, Flynn was as irrepressible as ever. He still had dreams he longed to implement.

NEW VISION

24

After the war John Flynn and Fred McKay, who had served with distinction as a command chaplain for three years in the deserts of the Middle East, had a joyful reunion.

"The war has really opened up the Inland," Flynn told him. "Roads have improved, water is more readily obtainable and some of the towns have grown. A number of men who served there say they plan to return to settle. I'm told the wireless network is really humming. For us, this means new challenges and new opportunities."

"Dr Flynn, I won't be coming back into the field immediately," McKay said. "Meg and I haven't seen each other for over three years. Even before that, we never had a home life. We need that for now. We've been married seven years and want to build a family. So I'll take a parish in Brisbane instead and see what transpires."

For once Flynn was speechless. After a few seconds he recovered, to a degree. "Yes, of course. That will be good, at least for the present."

McKay's decision was difficult for him to accept. He did not disagree with it; his problem was in trying to comprehend it. He knew Fred's heart was in the Inland: how, then, could he bear to stay away, regardless of the sacrifices which had to be made?

As part of coming to terms with the situation, Flynn told McKay he was sad he'd not had children of his own. His marriage to Jean late in life had its compensations, but there were no children. On top of this, he spent too few days with his wife because of his constant travelling. "As he mused over my decision," McKay conjectures, "I think he began to understand more fully the sacrifices his own patrol padres had made over the years." The work was less difficult and dangerous than when Plowman and Gibson had cracked under the strain, but separation from loved ones remained a stumbling block.

John Flynn got on with his plans. The plight of very old bushmen (and women) was concerning him, as it had over the years. These proud, independent men and women were miserable if they had to spend their final years dependent on relatives. They were even more out of place in old people's homes in the big cities. What could he do? His answer was to develop a "camp for old-timers", where they could spend their twilight years in the company of like-minded pioneers. Where best to situate such a camp? He chose Alice Springs.

He settled on a picturesque setting at the foot of Mount Blatherskite, on the edge of the Todd River. Flynn paced out the 30 self-contained units he planned, for those who could "do" for themselves. He also planned a community lounge, dining room and administration centre. For those who required it, there would be a hospital ward.

> This will be a place where the old-timers can remain or maybe rest awhile in a land they understand. Eventually, we will have similar settlements scattered through all the distant places of Australia. These will assure men who have lived their lives in the freedom of the great open spaces that they will not have to end them miserably in the cold confines of some Old Men's Home in the city.

The first building, designed by Flynn himself, went up in 1949. Flynn was excited as he watched the men erecting it. He wandered about and planned where vegetable gardens should be developed, flowers and shrubs planted and further extensions constructed. The dreamer was in his element. "This will become a model for the care of our elderly," he said.

He was right. The settlement became a showpiece, but only after sacrificial input by his staff. Flynn, though most appreciative, considered hard work as worthwhile in itself: "The reason so many people are not happy in their work," he would say, "is that they do not do their best at it."

One of the old-timers at the home was Dick Gillen, Bruce Plowman's faithful "camel boy" all those years before. It seemed fitting that old Dick, still fit and frisky, should benefit from the AIM home. Fred McKay later arranged a reunion between Dick and

Bruce Plowman, an emotional and joyful meeting. Dick sent Plowman a charming letter, an extract from which states:

> I am a thousand times please to hear from you ... Old Timers Homes is a wonderful place to live while we are alive ... We are having our show at Traeger Park on the 27th and 28th of this months. They are having all sports here now, not like when I was little boy ... I will always remember you and with all my heart because you grow me up and good to know you and Mrs Plowman. Kindest regards to you both. From your old camel boy. Dick Gillen.

Another of Flynn's projects came to fruition at this time. For years, he had wanted a film to be made that would present the reality of life in the Inland. "The media shapes our world," Flynn said. As a first-rate propagandist, he had always taken an interest in films. In fact, he was a pioneer member of the Religious Films Society, sending them a yearly donation and sitting in on their meetings whenever he could. He wanted films to be accurate, though, and had refused to help in the making of an early film on the flying doctors, because it had the makings of a "B-class romance".

In 1947 came the opportunity he had been hoping for – a black-and-white documentary based around one of Skipper Partridge's Outback patrols. Titled *The Inlanders*, it met Flynn's exacting standards for visual excellence and genuineness of content. *The Inlanders* became a support feature in town and country cinemas throughout Australia and in the United Kingdom. Flynn himself saw the film many times without tiring of it, and encouraged others to go along.

Flynn's compassion drove him to new endeavours. He heard of bush mothers, isolated and fearful, who died soon after childbirth for lack of after-care. Often their babies died with them. What he dreamed of was a home where they could be cared for and acquire the skills to enable them to stand on their own two feet, a home they could come to in confidence both before and after delivery. Where should such a place be located? The answer turned out to be Alice Springs. The hospital Flynn had built there in 1926 had become redundant in 1939 when the government erected its own. The original building was far too good to be left idle, so it was turned into a home for women personnel of the armed forces. At the end of the war, Flynn was free once again to decide on its use. It suited his concept perfectly! He turned it into the Bush Mothers' Hostel.

Flynn's social revolution had led to a great increase in the number of children in the bush. Their needs came to absorb more and more of his attention. The yearly AIM camp at Glenelg in Adelaide ministered to the physical, social and medical needs of disadvantaged children, but Flynn wanted to establish a bigger and more permanent ministry. He sought out a suitable site himself, deciding on the palatial residence "Warrawee" at the Grange, Adelaide, with its large beach frontage and easy access to good medical facilities, including nearby specialists who would give their services free of charge. When Flynn found his Board unenthusiastic about another large financial commitment, he set about arranging funds himself.

Over the years, Warrawee did a magnificent job. There was no discrimination of colour or creed and a feature of the camp was the bonding that developed between children of different races. For the majority of these disadvantaged youngsters – some of them handicapped – the camps were the highlight of their young lives, recalled with pleasure for years to come.

One of Flynn's enduring dreams for young people in the bush was to improve the education they received. In the 1932 AIM handbook he proposed that radio be used to help "in home education, to supplement excellent work already being done by Education Departments". He dreamed of children connected to a teacher at a "mother" station, and thereby to each other. A 1936 article in the Brisbane *Courier-Mail* shows how he envisaged this in practice:

> The work of educating the children of isolated Outback areas of the State, which is now being carried on by the correspondence section of the Education Department, will be supplemented by a two-way wireless service. The children will not only be able to hear their teachers talking to them and giving them lessons, but will be able to ask questions of their teachers, and so get an immediate answer.

The same article showed why Flynn had not yet been able to do more than dream.

> Work on this plan will be undertaken as soon as the medical
> section of the AIM has been properly provided for and the
> anxiety of establishing these services has been lifted.

Another obstacle was that Traeger was extraordinarily busy at the time and could not give Flynn's plans the attention they deserved. It was left to a good friend of Flynn's, the remarkable Adelaide Meithke, to bring the idea to fruition. Miss Meithke was the person who had decided to support Flynn's idea of starting a FDS base at Alice Springs. Typically, she served the Alice Springs base enthusiastically, becoming the first woman president of a state section of the FDS. It was through this involvement that she travelled to Alice Springs in 1944 and spoke to various Outback children en route. As a former teacher, she was appalled at the obvious deficiencies in their education by correspondence and determined to do something about it.

During her stay in the centre, Miss Meithke heard of the mothercraft lessons that were given over the FDS network. Would it be possible to use the network to help children with their schoolwork? The technical answer was "yes". So began the concept of the "School of the Air".

It took years of effort to set up because this was a new and untried field. Special techniques had to be devised for a classroom size of 50 000 square miles.

The School of the Air eventually began its experimental broadcasts in 1950 and has since grown into a network of bases. Now called Distance Education, it delivers a vastly improved education to the isolated children of the Inland, operating each weekday, mornings and afternoons, for several hours. Pupils may interrupt the teachers by asking questions during the lesson, and so benefit from direct interaction, just as Flynn envisaged. They can also tell stories, take part in radio plays, and speak to each other. Travelling teachers supplement the broadcast lessons.

In the post-war years, Flynn's view of the development of the Inland was at variance with those of political parties. His idea was not to replace the solitude of the Inland with smoking cities, but rather to take it as it was and to help the pioneers live reasonable lives there. Politicians saw it another way; for example, they applauded the fact that improved roads were increasing the tonnage of road transport and that many men who had served in the Outback during the war were returning there to live. Flynn saw that while such progress was potentially good, the changes could impact adversely on the pioneers. He stated:

> Pastoral holdings must always be large and neighbours must necessarily be many miles apart – 50 to 100 miles being commonplace. However, cutting up some of the former large company stations will not help. It will remove the communities that grew up around the old station headquarters, social interaction will diminish and men will "go it alone". I also fear the revolution in transport which is already starting. Outback towns will die as trucks and cars thunder past, no longer needing their services. This progress will increase isolation rather than solve it. We are in danger of condemning our brave Inlanders to be pioneers permanently.

Flynn reiterated his policy to his patrol padres.

> Do not pass by the lonely hut near the highway, but find its normal occupant. Then minister to him, so that he will know he is both loved and important to the Church.

In his seventieth year, in 1950, Flynn was asked to look over and make suggestions for the fourth edition of the *Flying Doctor Service* booklet. He arranged to have an evening at home with Jean in order to do this.

He settled into his comfortable chair, lit his pipe and chatted to Jean as he read over the manuscript. "I like the cover," he said. "What do you think of it?" He held it up for her to see.

"That must be Alf Traeger sitting at his transceiver with an aeroplane flying overhead, but what are the camels doing underneath the transceiver?"

"It's a composite, a theme picture, depicting communications in the Inland. I rather like it. Now let me see what it's like on the inside." He adjusted his spectacles and settled back to read.

They sat in contented silence for a few minutes. He was surprised that the booklet spent so much time describing his early vision and efforts: the nursing homes, the wireless network, the flying doctors.

"How are you finding it, Jack?"

"OK, but they make it sound as if I did it all by myself without the help of the Great Father and all my friends. My mythical self again," he grumbled. He himself saw his life as a stage on which a number of great actors had performed, but too often writers made it sound as though he alone had achieved everything.

When he reached the details of recent developments, he was pleased. "This is better, Jean. 'It must always be remembered that the FDS was born in a spiritual atmosphere; fostering the morale of the pioneer is a basic principle.' I like that."

A few minutes later, he held up a photograph for Jean to look at. "Here's a picture of Myra Blanch, crossing flood water between an aeroplane and a homestead. She's a game girl, our Myra. As our first flying sister, she is doing the work Adelaide Meithke wanted done. Adelaide must be pleased about it."

"What does it say about Myra?"

"It says, 'The work of the flying sister is not to assist the doctor on his flights, but to watch over the welfare of the womenfolk and the children at their isolated outposts.' It goes on to describe the many ways in which she does this. Her work answers the need that Jeannie Gunn brought to my attention way back in 1912, that women need other women to talk to from time to time. Of course, our radio network also helps."

A short while later, he read out the description of the work of the flying dentist, another recent extension of the services offered.

"Don't you think they should give more examples from people's lives?" Jean asked, when he had finished.

"I would, if I was writing it," he concurred.

A little later, he said to her, "They do quote a case history, right at the end of the booklet. It concerns some newcomers to the Inland. I'll read it to you:

> They had come from Victoria to a government job in the far north. Little did they dream of the rigours of dust and climate. Within six months, Jean, a fair-haired lass of five years, was developing trachoma – that dread disease of the eye. To whom could they turn but to the flying doctor? There was no other medical man for hundreds of miles.

'May I come too?' asked the distressed mother, as the doctor stepped out of the plane on the saltpan landing ground.

'I'm sorry,' said the doctor. 'We are overcrowded – another patient on board – a black boy with a broken leg.'

Picture that mother handing over her clinging child to a strange doctor, who was going to take her to a strange hospital 250 miles away! 'You'll look after her, won't you, doctor?' pleaded the mother between her tears, 'and see that she has her doll to play with in bed tonight?'

'Yes,' replied the doctor, 'I'll do that and much more. We'll bring her back to you well and happy.'

Jean did come back – well once more.

The FDS means much to the mothers of the Outback."

As he settled back to chat further with Jean after reading over the booklet, John Flynn felt a deep sense of thankfulness. His dreams had, indeed, come true.

He would have felt less at peace had he known about the storm that was about to break over his life.

25

LEGACY

As the forces gathered to shift him from office, John Flynn, always quiet and self-controlled in the midst of turmoil, retained his equanimity. He never lowered himself to bicker and squabble despite the virulent criticism to which he was at times subjected.

Opposition to his continuing as Superintendent had been gathering for a while among members of his Board, who felt he was too old and was losing his grip. True, he looked elderly now, and haggard, and his thin brown hair had silvered around the temples. At times his yarns became more rambling than ever, causing some friends to avoid his company unless they had time on their hands. Despite this, his mind was still razor-sharp and his vision for the future far ahead of any who sat in judgement of him.

Flynn realised he must make plans for future leadership. No one had acted as his deputy, so there was no obvious successor. He decided the AIM had more chance of survival if it did not depend too heavily on one new, unprepared leader, so he decided to divide the ministry into three areas: "regional seniors" would be appointed from among experienced patrol padres to oversee each section. They would carry out their task under his general guidance.

Flynn developed his plan carefully, consulting with many people in the AIM, and out of it, to refine the details. Then came the crucial debate at Executive level in March 1950. Flynn's plans were criticised, and when it came to the vote, not one member of the Executive supported his plan. This was tantamount to a vote of no confidence in his leadership. Later, a full Board meeting confirmed the decision with another unanimous vote. It was decided to nominate a new Superintendent and relegate Flynn to the position of Superintendent Emeritus from September 1951.

Privately, Flynn felt stabbed in the back, confused and hurt that no Board member had come to his defence. Obviously, much had been going on behind the scenes about which he knew nothing. Publicly, he handled his forced position with grace, making the point that perhaps a man should not hold onto high office beyond the age of seventy.

He applied himself immediately to the critical question of who should be the next Superintendent. If the wrong man succeeded him, the AIM could easily collapse due to financial straits and other serious problems. The successor must be a man not only respected throughout the AIM, but also possessing outstanding leadership and diplomatic skills in order to deal with the Board, businessmen and politicians. Skipper Partridge, who had the respect and leadership skills, could have been a candidate but was unwilling to do head-office work in Sydney.

John Flynn became convinced that Fred McKay was the only viable successor. McKay, though, was no longer in the AIM, but was happily settled in his parish in Brisbane.

Within weeks, he was to receive a letter from the Chairman of the Board inviting him to accept nomination as Flynn's successor. He immediately referred to Flynn, who sent him the following letter of endorsement.

> Our AIM is in rough waters, as we all are, and I know of no one who could handle the tiller better than you could, for others in sight are not rock-and-shoal conscious ... I hope ... you will accept – even though you may do so in fear and trembling. I don't think a man can succeed in a very responsible task unless he is afraid of it.

McKay was happy in his Brisbane parish and had no illusions about the difficulty of taking on the leadership after John Flynn. It would be an almost impossible task. Not surprisingly, he hesitated.

Flynn came to Toowong for a week and stayed with him. They did little else but talk about the situation. Despite what had happened to him, Flynn repeatedly encouraged McKay to take on the job, no matter what.

Skipper Partridge also endorsed McKay's nomination in a private letter to him. In it he expressed outrage at the way Flynn had been treated.

> Dare the Assembly decide to pension Flynn off? ... The AIM is Flynn, and Flynn is the AIM. He is the greatest asset we possess, and will remain such until he dies. Nobody can put him in a corner under a cloak and expect him to be forgotten and unheard. The paucity of leaders within our Church today is surely deplorable, and are we going to shelve the greatest?

In this period of turmoil, with the Board no longer referring to him regarding AIM policy, Flynn decided to commence leave prior to retirement. At a final "setting apart" service held in Brisbane on 11 March 1951 for two nurses, he delivered an inspiring address, his diction clear and concise. Several members of the congregation that day recorded afterwards how moved they had been by his sermon. At least two, though, noticed an unhealthy yellowing to his skin and how he seemed to drag himself about.

Flynn was obviously jaundiced by the time he returned to Sydney. He resisted Jean's advice to see a doctor, but agreed to "rest up a little" so that his strength could return. Early in May, however, as he entered the Ashfield church, he stumbled and would have fallen except for willing hands that supported him. "Silly me, I am so sorry. Thank you for your help," he said, embarrassed that he had caused anyone trouble. During the service itself he collapsed, and within minutes was being rushed to hospital by ambulance.

Dr George Simpson, Flynn's great friend, was at his bedside when he opened his eyes again later. He then passed into a coma. He was suffering from painless liver cancer and was beyond surgical help.

On the 5 May 1951, a unique soul left this earth.

John Flynn's death was marked by a two-minute silence over the national broadcasting service, a sign of respect unprecedented in Australian history.

Jean Flynn wandered about the house in a state of shock. She found it difficult packing her husband's things. She picked up his quart pot, blackened by countless campfires, and remembered the times they had lain under a carpet of stars, to awaken next morning to birdsong.

Flynn had left his desk in a typical shambles. Absentmindedly, she began to clear it. Underneath his teacup was a note, "I would like to meet this teacup at ten tomorrow morning". Flynn often left messages like this for her to find. It was all too much. She sat down and wept.

When she was able to resume her task she put to one side the business to which she would have to attend. This was when she discovered what she already suspected – his bank account was empty! Flynn had never accumulated money or material possessions.

At Flynn's funeral service at St Stephen's Church, Sydney, two women noticed one another. Each found the other strangely familiar. When they spoke together after the service, they discovered they had been friends and neighbours for 20 years over the wireless network without ever having met. It was out of profound gratitude for Flynn's ministry that they had attended the service that day. John Flynn would have smiled happily to hear their excited, friendly chatter.

Many were the epitaphs for John Flynn. A most appropriate one, though unintentional, had been written by the man himself in the 1916 copy of *The Inlander*. He was describing the four "chapters" found in many great lives:

CHAPTER I; Dreams
CHAPTER II; Struggles
CHAPTER III; Attainment
CHAPTER IV; Faith and Service

And somehow, all unite in assuring us that there was enduring sense in Grandfather's theory that every man needs to be born twice. It is not enough to be delivered into the world all ready to scream lustily. There must be a second birth – when the dreamer says with confidence "I WILL!"

Our forefathers held that this second life must be of such a quality and origin as to withstand the shock of "dust to dust"; which seems a very necessary view.

Flynn believed that by saying "I WILL" to Jesus Christ, he would experience that second birth of which he wrote so eloquently, and would thereby be assured, through God's promise, that his life would continue beyond "dust to dust" and "ashes to ashes".

His ashes, nevertheless, needed to be dealt with. What should be done with them? Flynn had once remarked to Jean while climbing Mt Gillen that it would be a lovely place to be buried, its stark landscape strikingly coloured in the crystal air. Mt Gillen was especially appropriate because its position, a few miles from Alice Springs, was close to the centre of the Inland.

His friends mobilised themselves to fulfil Flynn's wish. Kingsley Partridge was chosen to deliver the address at the interment of the ashes at the foot of Mt Gillen on 23 May 1951. The entourage of 80 cars slowly wound its way out from Alice Springs along a road graded and watered to prevent dust problems. Shops in Alice Springs closed for two hours as a mark of respect.

Jean Flynn chose not to be present, so Skipper wrote a description of the scene for her in a long letter:

> Over 500 people gathered on the little flat across Chinaman Creek ... a glorious vista to Mt Gillen and the range face is seen through a wide avenue of ghost gums.

Of the large crowd, one old bushman commented, "If it hadn't been for John Flynn, there would not likely be this many people in the whole of the Inland." There were miners in working clothes, Aranda Aborigines, cattlemen in riding boots, churchmen, families, children – everyone was represented.

Skipper looked out across the crowd for a few seconds from the flower-bedecked official platform before starting his oration; AIM nurses stood out in their smart uniforms, as did a V-shaped line of Northern Territory police. He was conscious that a utility packed with radio gear would take his words across the nation. He began:

> Within the Bible at the Gospel of St John appears this phrase, "There was a man sent from God whose name was John".

> Truly, John Flynn was God's gift to the lonely places within our great island continent.

> He came from God equipped with a capacity to dream, and this afternoon his dreams are in many a country homestead, their most prized and useful asset ...

As he continued his address, he noticed tears streaming down the cheeks of many people. He himself was greatly moved, and he told Jean Flynn later that "only God Himself" gave him the strength to continue.

I am conscious that this afternoon I am speaking either directly or per medium of the pedal radio to many a soul whose mind is full of remembrances of him ... of one labouring in the shadow of these ranges cutting firewood and burning lime for his newly-erected nursing home – which was to be the first, and for many a day the only, hospital in Central Australia. You remember him battling up through the Depot Sandhills with materials for that building, or there are men here this afternoon who accompanied him on midnight rush trips down along the Tragic Mile, or across the Chickeringa Stones with an accident case or a patient for the railhead and fortnightly train at Oodnadatta.

These memories of yours are all precious, for they crystallise within your minds the picture of a kindly, helpful soul who so made himself one with you in your problems that he will live with you while memory lasts ... .

You old-timers here will bear me out in this, that none of us ever knew him to turn one trick in his own favour. Like the Christ he acknowledged and served, he gave – and gloried in the giving ...

"He put hobbles on the bush." That was the phrase of old Queensland Jack, who was sitting outside the bough-shed store at Hatches Creek and listening to the first wireless messages go over the new pedal radio, the new pedal radio we had just installed ... Yes, John Flynn put hobbles on the bush. He tamed something of the harshness out of its isolation, made it safer for the establishment of real homes in the Outback, and so set lasting foundations for us and the generations who will come in our place. May we, and they, all be touched with something of that spirit of goodwill which John Flynn radiated through all his days.

I have been entrusted by Mrs Flynn to commit the ashes of her loved one, your friend, my friend, back to the land he loved and made his own. Here he dreamed his dreams under many a starlit sky. Here he worked with pride and joy in a task done well, so here he lies where he longed to be ... his memory is forever eloquent, for across the lonely places of the land he planted kindness, and from the hearts of those who call those places home, he gathered love.

His oration finished, the congregation sang "Abide with Me". As they sang the words, "Shine through the gloom and point me to the skies", they heard the sound of an approaching aeroplane. The policemen came to attention and saluted, and all eyes turned to the summit of Mt Gillen, which glowed in the bright sunshine. A flying-doctor aeroplane piloted by Captain Ian Leslie, its red cross shining clearly, approached the summit.

Skipper described what happened next in his letter to Jean Flynn:

He gradually lessened his height as he approached the Mount, so that when the wreath was dropped, it appeared to fall right on the very peak of the mountain.

Then he banked the plane and swooped down so that the range face was a background to the machine, then up again to make a complete circle round the cairn. He repeated this circle and each time he did so, THE SHADOW OF A CROSS WAS CLEARLY SEEN ON THE RUGGED FACE OF THE RANGE.

The sight of this cross, the shadow made by the flying-doctor aeroplane, was startlingly appropriate. Years later it was still a sharp memory for those who had been at that service.

———

Just how would Flynn's work survive him? That would depend on whether Fred McKay and the AIM could continue in the same spirit.

The day after McKay commenced work, sitting in Flynn's chair at AIM headquarters, he received a dramatic telegram: the Birdsville nursing home and contents had been destroyed by fire. The two nurses had escaped, uninjured, in their pyjamas!

McKay immediately called Allan Vickers at Charleville, asking him to fly at once to Birdsville and evacuate the nurses.

On arrival, as Vickers walked towards the burnt-out shell of the hospital, still reeking of wood smoke, an onlooker said, "Well, that's the end of Birdsville, I guess." That emotional statement revealed to him just how important the nursing home had become to the community. He was in for another surprise when he told the nurses why he had come. They both adamantly refused to leave with him!

"Mrs Rabig's baby is due in a few weeks and she'll be coming in any day now. We couldn't desert her or the others who will need us. We can use the isolation ward, which escaped the fire, until something better can be organised."

So Vickers flew back to Charleville, collected equipment and clothing for the nurses, and returned to set up their dispensary. Locals set up a bough-shed as a temporary cooking and laundry facility. They put extra branches on the top, as the midday temperatures averaged around 120 degrees Fahrenheit.

With the staff defiantly staying on, Fred McKay needed to make the rebuilding of the hospital a top priority. He contacted his brother, Les, up near Burketown. Les was a patrol padre who was especially gifted with his hands. He turned his truck around and sped towards Birdsville.

McKay next contacted Ben Hargreaves, who had helped him to build the Birdsville Hospital in 1936. Ben had retired in the interim, but nevertheless agreed to rebuild a bigger and better hospital.

So far, so good. Now, what about money? The AIM was in the financial doldrums and had no money for new projects. McKay launched a national appeal for funds.

Mrs Rabig's baby was born in the makeshift hospital three weeks after the fire. Mother and child both did well. For the next 18 months, the Birdsville nurses lived in one cramped bedroom while they carried on the work. Les McKay spent eight months there without spending a weekend at home with his wife and children in Toowoomba. He was too busy helping.

It was obvious, from what was happening at Birdsville, that dedication to Flynn's dreams continued undiminished. In fact the appeal to rebuild the Birdsville Hospital received such a great response that work commenced just 14 weeks after the disaster – an occurrence dubbed the "Birdsville Miracle" in the national news. Touching examples of support and sacrificial giving came to light: a young lass was observed emptying her whole purse into an offering plate for Birdsville, and then had to walk home without even a penny for the bus; two little children in a country town sent in the wool clip of their pet lamb ... and so on.

What, though, of Flynn's leadership? Could Fred McKay replace that? In many ways, he did. He knew Flynn so well that he consciously made decisions that he knew Flynn would have made, following in the great man's footsteps.

McKay and the Board had still to establish a satisfactory working relationship, though. The Superintendent was away on AIM work when the Executive decided on a number of drastic cost-cutting measures. These included shutting down Central Patrol, the organisation's very first patrol region, which would result in the loss of the outstanding services of Skipper Partridge. Further, they decided to close the Bush Mothers' Hostel and Old Timers' Home in Alice Springs.

McKay was highly disturbed to hear of these decisions. He wrote to Reverend Stewart Lang:

> Skipper's Patrol was closed in my absence ... This to me, and I know "Skipper", appears to be a tactical move to place "Skipper" in a position where he has no alternative but to resign ... The whole business, and other happenings, have made me feel like packing my own swag and getting out, BUT THIS WOULD BE CAPITULATION AND TRAGEDY. I AM GOING TO SEE THE WHOLE THING THROUGH − and you, with your knowledge of the personalities in question, will realise the goings on and the tactics that will probably have to be faced. My point is that a matter of major policy in relation to our oldest patrol and our senior member of staff was all finally executed, with no reference whatever to the Superintendent! From my point of view this situation is intolerable. Mrs Flynn says exactly the same used to happen with Dr Flynn, and he was grievously hurt, yet he "took it" in his last years, carrying the burden quietly.

McKay's determination to "see it through" meant confrontation was inevitable. A series of difficult meetings followed, the upshot being an agreement that no further important decisions would be taken without the Superintendent being present. The earlier decisions were reversed − Central Patrol stayed open (though Partridge still left), as did the establishments in Alice Springs. Meg McKay and Jean Flynn went to run the Bush Mothers' Hostel and Colin Ford, a patrol padre, offered to help in the running of the Old Timers' Home.

Jean Flynn stayed in Alice Springs long enough for the local population to get behind the hostel. The fact that John Flynn's widow cared enough to come and work, in an honorary capacity, to keep it going encouraged their support.

Jean wanted a bushman's grave for Flynn. These graves often had a pile of stones on top to discourage marauding dingoes, but she and her friends chose a large "devil's marble" granite boulder instead. She watched Fred McKay and helpers lower it onto the plinth, then walked over and congratulated them on a difficult job done well. Her own ashes would one day lie there beside Flynn's.

———

Not only had McKay succeeded in rescuing the AIM from a series of crises, he had established his leadership. "The old Flynn spirit under God's grace was like a guiding light on the hill to me," he observes. Moreover, he had gained clearer insight into Flynn's faith regarding finances. He recalls:

> As I reflected on the fears of the Board in the light of our God-given resources, I was amazed at the fallacy of their earlier pessimistic predictions! As it was, we closed nothing down. In fact, in the midst of everything, a successful appeal was launched to build the John Flynn Memorial Church. I learned, firsthand, what Flynn always maintained – that God does not fail to provide the rations!

McKay was to lead the AIM very effectively for another 22 years. Today, Flynn's dream of Christian service continues unchecked.

———

At an isolated mining camp, a man lay injured while his friends looked helplessly at his writhing form. His chest had been crushed in a rock-fall. The mine manager busily pedalled his transceiver into life in order to call the flying doctor. The whole scene would have been a little strange to Australian eyes: all the men involved were black and the circular huts in the background were unfamiliar. This was one of many similar dramas that have taken place in Africa, where Flynn's Flying Doctor Service has been successfully transplanted.

An interesting aspect of the work in Africa has been the revival of Traeger's pedal radios, as these are ideal for the rough and poverty-stricken conditions. Thirty sets were sent in 1962 to Nigeria with RFDS help, and to Tanzania and other nations since. As well as flying doctor calls, in Africa, the wireless network is associated with nation-building through transmission of expert information to rural areas.

One of the founders of the FDS in Africa was Dr Neil Duncan. He was the flying doctor at Cloncurry when he felt the call of Christ to establish similar services in Africa. In 1987, his wife Joan summarised the operational success of the mantle of safety in Nigeria:

> Hundreds of lives were saved and problems solved because Flying Doctor Service pedal radios had been installed in village dispensaries scattered over an area the size of England and Wales ... When the cholera epidemic hit the north-west corner of Nigeria, not a single person died of the disease for the first case was diagnosed over the radio network and within an hour the doctor and his team were on their way with vaccine.

By 1985, 20 developing countries were using Traeger's transceivers and a "school of the air" had started in Canada.

Thousands of transceivers still operate in Australia and are linked through the RFDS network. Referring to this, Fred McKay comments, "Flynn, though dead, yet speaks!" The RFDS now stretches its safety net over nine-tenths of the country, operating out of 13 bases. Each year, 40 flying doctors and 50 nurses treat about 150 000 patients, evacuating around 14 000 of them to hospitals. The service has 40 or so aeroplanes, including Kingair jets, its own pilots, maintenance engineers and support networks: in fact, it is recognised as a very efficient airline, winning the Civil Aviation Award for Excellence in 1990 as the Best General Aviator. Its annual budget approaches $30 million, more than half of which is raised by private donation. As 80 per cent of the Inland still has no routine medical services, the RFDS, which is still free and accessible day and night, remains vital to the health of much of Australia.

Flynn would be enthused by the technology used by the service today. Twin-engined jets are fitted with sophisticated navigational equipment and weather radar, and landing grounds have strip-lighting. Doctors fly with laptop computers able to access the most up-to-date medical information for any given emergency. The aeroplanes are hi-tech hospital units equipped to handle most emergency situations, including surgery. These days the most distant Inland location is only 90 minutes from its closest RFDS base.

The RFDS has assumed the role of a primary health provider. With the flying doctor may go a number of other professionals who extend the scope of the service provided by the RFDS: dental surgeons, opticians, physiotherapists, veterinary surgeons, social workers, occupational therapists and pharmacists.

Outbackers are now well served by modern communications systems that supplement radio and telephone: telex, facsimile and commander business systems are examples. Sadly, though, some of these modern developments have curtailed the "chats" between Inlanders that helped to lessen isolation during Flynn's lifetime. High costs are a factor in this. Loneliness has returned to areas of the Inland. Were Flynn alive today, no doubt he would be fighting to win special concessions for those who live far from others.

Flynn's patrol padres still combat the loneliness by distributing literature and providing the personal touch within their vast parishes. Under the new name of Frontier Services, run by the Uniting Church of Australia, they interpret Christ's love in the nuts and bolts of everyday living, giving flesh to His love on every Inland track. There is now an Aerial Patrol Padre, a giant step from Plowman's string of camels.

John Flynn explained that he never built a church because he was far too busy building people and families, which he considered of greater importance: "Earth holds no more beautiful thing than a young family," he once wrote. Despite this, he did dream of a "central AIM cathedral in Alice Springs", at which all denominations could worship.

With this in mind, he obtained a lease on land in Todd Street, Alice Springs, but when he died in 1951 his "Inland cathedral" was still just a dream.

After Flynn's death, Fred McKay revived the dream as a fitting memorial to the great man. A beautiful, interpretative cathedral was erected on the Todd Street block, designed to symbolise dozens of Flynn's visionary ideas and achievements. It is the only one of its kind in the world because Flynn was unique. The Prime Minister of the day, Robert Menzies, reflected this when he said at the opening:

> Dr Flynn possessed two qualities seldom found in one man. He had vision, and the executive ability to get things done. He was a modern Apostle Paul.